D0984266

AROUSAL

AROUSAL

THE SECRET LOGIC OF
SEXUAL FANTASIES

DR. MICHAEL J. BADER

THOMAS DUNNE BOOKS
ST. MARTIN'S PRESS ⚏ NEW YORK

For Margot

THOMAS DUNNE BOOKS.
An imprint of St. Martin's Press.

AROUSAL. Copyright © 2002 by Michael J. Bader. All rights reserved. Printed in the United States of America. No part of this book may be used or reproduced in any manner whatsoever without written permission except in the case of brief quotations embodied in critical articles or reviews. For information, address St. Martin's Press, 175 Fifth Avenue, New York, NY 10010.

www.stmartins.com

Title page art © Corbis

Library of Congress Cataloging-in-Publication Data

Bader, Michael J.
    Arousal : the secret logic of sexual fantasies / Michael J. Bader.—1st ed.
        p. cm.
    ISBN 0-312-26933-1
    1. Sexual fantasies. 2. Sex (Psychology) I. Title.

HQ31 .B185 2002
306.77—dc21   2001051290

First Edition: January 2002

10 9 8 7 6 5 4 3 2 1

CONTENTS

The Emperor's New Clothes and the Meaning
of Sexual Fantasy

ACKNOWLEDGMENTS

There are many people who have provided inspiration and support during the writing of this book. My agent, Amy Rennert, was the first to see the potential of a book in my writings on sexuality and guided me through the proposal stage. I also had the good fortune to have had several excellent readers who helped me clarify my argument and refine my voice: Benji Hewitt, Dr. Vin Dunn, Carl "The Hammer" Sommers, Chris Bigelow, Larry B. D. McNeil, Denny Zeitlin, Renate Stendhal, Lillian Rubin, Kim Chernin, and Michael Lerner. Kim Chernin and Michael Lerner were particularly supportive in helping me overcome self-doubts about the value of my ideas and my ability to express them in a book-length form.

If these friends and colleagues helped me strengthen my argument, my amazing editor, Alison Owings, helped me strengthen my prose. She helped me become a better writer and did it with a gentle, honest, and humorous touch.

I was trained as a psychoanalyst and have been shaped by this tradition. Owen Renik and Robert Wallerstein are two analysts who mentored me and were role models of critical thinking and clinical integrity. In the area of sexuality, however, there are but a few psychoanalytic thinkers whose work has inspired my own. Robert

Stoller, Ethel Spector Person, and Otto Kernberg are three who were important to me in this regard. Interestingly, the writer whose thinking about sex is most similar to my own and whose books have been a rich source of validation and inspiration to me is not a psychoanalyst at all. Nancy Friday has been writing about sex for over twenty-five years. Her collections of sexual fantasies are amazing sources of material for anyone interested in the meaning of sexual desire. Although I rarely quote her ideas directly, while reading her books I found myself repeatedly startled by how many of my own theoretical conclusions she had already anticipated.

Closer to home, my exposure to what is called "Control-Mastery" theory, a theory of the mind and psychotherapy first developed by the psychoanalyst Joseph Weiss and empirically tested by Weiss and Harold Sampson, has been the primary theoretical soil in which my ideas have grown. Hal Sampson, a teacher of mine for over twenty-five years, has been a nurturing mentor whose constant support has been what psychoanalysts call a "corrective emotional experience," counteracting my harsh internal critic time and time again. Most of all, however, it has been my twelve-year association with Joe Weiss—mentor, confidant, supervisor, and role model—that is primarily responsible for this book. Not only are my ideas about sexuality an extension of Joe's highly original theory of the mind, but he has tirelessly fostered my intellectual and emotional growth in areas unrelated to this particular project about sexuality.

Finally, I want to thank my wife, Margot Duxler. She not only edited and critiqued the content of this book, but has been there as my emotional anchor and my continual inspiration. Although friends tease me that Margot's contribution to my ideas about sexuality transcends the theoretical, I suppose that they are ultimately right. Margot has been the source of my passion for life in every area. This book is both about passion and a product of it. For that, I owe her my undying gratitude.

Introduction

A woman I was treating in psychotherapy—I'll call her Jan—reported that she frequently had this fantasy while making love with her husband. She imagines a large man sexually dominating her in an extremely rough and aggressive way. The man is a stranger, and he doesn't care at all about her pleasure. He holds Jan down and treats her body as a thing to be used for his own satisfaction. He fondles her in a harsh and painful manner and never looks her in the eye. He is exactly the type of man Jan loathes in her real life. However, this fantasy is very exciting to her. She finds that she needs it to have an orgasm with her husband.

Now, unless you're someone who has similar fantasies, the fact that pain, helplessness, and degradation can be sexually arousing is surely bewildering. Even if you do share similar fantasies of domination, or even practice them, the reason that they excite you is still probably equally mysterious. The fact is, most of us know *what* turns us on but not *why*. We may know what kinds of bodies we find attractive but not why. We may know how we like to have sex or imagine having sex, but not really why we prefer doing it this way and not some other way. We may know that sex is better in hotels or in public places, that leather pants or spiked heels are sexually arousing, or that group sex is an exciting fantasy, but we rarely know the real reasons behind these preferences.

My aim in this book is to draw back the veil of mystery surrounding sexual arousal and throw a bright light into those shadowy corners of our minds that determine what turns us on or off. This knowledge, I hope, will change forever our relationship to our own sexuality. No longer will we regard our fantasy life as a source of embarrassment or as abnormal. Rather than critically judging our sexual desires—and those of our partners—as appropriate or inappropriate, healthy or unhealthy, we will be able to see these desires as windows into the deepest levels of our psyches. By understanding the logic and purpose of our fantasies, we also will understand the bedrock of our personalities. Sexual fantasies are the keyhole through which we will be able to see our true selves.

I will offer a theory of sexual arousal that explains both the most theatrical scenarios of bondage and fetishism and the mildest preferences about sexual positions in the bedroom. The power of this theory is evident in the very fact that it is able to explain such an immense range of phenomena. Not only will it illuminate the meaning of our private fantasies and preferences, but it will make explicable the mystery of sexual chemistry—what ignites it and what extinguishes it. Couples will suddenly be able to understand the causes of their sexual compatibility or their sexual boredom. Instead of suffering in silence, couples who are frustrated in their sex lives will become better equipped to explore and communicate their true feelings to each other.

My theory about the causes of sexual arousal is grounded in my clinical experience as a psychotherapist and psychoanalyst. But while it draws from the work of many other workers in the field, it stakes out new ground. It draws from psychoanalysis, but it is not strictly psychoanalytic. It borrows from the field of cognitive therapy—an approach that emphasizes changing bad thought patterns—but is not a cognitive theory. It is sensitive to the concerns of sociologists and feminists, but it is not a social theory. For readers who are currently in psychotherapy, it will open up new avenues of exploration. For therapists whose patients talk to them about sex, it will offer a new model of listening and understanding. But this book is not only for professional use. It is a book for anyone who is curious about their sexuality or that of others or who has felt secretly aroused in ways that feel shameful.

MISUNDERSTANDING SEXUAL AROUSAL

Sooner or later, most of my patients talk about sex. They feel frustrated because they want to have more of it or guilty because they want less. They worry about performing during it or about feeling intimate after it. They may want to experiment with more varieties of it or feel ashamed of the wanting. They may feel guilty about having sex with the "wrong" people—the wrong gender, age, or marital status, for example—or feel bored having it with the "right" ones. They may worry about not reaching orgasm or about reaching it too soon.

The topic of sex arises in psychotherapy so often because its pleasures are both desirable and forbidden, a conflict that then creates psychological distress, and because sex is so often the vehicle through which we express a range of other feelings and satisfy a host of other needs. Through sex, we establish or avoid emotional connections, affirm or undermine our sense of masculinity or femininity, and ease everyday anxieties and tensions. Often, sexual arousal—or, more commonly, its decline—is the first sign of problems in a relationship, the proverbial "canary in the coal mine" (miners used to bring a canary down into the mines as an early warning system to tell them if oxygen levels were becoming dangerously low—if the canary died, the miners knew that it was time to get out). Our feelings about the how, where, and why of sexual excitement are often a window into the deepest levels of our psyches and the deepest sources of our suffering and pleasure.

Yet we still don't understand it. If you ask people why someone like my patient Jan would get turned on by being sexually used in a rough and insensitive way, some would shrug and suggest that sexual arousal, like love, is essentially mysterious, unmeasurable, a subject better explored by artists and poets than psychotherapists. Others would say that sexual preferences are simply biological in nature— hormones create desire. Some people, including many sex therapists and researchers, might argue that sexual preferences are *learned* in childhood through imitation and role modeling. Jan, for example, might have been abused when she was young and repeated this pattern in her fantasy life as an adult. Still others, including many feminists and sociologists, would point to the effects of gender conflicts, sexual stereotypes, and sexism in shaping the roles that women and men, both heterosexual and homosexual, adopt in a sexual relationship.

None of these theories, however, really explains the root cause of sexual arousal. Those who think it is an accident of the human heart, of course, discredit the search for causes altogether, implying that if we *explain* sexual excitement, we rob it of its power. They think that attempts at rational explanation do an injustice to the inherent spontaneity and mystery of sexual passion. The romantics are wrong. Explaining sex won't make it go away, any more than understanding the physical laws of the universe will ruin our appreciation of a beautiful sunset. Those who think that we simply *learn* how to get sexually stimulated through imitation eventually run into trouble explaining exactly how we transform what we see, or what's been done to us, into such compelling sexual excitement. Can we really learn about arousal by seeing it? How can the reenactment of painful childhood abuse produce such intense pleasure in adults? Similarly, those who account for sexual fantasies by referring to the power of gender roles and sexist stereotypes face the difficulty of explaining how we seem to go from being passive victims of the social order to active sexual agents who derive intense pleasure from these apparently oppressive social roles.

The dimension missing from all of these explanations of sexual arousal is a deep understanding of human psychology. For it is the imaginative power of the mind that transforms our biological imperatives into the actual experience of sexual pleasure. If we understand the workings of the mind, the mysterious desires of the human heart suddenly become more explicable. It is the mind that tells the heart who to desire and how best to fulfill that desire. The reasons that childhood abuse often produces adults who get turned on by sexual enactments of dominance and submission do not involve simple imitative learning but, instead, a deep psychological need to transform helplessness into power. The puzzling relationship between childhood abuse and adult sexual pleasure is immediately solved if we understand these dynamics. And the answer to the question of how patriarchal gender roles create adults who derive intense sexual gratification from acting out these roles in bed lies in the complicated ways our minds internalize social expectations and make them our own. Sexual politics are not implanted in our brains by osmosis or by force. Instead, sex role learning is filtered through the most primitive regions of our mental life and is mediated through the most intimate exchanges with our caregivers. Sex begins in the mind and then travels downward.

It is understandable why many people might be skeptical of psychological explanations of sexual arousal. Sexual arousal, after all, *feels* biological. It *feels* natural, spontaneous, almost like something that happens *to* us, not something that we are responsible for creating. Sexual pleasure seems to be so rooted in the body, so linked to the pleasurable stimulation of specific body parts, that any idea that our *minds* are running the show seems intuitively wrong. When we get aroused by a person on the street, an advertisement, a character in a film, or our partner; or when we discover that *this* feels good and *that* doesn't; or when we find ourselves thinking of a particular image during masturbation, we are not aware of feeling anything psychologically complicated. It seems like a simple case of stimulus and response. We are not aware of intermediate steps between a sexual image or behavior and the experience of excitement.

There are intermediate steps, however. A complicated process intervenes between stimulus and response. The thing itself—the exciting picture, story, position, or behavior—isn't automatically arousing. It arouses us for a reason, and reasons belong to the domain of the mind. After all, one person may get turned on by a particular picture or body type, while another person finds it boring. One person's Romeo may be another person's Quasimodo. Same stimulus, different response. My patient Jan got turned *off* by gentleness in her partner. Her best friend required gentleness. The most erogenous zones of our bodies can be touched without a hint of excitement (think of your last physical exam), while the slightest brush of an earlobe can be intensely pleasurable. Excitement is generated by the mind, a mind that endows images and sensations with just the right meaning to create pleasure. When it comes to sexual arousal, psychology makes use of biology, not the other way around. The key variable is always the unique psychology of the person who is responding. Only an understanding of that psychology can explain the wide variety of sexual preferences and fantasies that people enjoy, from the kinky to the so-called normal.

In order to understand the deepest levels of the mind, we have to turn to the quintessential "depth psychology"—psychoanalysis. My theory about the causes of sexual arousal and the meaning of sexual fantasies is a psychoanalytic theory, influenced by years of exposure to psychoanalytic studies of sexuality. However, psychoanalysis, too, often falls short in its efforts to explain sexual arousal. In the course of my training I came to feel that most psychoanalytic theories about sexual arousal did not seem to fit what I was seeing in my own clinical work. While psychoanalysis is unique in its attempt to explore the deep psychological wellsprings of sexual desire, its explanations of what it finds are often mistaken. (There were, and are, exceptions. Psychoanalytic theorists such as Robert Stoller, Ethel Spector Person, Jessica Benjamin, Nancy Chodorow, and Christopher Bollas have all made important contributions to our understanding of sexual desire and have been important in the development of my own ideas. Most of all, I have been fortunate enough to have studied with Joseph Weiss, whose contribution to my own thinking has been inestimable and will be discussed in detail later.)

Psychoanalysts tend to subtly pathologize sexuality, treating sexual fantasies outside conventional norms as unhealthy. The mind is depicted as a cauldron of dark and antisocial desires. Analysts tend to interpret "kinky," or what they call "perverse," fantasies as caused by inherently "kinky" or "perverse" wishes. My view is different. I do not think sexuality is driven by kinky desires. I think that it is driven by straightforward desires for pleasure and safety. "Kinkiness" is merely the complicated route that some people need to take in order to safely feel pleasure. Further, I hope to show that many of life's difficulties stem from irrational, unconscious beliefs, and their accompanying feelings, that were formed in childhood, beliefs that interfere with normal developmental aims and satisfactions, including sexual satisfactions. Most of us are held back, both in and out of the bedroom, by these beliefs and continually struggle to over-come and master them. Sexual fantasies and preferences represent a complicated attempt to counteract and master specific irrational beliefs in order to enjoy greater erotic pleasure.

Psychoanalysts, for example, tend to view many forms of sexuality as based on hostility. My viewpoint is that the hostility often seen in sexual fantasies is not inherently pleasurable but functions as a vehicle by which barriers to sexual pleasure—in particular, certain irrational unconscious beliefs—are momentarily overcome. Many psychoanalysts would be inclined to view my patient Jan's rape fantasy as driven by a primary desire to be dominated. My view is that Jan had a perfectly normal wish for sexual pleasure, but because of particular self-destructive beliefs, she had to use a domination fantasy to achieve that pleasure.

Freud's discoveries were monumental but also biased in many ways. He could be dogmatic as well as brilliant, misogynistic as well as revolutionary, and he left a confusing and complicated legacy. Psychoanalysis today does not speak with one voice. It is a veritable Tower of Babel, with many competing points of view.

The point of view that informs both my clinical work and my ideas about sexuality is one that was first articulated by the psycho-analyst Joseph Weiss. In collaboration with his colleague, Harold Sampson, Weiss founded a research program in San Francisco that has systematically tested and validated his theories about the im-portance of irrational, unconscious beliefs in the creation of psy-chological inhibitions and suffering, as well as the complicated ways in which patients in psychotherapy seek to master or disprove these beliefs in order to get more out of life (Weiss and Sampson, *The Psychoanalytic Process*, and Weiss *How Psychotherapy Works*). As I will discuss in chapter 5, Weiss's and Sampson's research has led them not only to pioneer a new approach to understanding psycho-logical problems, but to create a new approach to psychotherapeutic treatment, an approach that aims to affirm and facilitate the patient's innate drive toward health. In the spirit of Weiss's work, my theoretical and clinical approach to sexuality is an affirmative one, viewing sexual fantasy and arousal as resulting from an unconscious attempt to *solve* problems and not, as many psychoanalysts would have it, recreate them.

An individual's sexuality takes many forms, but the underlying meaning is always the same. Whether that person's sexual arousal is a response to a picture, person, sexual position, or elaborate daydream, it derives from the same set of psychological dynamics. Jan, for example, not only daydreams about being sexually dominated, but she also prefers to be on the bottom during the actual sex and is sexually attracted to men who look powerful and ruthless. The same set of core psychological issues generated arousal in all of these situations. In the end, sexual excitement feels the same and has the same meaning regardless of the situation that elicits it. A daydream about being ravished by a stranger might subjectively feel quite different from getting aroused by someone who merely looks strong and tough—the former feels like a private form of thinking, the latter a simple reaction—but the excitement connected to both comes from the same psychological source. *Sexual preferences are merely sexual fantasies that are enacted in the external world.*

But don't we commonly practice our sexuality differently than we daydream about it? Isn't it true that our behavior with a partner might not conform to our fantasies? Sexual behavior is obviously much more subject to social prohibitions and potential embarrassment than a private daydream, and sex with a partner requires compromise and accommodation in ways that are absent in fantasies. These differences account for the obvious discrepancies between our private wishes and our public behavior. Nevertheless, what we would most like to *do*, while sometimes secret, is similar to and derives from exactly the same source as what we like to imagine. We may make compromises in our actions (and even enjoy them), but the underlying causes of our pleasure are still the same as they are in our most private daydreams. And these causes are usually hidden from our view or, in the language of psychoanalysis, are *unconscious.*

Jan had no idea why simulating a quasi-rape scenario turned her on. As we were to learn later, there were reasons, but these reasons were not conscious, and initially she could not articulate why this fantasy was arousing. In fact, it embarrassed her because it contradicted her self-image as a strong and confident woman. Why would being roughed up by an insensitive man in bed bring her to orgasm, when such a man, and such a mode of relating, generally repulsed her? Jan worried that she must be a masochist. Yet something in this quasirape scene aroused her. That the "something" was entirely unconscious worsened her shame. She did not understand why domination aroused her and worried the fantasy came from some shameful place in her.

No one likes to feel driven by forces outside his or her control. One patient of mine announced in her first session that, even though she knew it was irrational, she had the belief that she could choose to feel any emotion she wanted. When we explored the origins of this idea, we found it arose soon after her father died. She remembered feeling completely overwhelmed by feelings of helplessness, desolation, and loneliness. Unfortunately, her family was in complete denial, barely reacting at all to the father's death, completely detached from any feelings of grief in themselves or others. My patient felt particularly helpless in the face of her grief because no one helped her with it. No one was attuned or sympathetic to how she felt. As a result, she became ashamed of her feelings. Because no one had understood her feelings, she felt that they were some kind of disgusting alien presence inside of her. It was in response to this feeling that she defensively developed the conviction that she could completely control her emotions. Her belief that her conscious mind was in total control was a response to the shameful fact that it was not.

We are always more vulnerable to feeling ashamed of our sexual feelings and fantasies when we do not understand them. We do not understand them, first and foremost, because they are unconscious. Freud once said that three scientific discoveries had irretrievably damaged our narcissism—the arrogant assumption that we are the center of the universe. One was Copernicus telling us that the Earth revolved around the Sun, and not vice versa. The second was Darwin showing that we were descended from the apes. Freud himself claimed the third, namely his discovery that powerful unconscious processes belied conscious rationality. Freud believed the cause of sexual arousal was unconscious. It is an affront to our vanity, our pride, to realize that something as personal and "natural" as sexual arousal is caused by something outside of our conscious awareness.

We all are, moreover, unconscious of a great many things. Some seem superficial, but our lives depend on them. We're not conscious, for example, of the many movements and reflexes required to drive a car. We take them for granted, and yet when we were learning to drive, they all seemed new and had to be exercised in a conscious and deliberate manner. Once acquired, the rules, requirements, and neuromuscular adjustments needed to drive became nonconscious or automatic. We simply could not drive if we had to be conscious at all times of our decision-making process.

Similarly, we are also automatically scanning other people in our environment and responding accordingly. We are constantly, but subliminally, reading the facial expressions, mannerisms, and tone of voice of other people for cues about what they are feeling and what they are likely to do. If we did not do it, we would be out of synch with the world around us. This process of "reading" other people, like driving a car, involves filtering and decoding a vast amount of interpersonal information and coming up with the appropriate response, all in the span of a heartbeat. Not only is this interpersonal process unconscious, it is *essential* that it be so. Unconscious thinking is much faster and more efficient than conscious thinking. If we had to be aware of the complexity of each interpersonal interaction, we would be paralyzed.

Recent research shows that this kind of unconscious information processing does not even require the use of the brain's cortex, usually seen as the seat of rationality and consciousness. Nonconscious awareness, learning, and responsiveness seem to be located in brain structures beneath the cortex. This subcortical system is constantly resonating with our social environment, intuiting the emotions, motives, and intentions of other people to help us connect to them securely and productively. It is always "on," and it does its job in the silent background of everyday life. (For an excellent review of this research, see Thomas Lewis, Fari Amini, and Richard Lannon, *A General Theory of Love*.)

In many ways the brain's nonconscious processing is often far more accurate and efficient than its conscious processing. We often see its workings in our choice of sexual partners. When the characters of Tony and Maria first saw each other across a crowded dance floor in *West Side Story*, they knew, in one magical moment, they were meant for each other. In real life a similar—albeit less magical and, we hope, less tragic—type of attraction happens all the time. My patient Jan, for instance, knew from her first date with the man whom she later married that he would be kind to her but not excite her sexually. She later admitted she intuitively "knew"—before they'd even held hands—that their sex life would be tame and tepid. She tried to hide this awareness from herself, rationalizing that it was enough that he was kind and sensitive—qualities missing in most of the men she'd dated—and hoping the sex would improve over time. She could also tell with equal speed if a man would "fit" and fulfill her aggressive sexual daydream. She told me that she didn't even have to talk to such a man to know that there would be good sexual chemistry. She could tell from a "look," a certain carriage, a special "energy" if he would be an insensitive and aggressive "taker" in bed. Such a "look" would trigger a familiar feeling in her, a feeling of alertness, of tension, and then of excitement. On the occasions she had sex with such men, she was invariably correct in her assessment of the man's sexual proclivities.

This kind of sexual intuition is not unusual. Certain images can stimulate us *instantly* because they contain the requisite subliminal information. Certain personality traits, however subtle, can do the same. If a man, for instance, gets turned on by being sexually dominated by a strong and aggressive woman, he will find himself "naturally" turned on by certain women and not by others. He does not have to have sex with them to know if they can and will enact his preferred fantasy. Certain aspects of a woman's appearance or manner will unconsciously "fit." He will feel attracted and not know exactly why. It is as if such a man is able to tune into a special channel that other people cannot see or hear. In contrast to men with other predilections, this man's nonconscious mind has read all the available cues, put them together in an instant, and alerted him with various arousal signals that this particular woman fits his special psychological bill. The end result of this complex process is the simple experience of attraction, an experience that feels entirely spontaneous.

To say that a particular trait or image "fits the bill," however, only raises again the central question that this book is attempting to answer: what determines each person's "bill," each person's particular set of requirements for sexual arousal? Why, in *West Side Story*, was Maria *exactly* whom Tony was waiting for and vice versa? Whether it's in the form of a real person across the dance floor, a fantasy we use during sex, or a preferred sexual position or style of lovemaking we all require specially shaped psychological keys to unlock the internal doors to our sexual pleasure. When we happen upon such a key in the outside world, or imagine one in our fantasies, the arousal that results feels entirely natural and absent of any premeditation.

Sexual fantasies might be likened to microchips in which complex information is reduced and contained in a tiny, nearly invisible space. A version of this metaphor was first used by the psychoanalyst and sex researcher Robert Stoller. Stoller used the image of the "microdot" to convey the idea that a complicated fantasy was condensed into the moment of sexual arousal. Stoller's microdot, having entered the computer era, has now become a microchip! My patient's sexual fantasy of domination is just such a microchip. A huge amount of psychological information is packed into a simple fantasy. Similarly, a man's preference for big-breasted women, a woman's attraction to men in authority, someone's excitement about anal sex, or the erotic appeal of youthful innocence are all sexual microchips. All are experienced as simple and inexplicable sexual reflexes, but all contain a great deal of unconscious information and processing. The erotic outcome is the tip of the iceberg that is experienced consciously. The rest lies beneath the surface.

The nonconscious mind is operating not only in our interactions with things and people, it is also constantly affecting our conscious state of mind and emotional well-being. Even in ordinary social life, well outside a therapist's consulting room, the evidence for the centrality of unconscious thoughts and feelings is everywhere around us. For instance, we all take for granted that during sleep we make up elaborate stories and reflect on complicated problems in our dreams while our conscious minds are completely asleep. If someone close to us consistently forgets our birthday, we intuitively will not believe his or her claims of innocent forgetting but instead infer some other unspoken, ulterior, and unconscious motive. A patient of mine got a headache every time he visited his in-laws but was unaware of the connection until I brought it to his attention. Another patient got depressed every May and didn't have a clue as to why. She eventually realized that the explanation lay in the fact that her mother had died in May. Many of our responses are explicable only if we assume the existence of unconscious thoughts and feelings.

The unconscious is all around us. We chuckle when we observe prepubescent boys and girls exaggerating their disinterest in the opposite sex because we intuitively sense their struggle to suppress and keep unconscious their real feelings of attraction. A friend of mine dropped out of college when she was one course shy of graduating, claiming that she was just "tired of school." Even the most psychologically naive of her friends knew she was responding to some other issue, more deep-seated, about which she was unaware. We've all had the uncomfortable experience of realizing that a mannerism, trait, or behavior of ours is *exactly* like that of a parent, even though we have consciously vowed never to be like that parent. The unconscious process of identification has slipped below the radar of our conscious will. The unconscious basis of sexual arousal, then, should not be startling. The fact that it feels natural and instinctive does not mean that it is without complexity or without psychological meaning.

While I have come to reject many assumptions of psychoanalysis about the nature of sexual desire, one fact is irrefutable: psychoanalysis, more than any other theory, has helped us appreciate the power of the unconscious mind and informed our attempt to unlock the meaning of sexual excitement. Its aim has always been to get below the surface of our conscious experience and explore the deepest levels of our personalities. Freud thought—and I agree—that the aim of psychoanalysis is to make the unconscious conscious. He felt that when certain kinds of thoughts and feelings are kept out of our awareness, they come back to haunt us. In my clinical experience, when people come to understand their sexual preferences and fantasies, they not only feel less embarrassment, but gain tremendous insight into other areas of their personalities as well. They realize that the forces that shape the objects of their sexual attraction and that draw them to particular sexual scenarios are the same forces that affect their professional ambition, their capacity to love, and their mood states. We do not lose our passion by understanding its sources. By delving into the deepest levels of desire and conflict that generate our fantasies, we can stop feeling as though we are the victims of alien sexual impulses and compassionately appreciate our own needs and foibles. As sexual shame dissolves in response to insight, our capacity to enjoy our sexuality increases. More than that, however, when we understand our sexuality, we understand ourselves.

NOTE ABOUT CONFIDENTIALITY

The identities of the patients in this book have been very carefully disguised in order to protect their privacy and the confidentiality of their therapy.

How Sex Works

Where is the love, beauty, and truth that we seek, but in our mind?
—Percy Bysshe Shelley

Sex is hardly ever about sex.—Shirley MacLaine

SAFETY: THE ROSETTA STONE OF PSYCHOLOGICAL LIFE

A thirty-two-year-old lesbian patient, Jenny, reported that she liked to be dominated during sex. She was a frequent visitor to sex clubs that catered to sadomasochists. In this particular scene, Jenny was a "sub"—sexually submissive—and engaged in elaborate scenarios of bondage, self-abasement, and submission. The true meaning of her sexual preference didn't emerge until we understood Jenny's family history. Her father had died when she was young. Jenny's mother was often depressed, spending days on end in bed, leading her daughter to feel worried, abandoned, and neglected. Burdened by these feelings, Jenny grew up feeling, among other things, sexually inhibited. She worried both that she would not be enough for her partner and that she might overwhelm her if she was too intense.

As a result of her growing self-awareness, Jenny was able to see that her sexually submissive role guaranteed two things—that she would be intensely connected to her sexual partner and that she could not, under any circumstances, hurt or overwhelm that partner. As I hope to explain, Jenny's sexual fantasies and practices made it *safe* enough for her to be sexually aroused.

Safety is the crucial concept needed to decipher the mysteries of sexual passion. Safety is the concept that functions as the key to unlocking the meaning of our fantasies, a kind of Rosetta stone guiding our attempts to translate the language of physical arousal into the language of psychological meanings. The quest for psychological safety is at the center of psychological life. And, as we will see, the unconscious mind is primarily concerned with ensuring our safety. Since our unconscious minds are continually working to help us pursue our aims in the safest way possible and since sexual pleasure is one of our primary aims as adults, we need to look below the psychological surface in order to understand the twists and turns through which our minds lead us in the pursuit of fulfillment and excitement. However, before we can understand how sexual fantasy and arousal are chiefly grounded in safety, we have to take a brief detour into the inner world of children and the complexities of their psychological development.

There are lots of ways we seek safety in our lives. On the most obvious level, we try to avoid situations that are physically dangerous. Safety, however, is also an important emotional state. Threats to emotional safety are as dangerous as threats to our physical safety. As we will see, sexual excitement often triggers feelings that threaten our sense of psychological security and, therefore, leads to sexual inhibitions.

The unconscious management of psychological safety does not begin with the onset of mature sexual desires. It begins in childhood, almost from the moment of birth. As research now tells us, the newborn baby is wired to form an attachment to its mother. The baby can recognize the mother's particular voice and face and prefers them over all other voices and faces. Evolution has guaranteed that the baby has the ability and desire to connect to the human being most able to help it survive. Furthermore, our brains and psychological natures are primed to make us love those people who are responsible for our well-being. We become attached, and we fall in love. Without such attachment, psychological research has shown that babies become frantic, disorganized, and depressed. A secure attachment is crucial to healthy human psychological development.

If a secure attachment to a caregiver is crucial to psychological survival, how do we ensure that we keep one? The answer lies in our unconscious ability to read our family environments and to adapt to those environments—to be willing to do whatever it takes to make sure that our parents love and protect us. We bring to this task our intuitive sensitivity and our highly refined ability to sense the moods of our parents and to do whatever is needed in order to stay connected to them. Loving our parents makes us *want* to do the very thing that we need to do—make our parents happy and avoid a rupture in our bond to them.

When we talk about the need to maintain a secure attachment to our caretakers, we are talking about psychological safety. An insecure attachment produces feelings of danger. When a parent becomes angry, intrusive, neglectful, or rejecting, the feeling of a secure attachment is threatened, and the child experiences anxiety. Similarly, when a parent appears weak, anxious, or unhappy, the child also registers danger. The child will do pretty much anything to avoid perpetuating these situations and to reestablish conditions of safety. The child's mind isn't necessarily even consciously registering these dangers. The child experiences danger on an intuitive level, quickly associating the loss of a parent, or of that parent's love and protection, with a "bad" feeling.

While we may intuit all sorts of things about the emotional state of our parents, always alert to disruptions in relationships with them and highly motivated to repair them, how can we, as little helpless children, repair anything? The answer is by changing ourselves. The only things that we have control over are our own thoughts and feelings.

A wide range of such thoughts and feelings are available for changing. As children we all need not only to connect with our parents, but also to progressively separate from them. We have a need to be admired, the center of our parents' lives; we also need to feel increasingly competent and strong in our ability to overcome obstacles and master challenges. We eventually want to feel able to compete confidently but also to take pleasure in affiliating with peers. As we develop, we will seek—and need—a special acknowledgment for our masculinity and femininity, a sense that our "girlness" and "boyness" are recognized and appreciated by our parents. We need to feel that we can have an effect on our parents, that our needs are important, but we also need to feel that our parents can maintain their own boundaries and interests in spite of whatever we might demand. We need to have parents we can admire and proudly identify with, to have happy parents who love themselves and each other.

People have many needs. None of them can ever be met perfectly, but all remain with us, animating our psychological development. However, all these needs are expendable in the service of the need for psychological safety. If we can avoid or repair a rupture in our relationships with our parents by suppressing or altering our feelings, desires, and even our perceptions, we will do it instinctively, naturally, without a conscious thought.

We adapt. Consider a child's experience of parental neglect. Can the child think, "Well, my parents are going through a tough time because Dad lost his job and Mom is an alcoholic. It has nothing to do with me. I'll be able to feel nurtured and appreciated elsewhere in the world"? Obviously not. The child doesn't know any reality other than the one that his or her family creates. The child can't just pick up and go live with another family. He or she has to make it "right"—to make the environment seem more normal in order to adapt successfully and safely to it. We develop a belief that deprivation is the normal state of affairs.

We also go one crucial step farther: we experience reality as if it were also morality. We begin to believe that any wish for special caretaking and love is forbidden, off-limits, as if it meant asking for too much, for something we aren't *supposed* to have. We not only have to accept neglect, but we must make it seem as if the fault lies with us, not with our parents. It's not that our parents can't give; it's that we need too much. A patient, Mark, recently told me in his first session that he felt misunderstood and unappreciated by his wife, but he never told her because he felt guilty for wanting something inappropriate. He said his wife had enough on her hands taking care of their three children. He later remembered that his mother had always seemed similarly overwhelmed and that, although he was lonely as a child, he often felt guilty about being too needy. Mark blamed himself for feeling neglected.

Why would a child develop such an irrational and self-defeating belief, a belief psychoanalyst Joseph Weiss terms *pathogenic* because it clearly works against the child's healthy aims and interests? The reason is to maintain the authority and virtue of our parents and, therefore, the safety of our relationship with them. It is well-known that abused children regularly refuse to condemn their abusive parents. Instead, they condemn themselves. With their parents safely exonerated, children are relieved of worry about the security of these relationships. It is said that most people would rather be sinners in heaven than saints in hell, continually excusing their parents, taking responsibility for their own mistreatment, and developing private unconscious theories to justify it. It is as if the child is unconsciously saying, "It's all right . . . I don't want much anyway. In fact, I probably don't even deserve it. It's not your fault; it's mine."

Children alter the course of their own needs and desires in the service of safety and adaptation all the time. One boy inhibits his normal competitiveness because he perceives that his father always needs to win, or he starts to fail at school because he unconsciously infers from his father's behavior that the father will be jealous if his son does better than he did. Children can be quite perceptive about their parents and never register these perceptions consciously. The boy with the competitive or envious father was worried about hurting his father with his strength and success, but he may never have consciously registered the thought, *My father is competitive with and jealous of me.* Still, the boy is highly motivated to read his father in order to make sure that the two stay safely connected. He may, in fact, be objectively *wrong* about his father's true motives, but the result is the same.

Freud would have focused on the boy's need to give up his romantic attachment to his mother because of the threat of castration from his jealous father, but the fact is that children sacrifice or inhibit their normal strivings for all sorts of reasons. One of my patients became extremely fastidious and polite as a little girl because she didn't want to burden her overwhelmed mother. She grew up feeling guilty about normal impulses to be messy. As an adult, if she felt any inclination to be lazy and get her boyfriend to do more of the cleaning, she would feel guiltily that she was "getting away with something." Another patient had a hard time as a child making friends because he felt guilty about abandoning his lonely mother. In response to his guilt, he used to stay home and keep her company, playing cards, cooking, and watching television, all the while sacrificing his normal developmental desire for a separate life with friends and the excitement of new challenges.

Experiences like these give rise to pathological beliefs that predict that if we pursue our aims, we will endanger our connections to our parents or otherwise threaten our psychological safety. We will somehow hurt them, or they will hurt us. Either way, we lose. Pathogenic beliefs cause psychological problems. Normal goals or developmental aims are sacrificed in order to preserve, maintain, and defend our relationship with our parents and their later proxies. If we have a pathogenic belief that becoming independent will hurt our parents' feelings, we'll have trouble functioning well on our own.

The trouble with pathogenic beliefs is that they are difficult to change. Highly adaptive at the time they are formed, these beliefs interfere with our lives. However, to give up these beliefs exposes us to the risk of being disconnected from our caregivers or being hurt by them. Consider the following common pattern: We grow up with the pathogenic belief that we are undeserving of love. Someone then comes along and loves us. Are we likely to see, accept, or value this positive turn of events? No. Instead, we give great weight to negative messages that mirror our self-criticisms and discount positive ones that might contradict these same criticisms. Because we tend to discredit evidence that contradicts our beliefs and overvalue evidence that confirms them, pathogenic beliefs are circular and self-reinforcing. This is why they persist into adult life.

Pathogenic beliefs often take a simple form. A man in therapy with me began to stutter whenever he was beginning to criticize me. The meaning of this was: if I'm critical, my therapist will get angry. The man was quite attached to me and highly sensitive to any imagined threat to our relationship. He had a pathogenic belief, derived from his experience with his parents, that if he was critical, the other person would be hurt and angry, thus jeopardizing the relationship. Other common pathogenic beliefs include such ideas as: If I'm dependent, my parents will feel drained. If I'm independent, my parents will feel left out. If I'm proud, I'll be humiliated. If I show off, I'll be criticized. If I'm selfish, others will feel hurt.

Such beliefs begin in childhood and often persist unchanged into adult life. Once these beliefs begin guiding our behavior, we simply take them as the way we—and the world—naturally function. We don't think, *I'm irrationally experiencing my spouse and friends as if they were my parents.* We operate according to the unspoken and unconscious assumption that the similarity between the past and present is true. Only if we are particularly psychologically insightful or have the benefit of therapy can most of us consciously appreciate the extent to which our present experience of the world repeats our past.

While pathogenic beliefs originally targeted dimensions of psychological life *other* than sex, the desire for sexual pleasure, is also present in some form in childhood. Children obviously feel physical pleasure, and it is well-known that this pleasure is sometimes connected to genital stimulation. Once experienced, such pleasure is sought over and over again. Unfortunately, sexual excitement is loaded with taboos in our culture and is inevitably fraught with conflict and complications. It is no wonder, then, that to a human mind in which psychological safety is such a primary goal, sexual arousal should present a particular challenge.

GUILT, WORRY, AND INHIBITION

Beliefs are felt and not simply thought. When pathogenic beliefs inhibit sexual excitement, they do so with great emotional intensity because they often involve feelings of guilt and worry. Guilt is indistinguishable from the conscious or unconscious belief that we are "bad" because we have hurt someone. Worry, in this context, is the feeling of anxiety that accompanies the pathogenic belief that someone important to us is hurt or fragile. These two feelings— guilt and worry—almost always occur at the same time. We worry about hurting others, and when we do, we feel guilty about it. We more easily feel guilty about hurting someone if we're already worried about them.

Guilt and worry are not only instrumental in causing sexual inhibitions, but are prime causes of psychological suffering and self-defeating behavior in general. Many people feel that if they are more successful than their parents, the parents will feel envious or betrayed. Consequently, they feel a tendency to feel guilty and worried about them. This kind of guilt can be aptly called *survivor guilt*—the pathogenic belief that being happier and more successful than those we love will harm them. Survivor guilt was originally considered the guilt that survivors of war, natural catastrophes, and concentration camps felt, a pervasive sense that one's survival was somehow purchased at the cost of someone else's death. It is also seen in people who have escaped dysfunctional families or harsh social conditions. Many of us suffer from the pathogenic belief that our gain is someone else's loss. Leaving our family or community behind can create feelings of betrayal of those we love. People tend to deal with survivor guilt by putting a lid on their level of satisfaction. Survivor guilt is frequently seen along with *separation guilt*—the pathogenic belief that if we leave our families, we will hurt or deplete them. In survivor guilt the crime is hurting our families by being happier than they are, while in separation guilt the crime lies simply in having a life of our own.

We all suffer from some form of survivor and separation guilt. Who hasn't felt bad about having more than others or leaving others behind? Who hasn't had or felt a whisper of illegitimacy and fraudulence about success because of the guilty sense that we're overreaching ourselves? Many people who cannot tolerate success unconsciously arrange to fail. A patient of mine from a poor family began moving up the ladder at his law firm. When he finally made partner, he became depressed and began drinking. He couldn't enjoy his success because he felt he didn't deserve it, a feeling often accompanied by memories of his unemployed and alcoholic father. Symbolically, he felt he was putting his father down by his success.

Another man I treated finally got married to a woman who adored him. She was sexy and exuberant, the polar opposite of his grim and inhibited mother. Although he was generally thrilled with his wife and had had great sex with her prior to their wedding, on their wedding night he was impotent. He reported to me that he had been preoccupied all day with whether his mother was enjoying herself at the wedding and was comfortable in her hotel room. These thoughts interfered with his sexual arousal and represented his intense guilt over leaving his mother out, as if he was, as he put it, "dancing on her grave."

Often the manifestations of survivor and separation guilt are subtle. A patient of mine, Helen, was constantly worried about her financial security, despite the lack of any solid reason. It turned out her mother was always worried about money. We came to see that Helen was unconsciously identifying with her mother because it made Helen anxious to feel so much better off than her mother had been. If she relaxed in the knowledge that she was financially secure, she would be faced with how sorry she felt for her mother and how guilty she felt for having something that her mother lacked. She did not consciously know this, of course, when worrying. Her subjective experience was that *objectively* there was a lot to worry about. It was only upon analyzing this trait in therapy that we were able to see its origins.

People "snatch defeat from the jaws of victory" all the time out of unconscious guilt toward their families. They cannot fully enjoy a separate, happier, or more successful life because they imagine that they will feel lonely and disconnected from their families. Because this fear threatens their feeling of psychological safety, they then have to work hard to stay connected to their handicapped families by being handicapped themselves. An athlete who escapes the ghetto to achieve success may self-destruct. People who get promotions sometimes get depressed rather than excited. Clichés like

"It's lonely at the top," or "The bigger they are, the harder they fall," injunctions against "getting a swelled head" or having too much "chutzpah," all suggest this same thing: success makes someone vulnerable to punishment. This reflects the workings of survivor or separation guilt. For someone with guilty pathogenic beliefs, success at work, love, and sex can all trigger unconscious alarms that motivate the person to attempt to restore psychological safety. Ambitions then fail, love sours, and pleasure is inhibited.

When a child feels survivor guilt because of the unconscious belief that he or she will hurt a loved one by having greater satisfaction in life, is this inference always accurate? Frequently, the child is *completely* correct. Spurred by feelings of envy, competition, or fears of abandonment, parents often do begrudge their children's success and happiness. The caricature of the martyred Jewish mother tormenting her child with guilt because the child wants to be independent is certainly often really present in milder forms. Parents routinely, and irrationally, hold their children responsible for their happiness. Thus, children are often astute observers of their parents' moods and *accurately* intuit their parents' internal weaknesses. When a child feels guilty about hurting a parent, or is inordinately worried about a parent's happiness, when a child feels that a parent needs to be bolstered, protected, or fixed, that child is often intuiting reality accurately.

But not always. Children also often *misunderstand* a parent's motives and intentions. Children do not have a fully developed capacity to see their parents as completely separate from themselves physically or emotionally, and cannot always accurately judge their parents' motives. Child psychologists sometimes describe a child's thinking as "omnipotent" or "egocentric" because, according to such thinking, a parent's comings and goings are primarily related to the child. We cannot easily comprehend the fact that the parent has a separate life that does not always involve us, a life for which we are *not* responsible. This egocentricity is understandable on a number of levels. First, it bears the stamp of the child's cognitive immaturity. Researchers in child development have demonstrated that the capacity to correctly assess cause and effect and to differentiate one's own intentions from those of others is only gradually acquired in the course of growing up. Second, the parents' feelings and actions do, in fact, have a larger-than-life impact on the child. After all, the child needs the parents more than the parents need the child. The child's need for the parents is absolute, while the parents' need for the child is only relative. It is adaptive, therefore, to regard the parents' moods in a self-referential way because these moods profoundly influence the child's security. To assume otherwise, that is, to fully face his or her own objective helplessness, would be too dangerous for the dependent child.

Even normal aspects of a child's thinking can lead him or her to make highly irrational inferences. For example, a parent can be depressed about something unrelated to the child, but the child might infer that his or her independence is the cause of the parent's distress. A parent may get sick, divorced, or even die, and children will regularly feel guilty. I had a patient whose mother died when he was seven years old. As a response to her earlier illness, her son, my patient, had been acting out aggressively in school. After her death, however, he completely suppressed any kind of aggression because he had acquired the pathogenic belief that his misbehavior in school had contributed to his mother's death. He was, of course, completely wrong, but he did not have the cognitive or emotional resources to know it.

Usually, the child's inferences about the parent combine elements of objectivity and misunderstanding. A patient of mine experienced his father as frequently irritated at home, especially when his son asked him to buy something. These interactions played a part in the development of pathogenic beliefs that my patient wanted "too much" and that his needs were a burden to others. He learned later that his father had suffered several economic setbacks when the patient was small, and that the father had felt terribly guilty about his perceived failure as a breadwinner. The son's view that his father was burdened by his son's needs was both right and wrong. His father was, in fact, taking his disappointment out on his son, even though it had nothing to do with him. His father did experience his son's needs as burdensome, but the irritation was not because he felt his son's needs were excessive but because he felt his own economic failure made him a bad father. His son couldn't possibly know this. The son's conclusions were entirely rational from his limited and subjective point of view but were irrational in a broader context.

GUILT, RUTHLESSNESS, AND SEXUAL EXCITEMENT

Because pleasure is such a highly prized aim, and one frequently missing from many people's lives, it will come as no surprise that survivor and separation guilt interfere with its experience. But before we explore the centrality of guilt in sexual inhibition and the role of sexual fantasy in overcoming this inhibition, it is important to remember that however much we repress and stifle our sexual desire, it is always with us. This contradiction presents the mind with an obvious problem for which the solution is sexual fantasy. The function of sexual fantasy is to undo the beliefs and feelings interfering with sexual excitement, to ensure both our safety and our pleasure. Our fantasies convince us that we're not going to harm or betray anyone, and that if we get fully aroused, no one will suffer.

But what exactly are we including under the rubric of sexual fantasy? Because many people report that they don't have sexual fantasies, that in fact nothing very elaborate occurs in their minds when they get aroused, one useful approach to this question is to expand our definition of sexual fantasy. Ordinarily, when we think of a fantasy, we tend to think of a story. We can easily see that when my patient got herself excited by imagining being dominated by a ruthless man, she was having a fantasy. In this sense, fantasies are like daydreams, mini-narratives that we use to generate excitement. However, fantasies are often hidden and not always obvious even to the person having them. If someone begins to get aroused by a particular personality trait in another person, say an air of arrogance or innocence, this trait is playing a role in a hidden fantasy. One patient I treated was aroused by the image of an innocent young woman because it negated his normal view of women as bitter and cynical. His experience of innocence had the same meaning as would an elaborate narrative fantasy that featured his seduction of such a woman. In both cases the imagination uses female innocence to overcome a conflict that was suppressing sexual excitement— namely, his guilt about feeling contempt for unhappy and bitter women.

The particular ways we like to have sex can also be understood as being similar to sexual fantasy. We all prefer enacting certain scenarios in bed—certain positions, seductions, verbalizations, aesthetic contexts, states of undress, or role-playing—because the details of such scenarios play a highly symbolic role in counteracting certain psychological forces that hold back desire. One patient, for example, always preferred being penetrated by his male partner rather than being the penetrator because this position reassured him that his partner was satisfied. He constantly struggled with a grim, unconscious belief that he didn't have much to offer a man and worried a great deal about the other's sexual satisfaction. Another patient got especially aroused when she and her boyfriend had sex in a semipublic place where there was a danger of being discovered. She ordinarily struggled with a great deal of sexual guilt that stemmed from a very repressive family environment. By flaunting her sexuality, risking exposure but *not* getting caught, she could dramatically, though temporarily, defeat her conscience. When we explore the meaning of sexual fantasy and its role in overcoming sexual inhibition, we are not limiting ourselves to the explicit narratives found in a masturbation fantasy, sexual reverie, or a collection of written erotica but are including the entire array of preferences and inclinations that are central to our arousal.

There are multiple ways that guilt can negatively affect sexual excitement. At the most general and obvious level, sexual feelings and interests are sometimes simply generically forbidden, first by one's family, and then by one's conscience and culture. The child grows up feeling guilty about "impure" thoughts of any kind. This is a simple but important form that guilt takes, one in which the child learns that he or she is not supposed to be sexual at all. It often easily blends with survivor guilt, in this case the unconscious belief that one isn't supposed to have more pleasure of any kind than one's parents had. All of the many familiar injunctions against sex that have riddled our culture for centuries create and reflect this general feeling that erotic pleasure is dangerous and forbidden. Ideas such as that masturbation is bad, children are asexual, good girls don't like sex, virginity is good, homosexuality is a sin, and premarital sex is bad reflect this generic type of prohibition. Many sexual fantasies contain elements that counteract or undo these limits.

A young man in therapy with me recounted his first sexual daydream, one he used during his adolescent masturbation. In this fantasy he had sex with one of his mother's young women friends, who in his fantasy worshiped him and would do anything to please him sexually. My patient remembered that he introduced an unusual plot device into this rather ordinary adolescent daydream. He gave himself the magical power to produce, with the snap of his fingers, amnesia in his partner about their sexual liaisons. We understood his fantasy in the following way: This young man had a mother who treated him with indifference and often made him feel very guilty about having too much fun (the mother was quite a dour and depressed woman). He grew up unconsciously inferring three things from their relationship: He wasn't very sexy or desirable, he wasn't supposed to have fun with girls, and girls didn't really like sex. These pathogenic beliefs greatly inhibited his sexuality. In his masturbation fantasy, he solved the problem by creating a woman who was the *opposite* of his mother—a sexy woman who adored him and enjoyed sex, and with whom my patient could lift his inhibitions and get excited. By giving himself the magical power to induce amnesia, his fantasy further protected him from guilt and ensured the safety he needed to get aroused and have an orgasm.

The magical amnesia is a good example of the creative way in which a fantasy attempts to solve a pathogenic belief that one is not supposed to be sexual. A fantasy in which one is forced to have sex is another. It is telling one's conscience, family, and culture "it's not my fault." Men have been using this excuse for centuries. They repeatedly claim that women "make" them lose their sexual control. Women, like the patient at the beginning of this chapter who fantasized being dominated by a narcissistic and brutal man, often resort to this excuse in their fantasy lives.

Many other fantasies involve secrecy, variations on the theme of "getting away with it," as a way of circumventing this kind of guilt. Fantasies of illicit affairs qualify in this regard. In others, the actors are pretending they are innocent, but something quite sexual is happening "under the table." A toe is felt inching its way up a pants leg, a hand on a knee slowly moves along a thigh, and all the while "proper" conversation is going on above the table. In this way the pathogenic belief that one shouldn't be sexual is subverted, while innocence is maintained. In still other fantasies, authority is being defied. A patient remembered an adolescent masturbation fantasy in which she and her boyfriend were having sex while her mother was in the room next door. She was aroused by the idea that they were doing it "under Mother's nose," reflecting again the unconscious intention of fantasy triumphing over guilt. Her fantasy was a way of reassuring herself that she could get excited without injuring or offending her mother. Sexual fantasies always find a way of turning the "no" of guilt into the "yes" of pleasure.

The relationship of sexual fantasy to guilt, however, is more complicated than this. Beneath broad moral prohibitions against pleasure are more intimate triggers for sexual guilt, triggers often found in the very nature of sexual excitement itself. One of these triggers involves the central role of selfishness in sexual excitement.

Popular wisdom has it that sexual desire is most passionate in the context of an intimate relationship with someone we love. Unbeknown to most people, however, the relationship dimension of sex is only half the story. *Sexual excitement also requires that we momentarily become selfish* and turn away from concerns about the other's pleasure in order to surrender to our own, that we momentarily stop worrying about hurting or rejecting the other person. We need to have the capacity to "use" another person without concerns that the other will feel used.

When I refer to "using" another person, I am not talking about actually disregarding the feelings of the other but about a quality of relatedness in which the other person does not need to be taken care of and, thus, can be taken for granted. "Using" the other, then, means that one is not obligated to worry about the other's pleasure and can surrender to one's own selfish excitement without guilt or burdensome feelings of responsibility. One patient described the most intense moments of her sexual excitement as feeling like waves crashing up against a shore that is steady, sturdy, and unyielding. She didn't worry about whether the "shore" could take it.

This aspect of sexuality can be aptly described as "ruthless." Ruthlessness is necessary for unbridled pleasure. Anything that promotes undue worry or guilt over the other's welfare will diminish excitement. A casual reading of the bestselling collections of sexual fantasies by Nancy Friday *(My Secret Garden, Men in Love, Forbidden Flowers, Women on Top)* reveals the centrality of the ruthless dimension of sexual excitement. Friday focuses primarily on women, because the kinds of coarse and explicit fantasies described in her books contradict popular notions that women's sexuality is always romantic and caring. Instead, one immediately notices in these stories a rough, urgent, and aggressive edge—either in word or deed— and a relative absence of explicit demonstrations of sensitivity and nurturing empathy. These popular collections of sexual fantasies illustrate the aggressive directness of intense sexual arousal and a notable absence of guilt, worry, or caretaking concerns for others.

The relationship of ruthlessness to guilt is obvious. We feel guilty about being selfish. Someone burdened particularly by survivor and separation guilt has the pathogenic belief that if he or she enjoys life, his or her loved ones will feel hurt or depleted. Surrendering to your own mounting excitement without regard for the internal states of your partner comes to feel insensitive and disloyal. It becomes difficult to "let go" and get maximally excited.

We can now see more clearly why guilt and worry are incompatible with sexual arousal. Sexual arousal inherently requires a capacity to be selfish, to turn one's back on the welfare of the other, to be all the things that a guilty person grew up unconsciously believing were bad and dangerous. Someone guilty and worried about others has difficulty being ruthless. The self-centeredness necessary for sexual excitement runs squarely into the inhibitions imposed by the forces of guilt, therefore making sexual pleasure problematic.

In emphasizing the importance of selfishness in sexual excitement, two objections will inevitably arise. First, if sexual arousal depends on curbing, rather than expanding, one's empathy, how can we distinguish a healthy sexual ruthlessness from the kinds of objectification of which women in particular are the victims in pornography, advertising, popular television and movies, and everyday social life? Second, since empathy and sensitivity obviously contribute to sexual excitement—connecting with the sexual rhythms of our partners and giving them pleasure are arousing to most people—how is this kind of attunement compatible with a desire to use the other?

To argue that some degree of objectification is necessary for maximum sexual arousal and that the capacity to use our real or imagined partner aggressively is necessary to let go of inhibitions is *not* to argue that objectification or selfishness should be a sexual ideal. At its best, sexual pleasure is deeply intertwined with a sensitivity to the feelings of our partner, in fantasy or reality, and a pleasurable desire to give him or her pleasure. Love is sexy, and sex enhances love. In other words, there needs to be a tension between selfishness and caring, between using and pleasing the other. If either pole is absent, there can be trouble. Most people would not like to be in an intimate relationship with someone who was *only* ruthless. The sex would eventually degenerate into an empty and mechanical release—masturbation with someone else in the room. A very common problem appears, however, when one or both partners *can't* be ruthless. Clinically, we often see sexual excitement breaking down under the weight of worry and guilt precisely because of conflicts over the selfish dimension of desire, conflicts that become worse, not better, with increasing emotional closeness. As we'll see in more detail later, familiarity may well promote intimacy, but it can also worsen the human tendency to worry and feel guilty about our loved one.

Selfishness and ruthlessness are often specifically addressed by a wide range of sexual fantasies and behaviors that we see in everyday life and in everyday clinical practice. Some of the most common erotic scenarios reported in sex surveys involve attempts to resolve guilt and worry-based conflicts, often centering on feelings of selfishness. Both men and women commonly report getting aroused by being dominated or by dominating someone else. Jan, the woman who required a fantasy of sexual domination in order to get aroused, was just such a person. She had grown up with a good deal of survivor and separation guilt. She saw her parents as weak and defensively repressed her own strength and sexual power because of the unconscious belief that her independence and exuberance had been too much for them. Jan had grown up feeling she had to hold herself in check lest she hurt her parents, and now she felt the same with her sexual partner. As a result, she could not get turned on by a man whom she experienced as nice but weak. In her sexual fantasy, however, she solved the problem by creating a male character so powerful and selfish that she knows she can't hurt him. His selfishness gives her a kind of permission to be selfish herself. She doesn't have to worry about him and thus can surrender to her own excitement without guilt or responsibility. Jan has found a way to feel safely ruthless, and her reward is intense sexual pleasure.

SHAME, HELPLESSNESS, AND SEXUAL EXCITEMENT

Another set of pathogenic beliefs that are addressed by sexual fantasy and preferences involve feelings of shame, rejection, defectiveness, and helplessness. These painful feelings are accompanied by ideas that one is bad or undeserving and often accompany states of low self-esteem and depression. Shame is different than guilt. Guilt involves beliefs that we're hurting others, while shame involves beliefs that we're exposed and unworthy in the eyes of others. Guilt arises when we reject others; shame when we feel rejected by others. As sexual excitement is incompatible with guilt, so is it incompatible with shame. But don't some sexual masochists seem to get aroused by being humiliated? As we shall see, the answer is no. In general, if we dislike ourselves or expect others to do the same, it is difficult to feel worthy of feeling either sexual desire or sexually desirable.

The frequency with which sexual fantasies seem to counteract in all of us shame and rejection derives from the frequent occurrence of such feelings in normal as well as pathological development. It is impossible to grow up without feeling rejected in some way. Our parents get angry, criticize us, have bad moods, at times want us to go away, or may not even like us. The only question is to what degree. No matter what the degree of rejection, the experience affects us. As children, when we feel criticized or rejected, we feel bad and unworthy. We may rebel and struggle against our parents' opinions, but in the end we will always comply with and internalize our rejection because, as we've seen, parents have the authority to define reality. When we feel that our parents don't like us or don't want us around, we feel disgusting and unlovable. Our parents *really* know us, after all, and feeling rejected by those we love and with whom we're so intimate automatically evokes shame.

While shame and rejection are common in development, every family enacts its own particular variation. Here the line between the normal and pathological gets blurred. Sometimes the themes of rejection and shame are mild. Other times they are traumatic. When the traumas are frequent and intense, the child's self-esteem is damaged, and psychopathology results. In some families the child's experience of neglect and hostility from the parents is so profound that feelings of humiliation, worthlessness, and helplessness dominate the child. When a parent is significantly absent—physically or emotionally—the child always feels rejected and infers that the parent's neglect or absence is due to something in the child that is defective or unlovable. When a parent is physically abusive, the child feels helpless and deserving of abuse. When the child is sexually molested, he or she often feels ashamed, believing that something bad about him or herself made the perpetrator lose control.

Most of us have experienced some form of shame and rejection, from the mild to the severe, and as a result, we all have pathogenic beliefs that we are unworthy. A woman in therapy with me remembered a daily ritual during her high school years that she enacted with her mother. The mother was quite depressed and stayed in bed until noon. However, every morning the mother would summon her daughter to the bedroom to inspect her wardrobe choice for that day. And every day the mother would criticize her daughter's choices. My patient felt ashamed and developed the pathogenic belief that she lacked the wherewithal to make her mother or anyone else happy.

Another patient reported that his brilliant alcoholic father frequently provoked competitions with him. Whether it was playing tennis or debating the relative baseball prowess of Willie Mays and Mickey Mantle, his father made most interactions into "fights to the death" and always prevailed. The son inevitably felt helpless, humiliated, and angry. He loved his father and wanted to be close to him but felt rebuffed and devalued. He grew up with worries about his masculinity and was likely to feel shame whenever he made a mistake.

Sometimes children's sense of shame and personal deficiency derives not only from how they were treated in the family but from identifications with that family. The shame they feel is vicarious. A patient of mine was ashamed of her alcoholic mother, remembering her as a slovenly, sloppy, depressed woman. The daughter grew up determined to be the opposite of the mother and to behave in a polite, controlled, and proper way. Her husband called her a "clean freak." Underneath, the patient was extremely sensitive to feeling shame and responded to almost any kind of criticism by becoming petrified that she was being seen as similar to her mother. It is a common observation of children growing up in chaotic or disturbed families that they feel a shame that properly belongs to their parents. The children borrow the shame of their families.

States of rejection, shame, defectiveness, and helplessness are inimical to sexual excitement. We can't feel ashamed and aroused at the same time. We can't feel weak and helpless while experiencing mounting excitement. We can *pretend* to feel ashamed or helpless during a pleasurable sexual scenario, but the reality is always otherwise—the manifest shame hides a deeper exultation, and the apparent helplessness is belied by control. The incompatibility of sexual pleasure with low self-esteem is so obvious that the bible of psychiatric diagnosis, the *Diagnostic and Statistic Manual of Mental Disorders,* Fourth Edition (American Psychiatric Association Staff), lists the symptom of *anhedonia*—the inability to experience pleasure—as an important criterion in the diagnosis of depression.

Sexual fantasy, then, has the challenge of surmounting these emotions in order for excitement to take place. Because shame and rejection are common experiences, many common sexual fantasies function to negate them. Characters must be drawn, details chosen, scenarios plotted, and roles defined to this aim. One woman I treated imagined seducing her very formal and proper professor, fellating him behind a podium while he was giving a lecture, eventually causing him to lose control. This woman grew up feeling criticized by a controlling father and became highly vulnerable to feeling demeaned and controlled by a male partner. In her fantasy she reverses the relationship that she once had with her father. The male professor is now helpless when confronted with her sex appeal, not vice versa, and she reassures herself that she's *not* an unattractive and rejected woman helplessly longing for attention but unable to draw a man to her. Men frequently have a similar fantasy of reducing a cold, controlled, domineering woman to someone sexually animalistic in desperate need of the man. He's not the beggar—she is.

Fantasies about genital worship are often solutions to the problem of shame, as are exhibitionist scenarios in general. The fantasy is that the other is enthralled by our body, not repelled by or indifferent to it. Our sexuality drives others wild and insulates us against shame and rejection. A patient of mine reported a sexual daydream in which she was being ravished by two men on stage in a nightclub, surrounded by excited men masturbating to the sight of her naked body. This woman had grown up plagued with worries about being unattractive, worries stimulated by her father's rejection of her.

Heterosexual foreplay in which a woman slowly strips for a man is another good example of a ritual unconsciously constructed in order to overcome feelings of shame. For the woman stripping the pleasure is in the reassurance of the man's excitement about her body, an excitement that counteracts any feelings of sexual shame that she might have, thus allowing her to feel pleasure. She's "strutting her stuff," not hiding it. For the man, the striptease is exciting because it features a woman who is shamelessly proud of her sexuality and her body, powerfully counteracting his everyday image of women ashamed of and inhibited about their sexuality, women toward whom he might tend to feel guilty and responsible. Many men develop such ideas about women through their experiences with depressed and inhibited mothers. Their tendency to feel guilty and worried about women's sexuality is momentarily negated by the clear evidence that the stripper is proud of her body, evidence that the man can use to free himself from his own inhibitions.

In this sense we transform the reality of our self-doubt and self-loathing into triumphant displays of sexual power and narcissistic glory. We weave together elements of real experience, cultural norms, wishful thinking, and pure whimsy into fantasies that allow us to feel excited. Pathogenic beliefs are neutralized, inhibitory dangers are circumvented, worries are assuaged, and shame-based insecurities are magically eliminated—all accomplished unconsciously, spontaneously, and in the service of erotic pleasure and excitement.

IDENTIFICATION, TRANSFERENCE, AND SEXUAL EXCITEMENT

Thus far, we have a picture of children becoming guilty, worried, rejected, and ashamed as a normal part of adapting to their family environment. We see them developing pathogenic beliefs that hold ambition and other developmental aims, as well as pleasure, in check. It must be remembered, however, that children don't comply with their environments in the same way that adults might. Children comply automatically and unconsciously, and do so, in part, through the crucial process of identification.

This process of internalizing our family environment is obviously most profound when we are very young. Much of what we experience of the world is transmitted through a kind of psychological osmosis in which, because we are not functioning yet as fully separate people, we directly absorb the feeling states and attitudes of our parents. Because we are so immersed in this intense relationship, we can't even easily distinguish between internal sensations and external ones. Our caretakers' moods establish the atmosphere that we breathe, moods with which we are physiologically and psychologically prepared to resonate. Gradually we begin to separate from our parents and claim ownership of our own separate experience. For example, we become increasingly able, as children, to differentiate between our mother's moods and our own.

This process of becoming independent, however, is a slow and

uneven one and can often be sidetracked. Often, for example, conflicts in the mother-child relationship can contribute to difficulties
in differentiation. Here is one variation of such a conflict. If mothers
are ambivalent about their children's separation from them, they
may give their children mixed signals about whether they enjoy or
dislike their children's autonomy. Children may come to feel guilty
about being different from their mothers, guilty about *not* taking on
in their mothers' feelings as their own. To resolve the tension of
being different from their mothers, children can and do intensify
identifications with them. They try to share their mother's moods.
It is an imaginary way of saying, "We're not different; therefore,
there's no problem." In general, it has been my observation that if
a parent is particularly rejecting, a child may hold on tighter, attempting to feel what the parent feels, becoming more *like* the parents in a desperate attempt to retain a connection.

We all use identification as a way of connecting with our parents.
We become "chips off the old block" out of love for and a desire to
be close to the parent. In many cases, particularly in response to
rejection, this process is exaggerated. It's the only way that, as children, we feel that we can get "inside" a parent who otherwise might
not be emotionally available. "If Dad is depressed, it may be hard
to feel any connection to him if I'm happy. If I'm depressed, too,
at least we're inhabiting the same emotional space."

The issues around identification don't end when we become
adults. Identification is still a basic way of connecting to others. It
underlies healthy processes of empathy. We put ourselves in each
other's shoes to understand each other. We identify with the victim
when we feel compassion for others. Psychotherapists as a group
use identification all the time in their work to figure out what's going
on inside their patients. Parents identify with their children, children identify with their parents, partners identify with each other,
and we all identify with heroes and role models.

Identification also is a crucial ingredient in sexual fantasy and excitement. Whether in bed or in our heads, we resonate with the energy of our sexual partners. We merge with them a bit, begin to vibrate to the same frequency. In fact, sexual ecstasy is often described as an experience of fusion, of losing our boundaries, of losing ourselves inside the other. In this sense identification works in the opposite direction of ruthlessness. Ruthlessness involves the ability to take the other for granted and be selfish. Identification involves letting your partner's feelings significantly affect your own. Ruthlessness means feeling separate. Identification means feeling merged. Ruthlessness means objectifying the other. Identification means seeing oneself *in* the other. Both can heighten sexual excitement. Both can also threaten it.

Identification also interacts in an important way with idealization. When we get sexually excited about another person, we initially idealize that person. The object of our desire is endowed with *only* positive attributes. His or her body is great, personality scintillating, manner and style exciting, and so on. Our desire blinds us to the other's flaws and exaggerates the other's virtues. At the same time, this exciting and idealized new partner pulls for even greater identification. We want to be as close as possible to such a person, almost as if our unconscious minds are saying such things as: "He's got a hot body, and so my body will get hot with him." "I'll bet she loves sex, so I can really let go of my inhibitions and love it, too." "He's probably rough with women, so I'll be able to be rough with him." "She's gorgeous, so if I have sex with her, I'll be gorgeous too."

At its best, identification fuels excitement; at its worst, however, it dampens it. If our partner is sad, identifying with him or her can lead to feeling sad as well, and sadness is inimical to sexual arousal. If our partner is worried or otherwise "down," the same problem exists. Feeling close to someone by feeling *like* that person, feeling intimate through sharing the other's moods, opens the door to feelings that directly threaten our capacity for pleasure. *We often experience difficulty in being turned on if we identify with the unhappiness of the other.*

The situation is made even more complicated by the fact that we identify with whom we think and feel the other person is, not necessarily with whom he or she actually is. We might experience our partner as inhibited and, because of a close identification with that partner, readily share his or her moods and feel sexually shut down. In reality, this partner may not be as inhibited as originally assumed but be superficially constrained and eager to open up. People may be inhibited only sometimes but not at other times, or simply be tired and not inhibited at all. Nevertheless, the fact remains that when our partners seem troubled, sexual excitement can be impaired.

One of the main sources of bias in the bedroom is what psychotherapists call *transference*, the shifting of long-standing images and feelings about a parent onto someone in the present. We partially experience all relationships, including those with sexual partners, against the template of our experience with the significant caretakers in our family. To some extent all people relive the past in the present. Furthermore, the more intimate and familiar we are with our partners, the more the channels of transference open up, and the more we begin to hear the echoes of the past in our present-day relationships. The more people know about each other and reveal about themselves, the more important the other person becomes. The more dependent they feel, the more that relationship will emotionally resemble the dependent relationships of childhood.

Transference becomes a problem when an unconsciously perceived similarity between our sexual partners and our parents leads us to exaggerate and distort certain moods and traits in our partners because they resemble problematic moods and traits in our parents.

When this type of transference occurs, as it often does in intimate adult relationships, sexual inhibitions can easily result. If we had a sad parent, we might be more sensitive to sadness in others. If we had a tired and burdened parent, we might be particularly reactive to such qualities in a loved one. A woman patient told me that her husband was extremely deferential during sex, which turned her off. She felt too responsible for his pleasure and self-esteem to be able to feel free enough to get really excited. However, I knew from her husband's therapist that he strongly wanted to be more aggressive but felt guilty about hurting his wife. His wife, on the other hand, felt that he was hopelessly timid and that this was wired into his personality. As a result of these assumptions, she felt inhibited and despairing. It turned out this woman had a very weak father who'd let her mother walk all over him. The daughter had grown up with the view that men were weak and easily bullied by women. She felt that she "knew" for a certainty her husband was just such a man and, thus, felt an aversion to him sexually. In fact, she was both right *and* wrong. Her husband *did* act deferential. But his deference was only a part of his story, a story that she couldn't see in its complex entirety. Because of the superficial similarity between certain traits in her husband and father, she transferred the feelings that she'd originally had for her father onto her husband. When she was able to more clearly see her husband's true desire, she was able to begin to open up sexually.

SOLVING THE PROBLEMS OF IDENTIFICATION AND TRANSFERENCE WITH SEXUAL FANTASIES

Many people use fantasies to unconsciously solve the problem of identification and transference by making sure that everyone in them is happy and aroused. In the unconscious, sexual excitement is in itself a powerful marker of health and happiness. The image of a happy partner not only alleviates our guilt and worry over hurting the other with our sexual excitement and reduces the chilling feelings of responsibility, but identifying with someone who is happy directly buoys us and makes us happy, too. If someone is prone to see his or her partner as depressed or is prone to transfer onto the partner the image of a sad parent, sexual scenarios in which the other is happy will be an aphrodisiac. The threatening identification with a sad parent is replaced by the exciting fantasy of a happy one.

Sexual fantasies are constructed in order to counteract the potentially debilitating effects of identification. If we had a parent who was detached, we might gravitate toward sexual fantasies in which everyone is intensely connected. If a man's experience of women was that they tended to be impulsive and out of control, he might feel imperiled by getting too close to such female sexual partners, whose excitement might feel frighteningly contagious. Thus, he might generate sexual daydreams and script sexual scenarios in which *he* is fully in control and detached from a partner who enjoyed or was even excited by the distance. He would therefore not only actively negate his fears of merger with a wild and impulsive woman but create, in fantasy, a reassuring partner who was in control of herself and happy with his self-control. Identifying with this kind of woman could then make it safe to experience pleasure.

A male patient of mine reported, with some shame, a recent masturbation fantasy. The fantasy involved having sex with a very coquettish and bubbly teenage girl who worked in a nearby health food store. He imagined that the sex was robust and playful. He fantasized—and was excited by—her smooth and youthful body and innocent and playful demeanor. Obviously, the sexual fascination among many men with young, nubile women is a widespread cultural phenomenon. At the same time, for this patient, these cultural messages were planted in fertile psychological soil. This patient had grown up with a depressed mother who felt cheated by life. He reported that his childhood home always had a "heavy" feel to it. He chose a woman to marry whom he perceived as similarly beaten down.

So how did his Lolita fantasy solve the problem of feeling pulled down into the dark moods he associated with women? He endowed a young woman with physical and psychological qualities that were the polar opposite of the grim and oppressed women whom he tended to see all around him. While his mother and current partner were weighed down and drained by the burdens of life, his sexual fantasy featured a girl who was sexually exuberant, unblemished by life, and entirely happy. At its deepest level, his sexually exciting identification with this teenage girl's idealized body and youthful spirit reassured him against an anxiety-provoking identification with the negative moods of his dreary mother. He felt safe and encouraged to get aroused.

OVERLAPPING FANTASIES

Sexual excitement, it seems, is exquisitely sensitive to and expressive of the deepest levels of the human psyche. The stories we make up to ensure our arousal reflect the reworking of our core fears and wishes. Some fantasies seem aimed at guilt and worry; some at shame, helplessness, and rejection; and still others at the problem of overidentification and transference.

The real world, however, is rarely this simple. Sexual fantasies and preferences don't usually fall into neat categories. People struggle against many different pathogenic beliefs at the same time. As a result, sexual fantasies often have to serve multiple psychological functions simultaneously. Consider, for example, the patient who fantasized about teenage girls. Once we got to the psychological bottom of things, we could see how this one fantasy simultaneously took care of a number of problems. He identified with the girl's youthful exuberance. The image of a happy and bouncy girl about whom he didn't have to worry negated his tendency to feel guilty and responsible for women. And by imagining her responsive adoration, he counteracted his fears of rejection. One fantasy simultaneously served multiple purposes and alleviated multiple anxieties. He was not unusual. There is rarely only one thing going on in any sexual scenario.

Sexualized rescue fantasies are another good example of a type of fantasy that counteracts several pathogenic beliefs at the same time. Many people become aroused by the prospect of healing or fixing a partner. A man I saw in therapy, for example, got excited when he thought that he could make a sad woman happy by having sex with her. The frequently seen desire in women to fix men is often acted out in sexual ways with the unconscious intent of making men feel powerful and desirable through various feminine displays of sexual awe and responsivity. And a common dynamic in therapists who have sex with a patient is the arousing, albeit self-serving, fantasy that their sexual attention is helping the patient's self-esteem. In all of these cases a fantasy of repairing someone through sex is tremendously exciting.

Upon analysis, such fantasies are usually serving several functions simultaneously. First, they are a means to overcome guilt. The hidden logic is: "I'm not hurting you; I'm helping you. I'm a good person, not a bad one." Second, sexualized rescue fantasies are usually a way of feeling important and are arousing precisely because they negate worries about being unimportant and useless. Having disproved feelings of both guilt and devaluation, rescue fantasies make it safe enough for sexual excitement to emerge.

In some cases the sexual appeal of a rescue fantasy seems to be more related to guilt, while in others, to rejection and shame. Usually, however, the reality turns out to be a complicated combination of both. When we're discussing the issues of guilt, worry, shame, and identification, and trying to understand how they contribute to the formation of sexual fantasies and preferences, we need to keep in mind that there is not a necessary one-to-one relationship between a certain conflict and a particular fantasy. Sometimes we can see cause-and-effect relationships on the most general of levels. Fantasies of being dominated usually have something to do with conflicts over guilt and worry. Exhibitionistic fantasies often involve attempts to defend oneself against feelings of shame and rejection. But to thoroughly understand any one fantasy in a particular patient thoroughly, we have to allow for a more complex explanation involving the interaction of many issues.

When D. H. Lawrence wrote, "The tragedy is when you've got sex in the head instead of down where it belongs," he meant that analyzing sexual desire can rob it of its proper instinctual intensity. Certainly sexual excitement feels entirely natural and spontaneous, utterly removed from the kinds of unconscious mental machinations I have been describing. Nevertheless, while our lust and capacity for pleasure are instinctual, the road to pleasure is a complicated one. Our families and culture place numerous obstacles along this road: guilt, worry, fear, shame, rejection, and identification all stand in the way of getting to what seems so natural. It is an extraordinary testament to the creative and adaptive capacity of the human imagination that it is able to weave together exactly the right story to overcome obstacles to arousal. Getting turned on involves transcending the past, counteracting dangers, disconfirming beliefs, undoing traumas, soothing pain, and finally, finally, laying claim to pleasure.

2

Sexual Fantasies as Antidotes to Guilt and Worry

Anxiety is love's greatest killer. It makes others feel as you might when a drowning man holds on to you. You want to save him, but you know he will strangle you with his panic.—Anais Nin

If sex isn't dirty, you're doing it the wrong way.—Woody Allen

We all feel guilty about something: survivor and separation guilt, guilt about having fun, about being selfish, ruthless, independent—such guilt is universal. Everyone grows up both wanting pleasure and independence while still caring about their attachment to their families of origin. The conflict between our attachments to our families and our wish to grow up and be happy often creates guilt. Even in the best of circumstances normal development introduces such problems and leads us to unconsciously put a lid on our desires. The solution is to be found in our sexual fantasies.

Women seem to be especially prone to guilt. They are socialized to be sensitive to the needs of their partners, to derive their self-esteem and validation from being "givers" and not "takers," to be objects of desire rather than desiring subjects. This can make it difficult to surrender to the pulse of one's own excitement, to be ruthless. Sometimes the very trait that enhances an emotional relationship undermines the sexual relationship. For example, I have found that in many lesbian couples, there is a special intensity to and emphasis on the empathy and interpersonal sensitivity of the partners. Such heightened attunement, however, can often lead to heightened feelings of guilt and worry in these couples, then to a dissipation of sexual excitement. The forces that breed emotional closeness are the same forces that inhibit sexual ruthlessness. Both ruthlessness and empathy are necessary in a healthy sexual relationship. When empathy breaks down, we are left with sex that is mechanical. When ruthlessness is inhibited, we can feel enslaved to the needs of our partner and lose touch with the fullness of our own desire.

Help is on the way, though. Sexual fantasies and preferences arise as elegant solutions to the problems of ruthlessness, guilt, and worry. The following are detailed case studies.

A RAPE FANTASY: THE CASE OF JAN

A clear example of the special difficulty women have with guilt and sexual ruthlessness can be found in a closer study of the case of Jan, who required a fantasy of being sexually dominated by a stranger in order to have an orgasm with her husband. Jan was an outspoken feminist who had, in fact, written numerous articles that critiqued traditional sex roles. In her professional life, she was usually viewed as strong and outspoken, someone who, in her words, didn't "take any shit." However, Jan's personal life was unsatisfying. She tended to get involved with "nice guys" who initially seemed to be extremely sensitive to her needs, almost maternal in their treatment of her. Her pattern was that she would eventually lose interest in these men and become critical of them as she began to experience their sensitivity and deference as weakness. Driven by her need for caretaking, she married one of them eventually and was inevitably plagued by sexual boredom. As she began to criticize her husband, she would frequently experience his injured feelings as a sign that he couldn't take care of himself. This made her feel guilty, "bitchy," an intolerable feeling that then led her to criticize him more, all the while hoping for some way out of this unhappy cycle. She hated being so critical but didn't want to be a typically deferential woman either. She felt pessimistic and depressed about her capacity to love.

During a discussion of her boredom, she first told me of the sexual fantasy that she used in order to have an orgasm with her husband, a fantasy that she'd used in some form since adolescence and that embarrassed her. To Jan, it suggested that while she defended women by day, by night she was a masochist, a pathetic woman who *really* wanted to submit to male power. Nothing could have been further from the truth.

Jan told me about her domination fantasy a little bit at a time, with many stops and starts. When we put all the pieces together, it went something like this:

I sometimes imagine that I'm sitting in my office, working diligently at my computer. It's late, and the building is empty. Suddenly my door opens, and a custodian enters, saying that he needs to empty the wastebasket, which happens to be under my desk. I'm curt with him and tell him to hurry up. I notice that he's quite big and well muscled under his uniform. As he reaches under my desk for the wastebasket, he suddenly runs his hand up my leg, under my skirt, and roughly squeezes my cunt. I start to resist. He grabs my hands, holds them together over my head with one hand, and with the other hand lifts me onto my desk, spreads my legs, and rips off my panties. He tells me that he's wanted to fuck me for a long time. His cock is huge. His whole body is massive. He's so strong that I can't move. He squeezes my tits hard. The thing is, while he's fucking me, he isn't even looking at me. Sometimes the scenario involves him grabbing my head and fucking my mouth. Other times, it's my ass. But it's as if he has to not only *have* a hard prick, he has to *be* a prick as a person. He has to not give a shit about my pleasure but instead just use my body as something to fuck and something to give him pleasure. He's exactly the kind of asshole I've hated my whole life, and yet this fantasy gets me so hot that I can reach orgasm with it in minutes.

The crude and raunchy language that Jan used in recounting her fantasy conveyed its essential meaning—namely, that what was happening had nothing to do with tender feelings, love, or sensitivity. For her fantasy to "work," the man had to be rough and insensitive—no whispering sweet nothings, no eagerness to please, no concern about whether the other person climaxed or not.

Why was this so appealing to Jan? Why would a fantasy rape bring her to orgasm while a real one would obviously traumatize her? Sometimes Jan would chalk it up to the effects of socialization—after all, society teaches girls and women to be passive and masochistic—but this offered her little comfort because she knew that there was something more than simple social learning going on here. Was she some kind of a masochist? Were her feminist opinions about the importance of female empowerment simply defenses against her private longings to be taken over by a powerful man? These were the doubts that haunted Jan and made it difficult for her to reveal and analyze her fantasy.

What Jan and I learned was this: Her deepest view of men was that they were, as she put it, "paper tigers." Outwardly, men acted macho and strong, but beneath this facade, men were really fragile and insecure. We all have a basic image or belief system in our minds, usually unconscious, about what constitutes a typical man and woman, what goes into the formation of masculinity and femininity. These beliefs are, to use computer language, "default" beliefs, beliefs that the mind automatically returns to unless the person makes a conscious effort to override them. With effort, we may develop other, more conscious and rational beliefs about masculinity and femininity, but there is always a pull back to our original constructions. A man might consciously believe, for example, that women like sex as much as men, while unconsciously believing that they don't. Jan's primary construction of masculinity was that it was hollow and weak. She unconsciously believed that if she fully experienced and expressed her sexuality, most men would feel threatened and overwhelmed. She chose kind and gentle men as partners because they offered the promise of satisfying other needs of hers, primarily needs to be loved and understood. But these men frequently confirmed her view that men were weak and unable to stand up for themselves, and she would test them by criticizing them. She secretly wanted them to assert themselves and not be affected by her attacks. Instead, these men would often get hurt. She would feel terribly guilty. The guiltier she felt, the more she wanted them to stand up for themselves and not be hurt by her, so she would up the ante and become even more "bitchy." The cycle would escalate.

At one point I playfully suggested that she seemed to feel that a man would have to be a giant in order to stand up to her. Immediately, Jan recognized the implied reference to her sexual fantasy. Its function became clear. She takes care of her problem of guilt by creating a man so strong that she can't hurt him. She arranges for him to be hurting her, not vice versa. In so doing, Jan reassures herself that *she's* not the destructive and powerfully ruthless one— he is. No matter how strong she is, no matter how excited she gets, no matter how out of control her impulses might be, her fantasy partner will never become overwhelmed. Since he is selfishly taking exactly what he wants, Jan can be confident that he's happy and satisfied, and she does not have to worry about buoying him up. Her fantasy counteracts her pathogenic belief that she overwhelms and hurts fragile men with her strength and needs. He's taking what he wants, and so she can get what she wants.

These discoveries about the meaning of Jan's sexual fantasy helped her tremendously. First of all, they helped reduce her shame; her fantasy didn't mean that she was a secret masochist, but rather that she felt guilty about being too powerful. Second, Jan was now able to review and revise her fundamental picture of men. Perhaps being sensitive didn't necessarily mean that a man was weak. Perhaps a man could be caring and still be strong enough to take care of her. And finally, Jan was able to use her insights into her sexual conflicts to feel less guilty about being strong with her husband and not have to test him so frequently. She began enjoying him. She still had fantasies about being sexually dominated, although they increasingly starred her husband as the dominator. In addition, Jan could now sometimes allow herself to enjoy fantasies and scenarios in which she was openly the aggressor.

Domination fantasies frequently involve attempts to circumvent the chilling effects of guilt and worry on sexual desire. Such fantasies are prevalent among both men and women, and obviously entail two roles in such scenarios, the "top" and the "bottom." Fantasies of being the dominator (or dominatrix) are also common. Perhaps because our society tends generally to discourage public expressions of aggression, self-assertion, and ruthlessness in women, it has been my clinical experience that in the heterosexual world, the submissive side of this type of sexual relationship seems to be slightly more preferred by women, while the dominant role in the fantasy seems to attract more men.

Jan's fantasy is not uncommon among women. There are many variations on the theme of a woman arranging a fantasy in which she can let go of her inhibitions about being too strong. Though the manifest script often puts her in a passive position, the underlying unconscious message is that she is guilty about being too much for a weak, limited, or inadequate man. Consider the following fantasy of Gina's, a fantasy that she, too, uses to have an orgasm with her sweet but boring husband:

> Fred is a nice man, in and out of the bedroom. When we're screwing, he always comes before I do. When I'm having sex with him and want to make sure I come, I will often have a fantasy in which he takes me to a romantic and private spot in the woods and, to my surprise, has arranged for his tennis buddies to meet us. Fred tells me that they're going to "wear me out." They're all over me, first one, then the other, taking turns fucking me. One will play with my tits and make me jerk him off while the other eats me out. Every hole gets filled up. I go wild and completely lose control. •

Gina felt that in reality she wore Fred out, that he couldn't keep up with her. To some extent this was confirmed by his tendency to ejaculate quickly, but it also reflected Gina's view of herself in relation to men in general, namely that she overwhelmed them with her sexual energy. Gina's guilt about being too strong in bed is perfectly counteracted by a fantasy in which she finally meets her match in the form of two men. The story line of her fantasy seems to feature her degradation—the men are going to "wear [her] out," she's being gang-banged, they "make" her jerk one of them off—but the result is that Gina has an orgasm because, in her unconscious reality, she finally has enough "man" to fill her up and satisfy her. She is so sexually voracious that it takes two of them to do the job.

As noted earlier, even a casual perusal of the bestselling collections of sexual fantasies by Nancy Friday provides lots of anecdotal evidence of the relationship of guilt and worry to sexual arousal. Many of Friday's respondents, women who sent her their sexual fantasies, describe their daydreams in direct, coarse, and aggressive language. The men and women who populate these fantasies get carried away with their excitement and do so with exuberance, force, and lusty aggression. Men "thrust with savage hardness," while women ride their "cocks." These fantasies aren't Harlequin romances in which sexual excitement is conveyed through a soft focus. The ruthlessness of these fantasies is important because it eliminates the need to feel guilty or worried. Everyone is having fun, no one is fragile, and the result is sexual pleasure.

Having illustrated common scenarios in which a woman uses a typically passive feminine role to enact and fulfill her active and powerful sexual aims, I want to say again that heterosexual gender roles do *not* translate neatly into sexual fantasies. There are countless cases in which the roles are reversed, situations in which the man wants to surrender sexually to a woman, to be "done to," and others in which women are aroused mainly by fantasies of explicitly and aggressively sexually dominating a man. Gender differences, though real, are not as profound as one might expect. The only relevant question is: what pathogenic beliefs do dominance and submission solve?

Since all of us have pathogenic beliefs of some kind, and since all sexual fantasies are attempts to correct such beliefs, we should not conclude that analyzing fantasies necessarily means that they are especially unhealthy. Sexual fantasies can and do have complicated psychological meaning without being pathological.

When it comes to its meaning, it doesn't matter if the scenario involves two men, two women, or a man and a woman. Someone is dominant, and someone is submissive, regardless of gender or sexual orientation. In any of these situations both parties are getting aroused by their respective roles. The point is to understand this arousal, the centrality of guilt in the scenarios, and the psychologies, not only of the one being "done," but also of the "doer."

TOPS AND BOTTOMS: THE CASE OF MANNY

It is common in my clinical practice for a patient to tell me about sexual practices about which he or she has little conflict. There seems to be no correlation between the type of sexual practice or fantasy that someone has, and the extent to which he or she feels sexually frustrated or confused. On the other hand, I have never seen a patient whose sexual practices and fantasies didn't shed an important light on what ailed them emotionally. While sex might not always be presented as a problem in and of itself, it almost always helps us understand things that clearly are problematic.

Manny entered therapy with one of my supervisees for help with depression. In the middle of his one-year treatment, he revealed details of his sexual life. Manny considered himself a "top" in the gay sexual scene in the city where he lived. In Manny's world, elaborate and formal rituals of dominance and submission were routinely enacted. He told his therapist about the "slaves" he had had over the years, some of whom had been given to him by a "master" from another city. One of these slaves had been "sent" to him from Texas and moved into Manny's house to serve as his houseboy. Manny described his sexual pleasure in whipping, slapping, beating, and humiliating this man, and he recounted in detail the slave's intense excitement at his beatings. Manny was not embarrassed or conflicted at all about his sexual preferences. He was mainly concerned about feeling depressed.

Manny had had a very traumatic and painful childhood. His father had beaten him for no apparent reason, often leaving bruises and welts all over his body. The father died when Manny was twelve years old. His mother had made excuses for the father and had never protected Manny. She was a depressed woman who made comments to Manny like, "If it weren't for you, I'd kill myself." She couldn't take help from anyone and saw herself as a martyr. When she was dying of cancer, she once told Manny, "Don't worry, I'll just die soon, and you won't have to worry about me." On her deathbed, hours before she died, she pleaded with Manny to "save" her. Manny subsequently blamed himself for his mother's death. He had always felt intensely responsible for her, calling her twice daily throughout his adult life and quitting a lucrative job so that he could care for her full-time during her illness.

It was clear that Manny had numerous reasons to be depressed. He came to understand how identified he was with his mother in his everyday life. He suffered from the belief that he lived only to give and not receive. When he was depressed, Manny felt like his mother was inhabiting him. He daydreamed about joining his mother when he died. Once, after he had stood up to a belligerent store clerk, he became depressed and feared that he was going to die of cancer. His therapist told Manny that he felt guilty about being stronger than his mother and was punishing himself by putting himself in the same boat as his mother. Manny instantly felt somewhat relieved by this clarification of the role guilt played in his unhappiness. His depression lifted somewhat but was still lingering in the background.

When Manny later told his therapist about his sex life as a "master" and described some of the sexual scenarios that turned him on, several lights went on for both of them. Manny had made a point of recounting how the "slaves" with whom he trafficked got extremely aroused by being dominated and abused. Their arousal was essential to his. In the world of sadomasochism, one usually can't enjoy being a master unless one's partner enjoys being a slave (exceptions to this rule where someone's pleasure depends on someone's actual fear and suffering will be discussed later). Manny and his therapist came to see how this fact enabled his sexual dominance to negate his tremendous guilt and worry about his mother. Manny was prone to think of himself as a bad son who had let his mother suffer and die, and this survivor guilt that squelched his passions. In the master/slave relationship, Manny created evidence that he was not a bad guy, a disloyal son, by beating someone who enjoyed it and therefore did not suffer from his abuse. His slave was happy and aroused by being hurt and dominated, a fact that Manny's unconscious mind employed to counteract his guilty belief that he was always hurting his mother.

Though this explanation helped Manny, it did not seem completely adequate. Why a master? Why not a slave? The answer emerged as Manny talked about his father, a man he described in such terrifying terms that, at first, neither he nor his therapist could see how much Manny had identified with him. Eventually, however, they came to see that, in his role as a sexual top, Manny symbolically became the abusive father and not the helpless victim. In psychoanalytic terms, he "identified with the aggressor." By enacting the role of a frightening parent, Manny momentarily negated the pathogenic belief that he was helpless and counteracted the terror of being overpowered. Manny and his therapist eventually described this process in terms similar to those used by Pres. Lyndon Johnson to describe why he placated FBI director J. Edgar Hoover: "I'd rather have him inside the tent pissing out than outside the tent pissing in." In his mind, Manny reversed the traumatic feelings of helplessness that he'd endured as a child.

In addition, by identifying with his father, he remained connected to him—a father whom he also loved. This is a common dynamic. We identify with hurtful parents out of love as well as fear. The psychological dynamic is: if you can't beat 'em, join 'em. The problem for Manny was that he was not only a slave driver to his slaves but to himself as well. He was as harsh with himself as his father had been with him. This harshness was a crucial ingredient in Manny's depression, and when he understood it, his depression lifted.

In sum, Manny was a "chip off the old block" during the S-M scenes and thus preserved a connection with his father. By counteracting the helplessness in his relationship with his father and the guilt in his relationship with his mother, Manny's sexual practices enabled him to feel intense pleasure. Further, by understanding how these dynamics affected the rest of his life, Manny began to get some relief from his depression. He had tormented himself with both the guilt about abandoning his mother "in her hour of need," as he put it, and with the self-blame and self-hatred that his father's abuse had created.

In therapy, Manny was able to begin to be more compassionate toward himself, to feel less like a disloyal or bad son and more like an innocent victim who deserved sympathy and self-love. His self-esteem began to improve. Manny's sexual practices, however, had not changed at the time he left therapy. He had created an entire lifestyle for himself out of his sadomasochistic tendencies and derived a great deal of pleasure and satisfaction from it. Although he better understood its origins, he had little motivation to change it.

TIED UP IN KNOTS: THE CASE OF ROBERT

In an article about beating fantasies ("Bondage Fantasies and Beating Fantasies," in *Psychoanalytic Quarterly*), the psychoanalyst Joseph Weiss presents a clinical case that perfectly illustrates the centrality of guilt in sexual fantasies. Six months into his therapy, Robert told his therapist about his bondage fantasies. During sex with his wife, he would often imagine a strong, happy woman tying him up and playfully having sex with him. She would pinch his nipples and seductively tease him. His fantasy woman was quite different from his experience with the actual woman lying next to him. In reality Robert was excessively worried about her. He felt that he had to work hard to bring her into social conversations lest she feel left out. He felt guilty when she was upset, and he saw it as his job to cheer her up. He admitted to being worried about his wife during intercourse because he feared that she had sex only to placate him. His belief that his wife wasn't interested in sex made it difficult for him to become sexually aroused.

Robert's therapist made the following interpretation: he told Robert that he used the bondage fantasy to reassure himself during intercourse that he was *not* hurting his wife. This made immediate sense to Robert, who confirmed that the fantasy of a strong, cheerful woman tying him up turned him on and that, in fact, during sex he blotted out what he saw as his wife's grim expression and substituted the image of a woman who was confident and enjoying herself. Robert was immediately relieved and responded that he was tremendously sensitive to every nuance of his wife's moods and could tell in an instant if she was unhappy. Since he often saw her in much this way, Robert was often downcast in her presence.

Robert was curious about the origin of his fantasy solution to the problem of a grim wife. He had never actually had a woman tie him up during sex and couldn't understand how he had developed this particular fantasy. Was he simply a masochist at heart? His therapist wondered if Robert's childhood might hold some clues. Robert was an only child. He remembered his mother as nervous, possessive, and easily hurt, completely unable to exert any authority. Robert felt that he had to "walk on eggshells" around her. He often felt nervous around *her* nervousness and had a lot of trouble separating from her. As an adult, he called his mother almost every day and twisted his own travel schedule to visit her regularly. Robert remembered his father as calm and warm. The two of them would play together, and his father read to him. Robert remembers his father showing him how to fix things around the house, and spending hours with him in his workshop.

Robert recovered an interesting memory almost immediately after the therapist made his interpretation that Robert's bondage fantasy reassured him that he wasn't hurting his wife. When he was about three and a half years old, he used to become restless and would often dash around his family's small apartment, engrossed in his own imaginative games and adventures. His mother would get upset, develop a headache, and retreat to her bedroom. On one such occasion, his mother's buoyant younger sister, who was visiting, ambushed him as he ran down the hallway and playfully held him down so he couldn't move. He enjoyed the attention of his vivacious aunt and remembers becoming sexually aroused. This memory was extremely clear to Robert, and he and his therapist immediately saw its relevance. Robert's early childhood experience with his mother led him to develop a frightening unconscious belief that he posed a danger to her. When the aunt playfully held him down, he was temporarily assured that he was not dangerous to a woman. He didn't have to worry about his aunt; he could also borrow her strength and sense of fun and so became sexually excited. As Robert became an adult, he often experienced his sexual partners as he had experienced his mother. He imagined that his self-assertion and exuberance would hurt them, and so he tended to suppress his sexual feelings. The mental image of a woman binding and dominating him helped him momentarily overcome his fear of hurting women, and this made it safe for him to become aroused.

Although Robert only imagined himself tied up, many other men, heterosexual and homosexual, frequently enact some version of a bondage fantasy. Such a man might get especially turned on when his partner is in complete control. Another man might like to be spanked or tied up. The essential psychodynamics of the situation are often exactly the same in both heterosexual and homosexual sex. The person being dominated, whether man or woman, is unconsciously reassured that he or she is not hurting the dominant partner and is not responsible for making sure that the partner is happy. Absolved of guilt, responsibility, and worry, the submissive partner can finally "let go" and experience intense sexual pleasure.

Thus far we've been emphasizing the aspect of guilt that involves worry about hurting a partner. There are, of course, many ways of hurting a loved one that are not immediately obvious, such as draining or overwhelming him or her with real or perceived needs, as the following case illustrates.

THE "MOMMY THING": THE CASE OF MATT

Matt was a thirty-eight-year-old phone-sex addict, but I didn't know it until two years into his therapy. I knew that his sex life with his wife of fifteen years was tepid and infrequent—he said that it had come to feel like "it was too much work"—but I didn't know that he was using phone sex to masturbate almost every day at work. When he finally worked up the courage to tell me, it was clear that he was terribly ashamed of his compulsion, didn't understand its appeal, and desperately wanted help to stop. He also was running up phone bills of more than seven hundred dollars a month at work and had to concoct elaborate stories to explain them.

Matt was a man who came across as eager to please others— sometimes to a fault. He had come into therapy originally because his sales job occasionally required him to act in a cutthroat fashion in his dealings with his peers, and Matt was so guilty and nervous about these situations that he had developed panic attacks. As a result of our work together over time, he began to feel more comfortable with his aggressiveness and to enjoy his job more. While proud of his success at work, Matt became particularly embarrassed when he admitted to me that he had been calling phone-sex services and had been having erotic conversations with women as an accompaniment to masturbation. He found that he could act out, at least verbally, what had always been a private daydream. There was one central fantasy to which he always returned:

> I tell the woman on the phone that I want her to have big tits. We pretend that she works for me, perhaps as my secretary. She comes into my office one day and closes and locks the door behind her. She tells me that she's been noticing that I've been staring at her tits. I nod. She asks me if I'd like to see them. I tell her yes. She takes off her blouse and bra and sits on my lap facing me so that her breasts are only inches from my face. "Do you like them?" she asks. I tell her I like them very much. She asks me if I'd like to suck them and adds that she loves to have a man suck her nipples and squeeze her breasts. I tell her that I must have a "Mommy thing" because I love the idea of nursing. She tells me that her breasts are full of milk and that I should milk them. So I start sucking and squeezing, and her breasts start expressing milk. She's getting incredibly excited and reaches down to unzip my pants and starts jerking me off with one hand while she is offering a breast to me with the other. She is moaning and gyrating on my lap, and I climax.

Matt was embarrassed about revealing this fantasy. He assumed that it meant that he was "really screwed up" and must have had a disturbed relationship with his mother, since breast-feeding seemed to be such an important theme. He wondered if there had been something sexual in his relationship with his mother or if he had been weaned too early.

Despite frequent inquiries about, and reconstructions of, his childhood experiences, however, it did not seem to be seductiveness or weaning that troubled Matt when he was growing up. Instead,

Matt saw his mother as an anxious woman who was constantly complaining about various physical ailments. According to Matt, she took lots of pain medication, tranquilizers, and antidepressants, and she was frequently in bed with headaches, stomach aches, muscle pains, or gynecological problems. Matt saw his mother as weak and fragile, rather than seductive, and he worried about her a lot. In addition to being worried, he was also a rather lonely boy. An only child, Matt remembered many days playing alone in his room, his mother holed up in hers, having to be quiet so as not to disturb her. Matt's father was often away on business. When he was home, he was frequently withdrawn or drunk in front of the TV.

As Matt came to see that he felt neglected, not seduced, by his mother, he realized that as a child he must have felt that she was too preoccupied with her physical suffering to tune in to him very much. Matt became his mother's caretaker. He would bring her medicine, listen to her complaints, sometimes call the doctor on her behalf. He became sensitive to her moods, could tell in an instant if she was in pain, and could shift immediately into a solicitous, caretaking mode. All the while Matt felt disconnected and rather grim inside. He developed the pathogenic belief that he was undeserving of caretaking, that his needs were burdensome and greedy, that a woman would experience giving to him as depleting, and that he would have to prove himself worthy of any caretaking he received from that woman. He felt tremendously guilty about need of any kind. Since his mother's emotional tank was empty, Matt experienced his normal and legitimate needs for nurturing as coercive. This was why his sexual relationship with his wife felt so onerous.

In this context it is easy to understand how Matt's fantasy worked. In his phone-sex scenario the woman wants to give to him and is gratified by giving. She *wants* him to take from her, to suck from her breasts. Maternal nurturing doesn't hurt or deplete her.

His wish to take is exactly matched by her wish to give. To Matt, large breasts symbolized women who had a lot to give to a man. Matt liked the image of a baby suckling because it evoked an image of a woman who herself felt nurtured in the process of nurturing her child. In Matt's unconscious mind, such an image nullified his picture of a mother who was too preoccupied, too burdened, to take pleasure in giving to her son.

When Matt was able to see why his phone-sex fantasy was so gratifying, he felt more sympathy about his own sadness and loneliness as a child. Self-compassion often increases when a patient comes to see how a disturbing behavior or feeling was formed in childhood. Matt's primary experience of women was that they were depressed and preoccupied, an experience that would make it difficult for him to sustain any kind of sexual excitement in a relationship. Since Matt expected that women didn't have the capacity or inclination to devote themselves to a man's pleasure or to their own, he felt guilty about wanting such a thing.

Matt didn't want to have sex with his mother. In order to get excited, he needed to create a woman who was turned on by mothering him. Unfortunately, he believed a real woman with whom he had a real relationship couldn't perform the same function. His pleasures required a toll call.

Matt's relationship to phone sex had many of the characteristics of an addiction. In a sense, our sexual fantasies can sometimes seem to have addiction-like properties, not simply because we feel desperately driven to have them or because abstaining from them produces uncomfortable feelings of withdrawal, but because sexual fantasies, like other addictive substances, are intended to tranquilize the anxieties associated with pathogenic beliefs. In some cases the parallels to addictions are striking and obvious in the sense that the person simply cannot get aroused at all without the use of the fantasy, or that without it the person feels incapable of pleasure and excitement. Most of the time, however, our fantasies and preferences are not obligatory. We can and do get aroused by a variety of stimuli and scenarios. Our libidos are somewhat flexible but not infinitely so. Sexual fantasies and preferences are unconsciously created because they are the *best* solution to the psychological problems associated with our pathogenic beliefs. Therefore, we are drawn, either in practice or in fantasy, over and over again, back to some version of these particular stories.

Unlike other addictions, sexual addictions can often lose some of their compelling power as a result of understanding them. In Matt's case, the key was not only understanding what drove him to the phone, but his gradual and, at first, tentative willingness to talk to his wife about his inner experiences of loneliness and guilt. Matt explained to his wife about his sense that his needs would burden her, that she'd feel drained by him. His wife, to his surprise, was receptive to Matt's newfound honesty and proved it in an interesting way. She greeted him one evening in sexy lingerie and told Matt that tonight he wasn't going to have any say about what happened in bed. She was in control. She made him lie down, completely still and silent. She made love to him, and Matt had an intense orgasm. Matt's wife was able to fulfill the same needs as his phone partners, namely that he be able to receive pleasure without any responsibility, without having to make a woman happy, without worry or guilt. Like his fantasied phone partner, his wife now seemed happy to give and expected nothing in return. It turned out that, for her own reasons, this kind of sex was quite exciting to his wife, and Matt was gradually able to increase his sexual pleasure in his marriage, which brought him and his wife closer.

FETISHISM AND SEXUAL AROUSAL

People who inhibit their sexuality as a result of feeling unconsciously worried and guilty about hurting their partners can free themselves up with a wide range of fantasies and sexual preferences. Jan's rape scenario, Manny's slaves, and Matt's phone sex are but a few of these sexual remedies. Another class of solutions to the problems of guilt and worry are called *fetishes*.

When we reduce something human to the status of a thing, or imbue things with human qualities, we are said to be *fetishizing* them. People often use fetishes to become aroused. In these cases, the function of fetishes is to eliminate any guilt and worry that might interfere with sexual excitement by eliminating the human dimension of the other person. Consider an example of an extreme sexual fetish: the fantasy or enactment of sex with animals. Whether it's Catherine the Great with her horse or shepherds with their flocks, the idea of sex with animals has long existed in Western culture. Often, for women, the focus of such a fantasy is on the size of the animal's penis or, more generally, the "animalistic" nature of the beast's desire. We think about "animal" passion as an intense passion that doesn't obey social rules or restraints. It is pure sex, its crucial ingredient being that there is no pretense of an exchange between two complicated and consenting people. As a result, the woman can surrender to her own sexual passion with impunity. For a man, the appeal—when there is one—is similar. He can use an animal without having to worry about his partner because his partner is not human. The animal's passion and genitals are fetishes. A fantasy of sex with an animal negates any irrational beliefs that we are obliged to feel empathy and responsibility for the interior states of others, beliefs that put a damper on sexual excitement.

A more common example of a fetish is clothing. Many people find articles of clothing arousing. Some people, usually men, find shoes especially exciting, particularly high heels. In the man's un-conscious mind, it is not the shoe itself that is arousing but what the shoe represents. What does a spike heel symbolize? Usually, in the unconscious mind of the shoe fetishist, it represents a strong, powerful woman. Sometimes such a woman is called a *phallic* woman because in our culture a powerful woman is seen as having a masculine edge. In addition, the high-heeled shoe is fetishistic in this way because its long, pointed form can unconsciously suggest the image of a penis. Obviously, such "phallic" women need not be masculine in any conventional sense. It might be more fair to say that, in the mind of the shoe fetishist, the femininity of the phallic woman is a tough and pointed one.

Although the excitement is triggered by the image of a high-heeled shoe, ultimately the shoe itself is not the cause of the man's sexual arousal. The shoe is only the tip of the psychological iceberg. The man is actually getting turned on by the fantasy of a strong woman because such a woman is tough enough to stand up to the in-tensity of the man's sexual desire and consequently isn't a woman for whom the man has to feel responsible and worried. The masculine toughness that the high-heeled shoe symbolizes helps the fetishist feel safe from the debilitating effects of his guilt toward women.

Other people fetishize parts of the body. He's a "tit man" or "leg man." She likes men who are "well hung." Any quality of appearance or manner can be fetishized. Someone might get turned on by hard-ness, size, youth, or a certain kind of hairdo. In all of these cases, a great deal of meaning and energy are packed into something that might be quite trivial. The *part* is treated as if it were the *whole,* or, conversely, a whole being is reduced to a part. The relationship with another person is mediated through that partial characteristic, that thing.

There are fetishistic elements in the sexual fantasies of most peo-ple, people whom one would never describe as fetishists. While some men—shoe fetishists—live for the sight of a woman's shoe, for others the attraction might be more subtle or subliminal. While some women *only* get aroused by being sexually involved with a "bad boy," many women might find certain aspects of ruthlessness attractive but do not *need* them to become aroused. In other words, there are often fetishistic qualities to someone's preferred route to sexual pleasure without that route being dominated by these qualities. We can learn a lot about the general issue of sexual arousal by looking into its more extreme or flamboyant forms.

An interesting example of a fetish is the attraction some people have to shiny leather, rubber, or latex clothing. This clothing, usually tight and formfitting, suggests some a kind of second skin, but one that is hard, tight, smooth, and shiny—not soft, vulnerable, shaggy, blemished, or otherwise imperfect. The image of such a skin, to its wearer and audience, unconsciously counteracts feelings of worry or guilt, as well as feelings of shame or insecurity. The reassuring fantasy that one of my women patients had while wearing such an outfit was that she was strong and invulnerable, not weak and insecure as she actually felt. Thus reassured, she could get turned on. A gay male patient of mine was attracted to leather on men because he associated the look with a hard-edged "top," who could dominate him and thus counteract his guilt about hurting others. Another patient had a fantasy of being completely bound up in a rubber suit. This man also had fantasies of being playfully tied up by young boys while they excitedly danced around him. For him, the issue was his fear of his own power to hurt others were he to let go of his self-control. The rubber suit, as well as the scenario in which he is tied up, served as antidotes to his feelings of destructiveness and guilt and thus led to an unleashing of his sexual excitement.

Race is also often fetishized in our society. Skin color, like clothing, hardness, or body parts, can be a "thing" that the unconscious mind uses to represent human qualities. Some Caucasians have a fetishistic relationship to African-American men. A black man is consciously and unconsciously associated with large, phallic sexuality. Blackness itself becomes the fetish, evoking meanings unrelated to color. These meanings don't have to be sexual but often are. A white woman may be sexually drawn, in fantasy or in reality, to a black man precisely because she fetishistically invests his skin color with meanings that permit her to get aroused. The real man becomes a one-dimensional stereotype in her mind. His "blackness" means that he is "other," different and separate from her known universe. In addition, his color is also associated in the white woman's unconscious mind with an inferior social status. Because of these differences, she allows herself to experience him as if he did not have a complex internal life that contained feelings and vulnerabilities just like her own. In her unconscious, he is alien, almost thinglike. Furthermore, the black man is often psychologically represented as primarily a sexual being, a creature with a large penis with whom the white woman can become extremely aroused. She doesn't need to worry about being judged by him because of his lower social status. She doesn't have to worry or feel guilty about him because he's not like her, fully human, familiar, and knowable. A white man is *like* her; a black man is not. She can surrender to her own excitement because she has reduced him to the level of pure animal sexuality. She uses her racial stereotype to overcome a pathogenic belief about hurting or overwhelming men and is therefore able to get excited.

These fantasies, racist as they are, suffuse our culture. For white men, the perception of African-American men is often similar to that of white women—large, phallic, and frightening. To the heterosexual white man, however, this perception is usually tremendously threatening. In addition, white men may also have a fetishistic view of African-American women as primarily sexual in much the same stereotyped way. A male Caucasian patient of mine occasionally went to see a prostitute and would choose only a black woman. He created and maintained the fiction that the prostitute "really had a good time" because, in his mind, black women really liked to have a good time. Her skin color symbolically represented a capacity for unbridled pleasure. He also always chose women with large breasts because they symbolized to him a woman who wanted to give her man pleasure. His own mother was an incredibly bitter woman, and, most of the time, his wife seemed worn and haggard to him. He grew up burdened with a sense of helpless responsibility for making women happy—a pathogenic belief that threw cold water on his everyday sexual interest. His fetishistic fantasy about race—embodied in his choice of a large-breasted black woman—was an antidote to his view of women as highly desexualized, stingy, and unhappy, and, thus, permitted excitement to emerge.

A racial stereotype, an animal, hardness, particular body parts, sexual positions, all are details woven together into sexual fantasies to permit excitement. They are like tricks we play on our consciences, illusions we pretend are real. All of them make it safe to experience pleasure by negating certain imagined dangers—in these cases, the danger of hurting or worrying about the internal states of the other person.

We've seen that people often feel guilty and worried about hurting their partners with their aggressive intensity, the strength of their needs, and the ruthlessness of their desire. There is also an entire class of sexual phenomena in which the unconscious purpose is to make it safe to look. We call this phenomenon *voyeurism*. Let's examine one case of it.

VOYEURISM: THE CASE OF BOB

Bob, a twenty-seven-year-old graduate student in history, came to see me for help with his relationship with his wife of three years. Bob was worried about the fact that he rarely wanted to have sex with his wife and, when he did, was unable to perform in a way that satisfied her. The situation had gotten so bad that both he and his wife came to expect disaster whenever sex was a possibility. Bob loved his wife and desperately wanted to please her sexually, but his failure to do so haunted him and made each attempt highly charged with significance. Would he please her or wouldn't he? Would he make her happy or have to face a feeling of shameful failure? He became increasingly tentative, searching her body language for cues about what to do, and the more he worried, the less he was able to get excited and the more critical and unhappy his wife became.

Bob thought of himself as a sensitive man and felt superior to men who weren't. His wife had been in a physically abusive relationship for years prior to their meeting and repeatedly told Bob that she fell in love with him because she knew that she could trust him and that he would never hurt her. Bob had grown up in a neighborhood filled with street gangs and always fancied himself as the polar opposite of these men. "I respect women," Bob told me, "rather than objectify them like those pigs I grew up with."

Bob eventually told me that although he rarely initiated sex with his wife, he masturbated almost every day. His masturbation fantasies varied, but most of them contained a common theme: he was having sex with or, more commonly, lusting after a woman who couldn't see him. In one scenario, Bob was watching a woman dancing in a sexually provocative way behind a two-way mirror. In another, the woman was blindfolded while Bob was having sex with her. In yet another fantasy, Bob was able to make himself invisible and spy on women while they undressed. He wasn't sure why these particular fantasies turned him on so much, but he knew that the essential detail in all of them was the fact that the women couldn't see him, while he was free to inspect their bodies with prurient curiosity or lust after and touch them. He admitted these fantasies to me with embarrassment. What kind of person was he? Bob wondered. Was he some kind of closet Peeping Tom?

Bob, who was visibly uncomfortable as we spoke, went on to tell me that he also felt uncomfortable with crude sexual language. He never described having sex with a woman as "fucking" and felt uneasy with words like "cunt" or "cock." He felt that these words degraded women and reduced lovemaking to something animalistic. He admitted, however, that when a former girlfriend once responded to the slow pace of their lovemaking by whispering, "Fuck me," Bob felt at once both repelled and excited. He consciously abhorred "dirty" language, but he was aware that something in the experience of a woman using such language was also extremely arousing. He didn't understand why. Like most people, Bob knew what turned him on and off, but he didn't have a clue about the meaning of these conflicted feelings, and not knowing bothered him.

As our work proceeded, however, the secret behind Bob's sexual inhibitions and fantasy life began to emerge. Bob admitted that, deep down, he felt that if a woman were to see the extent of his lust, she would be offended. She'd be offended by the fact that he was primarily turned on by her body and not her mind, that he wanted to fondle her, to stare at her genitals, to use her body for his own pleasure, and that he didn't always want to kiss her and be gentle but to "fuck" her and do it without regard to what she wanted. He imagined her thinking, "He doesn't like me as a person; I'm just a piece of ass to him." He remembered a childhood game that the rough-and-tumble neighborhood boys used to play in which they'd boast that they were part of the "4-F Club": Find 'em, Feel 'em, Fuck 'em, and Forget 'em. Bob felt that if a woman saw his true sexual desire, she'd perceive him as just like these boys: callous, narcissistic, and indifferent to the feelings of women. Bob told me about a girlfriend who'd asked him plaintively in the morning after their first sexual encounter, "Are you going to leave me now that you've gotten what you wanted?" He described how horribly guilty this had made him feel and how extreme and anxious his reassurances were.

Bob was dimly aware that his guilt and worry about women were exaggerated. He reported that he was embarrassed to look at his naked wife, even though she explicitly invited him to do so. He felt that somehow his interest would be experienced by her as sordid, even though she told him it wouldn't. This is a good example of how a pathogenic belief can persist despite conscious awareness of its irrationality. Another example involved Bob's description of the experience of accompanying a friend of his to a whorehouse. Bob had decided that he would have a drink in the bar while his friend went to a room with a prostitute. He explained that the most uncomfortable part of the whole experience was entering the bordello. Whenever a customer entered, a bell would sound that signaled all of the women to assemble in a "lineup" and display their wares while the new client inspected them. They were dressed in revealing lingerie, spike heels, flimsy bikini underwear, and the like. The entire point of the lineup was for the customer to look at these women, scrutinizing body types, body parts, height, weight, manner, and color to decide which one was most appealing. The man was not *supposed* to care about them as people. Bob became acutely embarrassed and rushed off. Even though the situation sanctioned exactly what Bob most desired—prurient looking and lusting—he felt ashamed and fearful that acting on his desire would be offensive to the women. He reported a similar dynamic occurring at a strip show where a woman would dance up to where he and his buddies were sitting and, in exchange for a tip, spread her legs so that they would have a clear view of her genitalia. He felt embarrassed and then felt silly for his reaction. His rational mind knew that she was explicitly inviting him to objectify her, to use a part of her body as an object of excitement without any expectation of "respect." But his unconscious mind rejected this knowledge. Instead, Bob felt that he would be violating and degrading her if he did what, clearly, he was supposed to do at that moment. Bob could analyze these situations and realize that his worries about women were not altogether rational, but he couldn't help but feel them.

Bob's fantasy of looking at or having sex with someone who couldn't see him is actually a common one. It is the stuff that voyeurs are made of. Voyeurs symbolically penetrate and have their way with their imaginary partners without the latter's knowledge. The objects of their desire can't object, take offense, or retaliate in any way. It's safe for both parties. An interesting version of this fantasy was fictionalized in a book, *The Fermata,* by Nicholas Baker. The narrator has the power to stop time, to freeze all motion in the world except his own. He uses these moments to perform various perverse sexual acts on women who have no awareness of his presence. Baker's hero, like Bob, likes to watch.

There are many other versions of this kind of fantasy in our culture. There are peep shows where men enter private booths and masturbate to the gyrations of naked women seen through peepholes or two-way mirrors. Some people fantasize about their partner wearing a blindfold. Many sexual scenarios involve relating to the other's body without any connection with his or her gaze. Some people like to be sexually penetrated—and penetrate—from the rear, or fondled from behind, in part because of the lack of face-to-face contact. Eye contact can present unconscious dangers. If someone can see you, they can judge you, can see the true intent in your eyes. If Bob's wife sees him lustily watching her, she can feel hurt and used, and Bob will then have to see it in her eyes. Feelings of shame are often symbolically represented by situations in which one is on display, exposed to another's gaze. Bob's shame about his sexual peeping could be alleviated by avoiding eye contact.

If fantasies help avoid the guilt of hurting and the shame of desiring the other, how do such irrational feelings arise? In Bob's case we had to look into his childhood. In the course of growing up, Bob had developed certain ideas, often unconscious, about who he was and who he was supposed to be. We discovered he had come to feel that his wish to be a rough-and-tumble boy—a boy confident in the world and with the opposite sex—would hurt his mother. This was never explicitly stated, but Bob inferred it from her hurt reactions to his going off to play "with the boys." His memory of his mother was that she was something of a martyr. Her husband, Bob's father, had run off with a younger woman when Bob was ten years old, and his mother had struggled to support Bob and his younger brother. She couldn't ask for help from anyone, even when it was clearly available. When Bob's brother was in the hospital for a serious childhood illness, his mother, who couldn't drive, walked five miles to and from the hospital every day, even though her neighbors had repeatedly offered to drive her.

Bob grew up determined to be a "good boy" so as not to add to her burdens. He remembered vowing that he wasn't going to hurt her like his father had, unconsciously inferring that his normal masculine assertiveness and boyish exuberance were equivalent to rejecting her. If his mother wasn't having any fun, why should he? He felt that his mother didn't really love and admire men very much, and Bob unconsciously worked hard *not* to act like too much of a confident man lest his mother become threatened.

As he grew up, Bob generalized from his mother to other women. He assumed, in obedience to his pathogenic beliefs, that no women would want him to act too sexually confident, masculine, and assertive, that women were instead sensitive creatures who might easily feel offended. It was almost as if he suppressed his normal phallic masculinity and became "one of the girls" in order to reassure the woman he was with that he didn't pose a threat to her. According to Bob's sense of how the world worked (formed in large part through his experiences with his mother), women felt threatened by men's sexual interest unless such interest was balanced by a corresponding interest in the woman's interior world. Therefore, unabashed staring at a woman's breasts or genitals would be inherently offensive to a woman because she would interpret this interest as selfishly indifferent to other aspects of her life.

It is easy to see, then, how Bob's sexual fantasies functioned perfectly to allow him to get excited. By insulating himself from the woman's direct perception and awareness, he could feel safe enough to stare and play to his heart's delight. He could be as randy, prurient, and self-centered as he wanted without the woman feeling offended or hurt. The details of the daydreams might change, but the essential theme of his invisibility was present in all of his fantasies.

Understanding these dynamics was liberating for Bob. In a sense, he "came out of the closet" and felt less "dirty" and "perverse" about his fantasies. Now that he understood them, he was able to talk to his wife about some of his inhibitions, which then enabled her to reassure Bob that she *liked* to be watched and aggressively desired. With the help of his new insight and his wife's reassurance, Bob and his wife's sexual relationship greatly improved.

In a social atmosphere of apparent permissiveness, in which we are being constantly stimulated by images of hedonistic consumption and sexual freedom, it may seem as if guilt is no longer as central to human psychology as it once was. My clinical experience tells me that this is not so. The forms that guilt takes might change with time, but the importance of it remains. I would speculate that while conscious feelings of sexual guilt may have decreased historically, as cultural mores have become more permissive, unconscious feelings of guilt, worry, and responsibility for others have not. Sexual fantasies still have an important job to do.

3

Born to Lose: Sexual Fantasies as Antidotes to Shame and Rejection

An absence, the decline of a dinner invitation, an unintentional coldness, can accomplish more than all the cosmetics and beautiful dresses in the world.—Marcel Proust

It is human nature to overestimate the things you've never had.

—Ellen Glasgow

Guilt is not the only feeling that stifles sexual excitement. Self-critical and deprecating feelings of all kinds can inhibit our capacity for pleasure. In fact, "loss of sexual interest" is considered by mental health professionals to be a primary symptom of depression. As I hope to illustrate in great clinical detail, there are special fantasies that function to counteract depressive feelings in the same way that special fantasies seem specifically to counteract guilty ones.

We do not need experts to tell us that it is difficult to feel sexually alive if we don't like ourselves. Because sexual arousal and self-hatred are so inherently contradictory, we not only see sexuality dampened by depression, but we frequently see sexual excitement actively sought as a means of lifting depression. Whether it is promiscuity or the compulsive use of pornography, sexual activity has the property of providing a pleasurable, albeit temporary, relief from self-loathing. A person in the grip of sexual tension and excitement tends not to feel inadequate, to ruminate about mistakes, or to feel embarrassed about his or her weight. It is not only that the sensation of pleasure cannot comfortably coexist with shame and depression, cognitive beliefs that accompany these sensations are also incompatible.

Perhaps it should go without saying that we don't feel sexy when we're depressed, or that if we don't like ourselves, we won't easily feel attractive to others. However, since many sexual fantasies and preferences are unconsciously devised to overcome this type of negativity, it is important that we understand the deep level at which shame, rejection, and helplessness extinguish sexual desire. Shame involves a feeling of being repulsive to others, while sexual arousal involves a sense of being connected to others. Shame evokes an image of being judged critically from the outside. Sexual excitement feels more like a powerful current in which one is swept up. We feel shame in response to someone's contempt. We feel aroused in response to another's desire. Shame makes us want to hide. Excitement makes us want to come out and play.

Shame is but one facet of low self-esteem. Feelings of rejection, unworthiness, inferiority, self-hatred, and even helplessness are also all dimensions of low self-esteem, and they all negate sexual excitement. Consider the feeling of helplessness and its antagonistic relationship to sexuality. Helplessness is a feeling that we can't have any impact on the world. Sexual arousal is usually part of an intimate give-and-take with a real or fantasied other. Helplessness makes us want to give up, while sexual excitement makes us love life, however temporarily. While it may appear that in certain masochistic fantasies helplessness itself is arousing, it is crucial to differentiate between true and fantasied helplessness. The helplessness of a masochist being tied up or forced to submit is scripted. It is staged in the theater of the imagination. In this sense, it is completely under control and actually functions as a way to help the masochist feel safe. True helplessness is another story. True helplessness is almost always traumatic and always neutralizes sexual passion.

Feeling desire, but faced with the inhibiting powers of shame, helplessness, or other forms of low self-esteem, our unconscious minds seamlessly weave a solution through the use of sexual fantasies. In ways similar to fantasies involving guilt and worry, we construct particular sexual fantasies and sexual preferences that negate self-denigrating beliefs and feelings, thus allowing sexual excitement to emerge. In order to feel aroused, we temporarily transform ourselves from frogs into princes and princesses. Sexual fantasies undo rejections, turn helplessness into power, redeem feelings of unworthiness, and stamp out even the slimmest vestiges of depression. For just a few moments, just long enough to have an orgasm, the Walter Mitty in all of us—the ordinary person with dreams of grandeur—imagines him or herself to be sexually powerful.

LETTING IT ALL HANG OUT: THE STORY OF ESTHER

Esther came to see me because she was depressed about getting older. She reported being married to a wonderful man who adored her and deriving much satisfaction from raising three beautiful sons. "I know that to other women it must look like I have it made," Esther told me, "but I feel shut down and blue inside." She revealed that, despite her husband's reassurances that she was attractive (reassurances that I noted to myself were entirely accurate), she felt ashamed of her body, secretly mortified that she was becoming "old, saggy, floppy, and fat." Her overall self-image suffered as Esther came to feel that she had little of value to offer anyone. She didn't "bring anything to the table," as she put it, other than her ability to be a good mother.

Esther dated the origin of these feelings to the aftermath of the birth of her third child. The delivery had been difficult, and Esther had been bedridden for several weeks. She felt that while her body had "bounced back" from her first two pregnancies, this third one had permanently damaged her. She gradually lost interest in sex with her husband, despite the fact that her husband was a sensitive lover. She reported that she even felt guilty about her low self-esteem, since there was "no rational reason for it." "Isn't this ridiculous?" she asked. "I'm ashamed of feeling ashamed!" In a previous therapy Esther had been given antidepressants, but to little avail. Drugs like Prozac made her feel even more numb and flat inside.

The depth of Esther's shame about her body was revealed one day through the details of a sexual fantasy that she revealed to me during a therapy session. As has often been my experience, a patient's fantasy can almost instantly throw his or her psychological dynamics into sharp relief. Esther had been talking again about her shame about her body, offering up a harsh inventory of its flaws. "Who would want to touch such a body," she lamented. "How about yourself?" I asked her. "Do you ever enjoy touching yourself?" Esther became embarrassed. We had never talked about masturbation. "Well, sometimes," she said in halting tones. "And what do you think about then?" I asked. There was a long silence.

Esther sighed and wouldn't look at me for a long time. Finally she said that she did have one particularly powerful fantasy that she used during masturbation. She said that she was very embarrassed to tell me because "it's a young woman's fantasy, not one appropriate for an aging mother like me." Eventually, after much hesitation, with frequent stops and starts, Esther told me about her fantasy:

Two men are fucking me on a stage. It might be in someplace like New Orleans, because there is a parade, like Mardi Gras, outside, in which people are dancing naked and being very sexual, and the club is packed and rowdy. It has this intense hedonistic feeling to it. I'm on my back. One man is fucking me while the other man is kneeling at my head, leaning over to massage my breasts, and I'm writhing with pleasure. There is a master of ceremonies, an MC, a black man, and he is describing the scene for the audience, recounting in detail what's being done to me, urging the audience to notice this or that detail of what each man is doing to me, focusing on various erotic details of my body. He's dressed in leather and has a huge erection. The audience, mostly men, are incredibly turned on, surging forward to get a better look.

Despite her embarrassment, Esther intuitively knew why her fantasy "worked." She knew that her belief that her body was disgusting was counteracted by the details of her fantasy. In her imagination Esther has a body that is *so* sexy that two men are enjoying it directly, while others are enjoying it vicariously. The attention she's getting is exquisitely intense. The MC is describing everything in *detail;* the audience is *surging* forward to look. In her fantasy Esther completely and shamelessly deserves the attention.

Even though Esther was able to see how her sexual fantasy neatly circumvented a painful reality, she didn't understand all of the levels at which it did so. She didn't understand, for example, that it made her feel psychologically safe enough to feel aroused. Esther didn't understand that her underlying self-criticisms made it impossible for her to feel sexual. She felt, instead, that her shame was warranted in reality, that she didn't actually deserve to be sexual, and that her fantasy was a pathetic attempt to escape that reality.

But Esther did not, in fact, have the body she thought she had. As her husband's sexual interest clearly indicated, she wasn't undesirable. So how and why did Esther maintain her shame about her body so strongly in the face of rational evidence to the contrary?

Even if her body had changed somewhat as the natural consequence of aging and childbirth, why were these changes such a source of self-loathing and, therefore, sexual inhibition?

A particular detail of her fantasy gave me a clue to the origins of Esther's shame. I kept thinking about the MC, the only authority figure in Esther's fantasy. Why was he there? What was his importance? I realized that I knew little about Esther's relationship with her father. I found myself wondering if she was using the MC to correct something painful in her relationship with her father. So I asked her about it. Esther told me she felt that her father was disappointed in how his life had turned out. He had been a well-respected intellectual in his European homeland, but after immigrating to the United States in the 1930s found it impossible to get an academic job. Instead, he opened an antique furniture store to which he went every morning in bad humor and from which he returned every night in a similarly bad mood. While he was emotionally distant from both Esther and her mother, she perceived him as deriving vicarious satisfaction from the financial success of his sons. She inferred, as any child in her situation might, that something about her femininity repelled her father.

Esther's belief that she deserved her father's rejection is an example of a pathogenic belief formed in childhood that persists into adult life and interferes with optimal functioning. A child cannot fully understand and face the pathology of his or her primary caretaker. Esther couldn't face her father's rejection directly and so developed the painful belief that something about her femininity provoked her father's rejection. Something in *her* caused her father to act the way he did. Beliefs such as Esther's are usually unconscious and, thus, are not available for conscious review and revision. Most of us don't remember how and why we formed these types of painful childhood beliefs. They operate silently in the background, sometimes emerging into consciousness, other times doing their dirty work behind the scenes. Esther's childhood self-doubts made her prone to experience the minor physical changes wrought by childbirth as confirmation of her father's apparently low opinion of her.

As a result of analyzing the meaning of the MC in her fantasy, Esther and I saw further how her sexual daydream elegantly and theatrically corrected the pathogenic beliefs originating in her relationship with her father that generated her low self-esteem. She realized that the defining characteristic of the MC was that he was focused entirely on her femaleness. His erotic narration repeatedly drew attention to her breasts and genitals, and it was to these markers of her femininity that the crowd was irresistibly drawn. Her femininity was the star of the show. In this way, her fantasy was an antidote to the shame and self-criticism that she'd grown up feeling in the wake of her father's rejection. On the stage of her imagination, her femininity drove men wild, while in reality her father seemed to prefer boys. In her fantasy, the MC was completely attentive to her while her real father ignored her. Even the racial features of the two men were polar opposites. Rejection is white, while sensuous adoration is black.

When Esther was a young adult, she was extremely active sexually. After she got married, however, and began having children, she felt that she cut off this sexual side of her. Because of her devotion to her family, Esther felt that she no longer could behave in ways that garnered constant male validation. She was now a "Mrs." and not a "Miss" and felt increasingly desexualized. She felt that she had purchased security and love at the price of passion. As Esther aged, she felt that she had less of a natural defense against depressive self-doubts about her femininity. This is a common problem in a culture that celebrates youthful beauty and physical perfection. The natural processes of aging take away an external source of evidence that we can use to reassure ourselves against internal self-doubts.

As she increasingly dissected the microscopic details of her changing body, Esther felt a growing sense of unworthiness. Esther and I understood this as a capitulation to her father's rejection of her femininity. "Father was right," Esther's unconscious mind told her. "You aren't really deserving of a man's love." Her depressive childhood reality was her default position; and when she was no longer fighting against it through frequent sexual activity that garnered male approval, its power again held sway.

People use all the resources at their disposal to defend themselves against and to transcend painful childhood beliefs. We may become quite critical and blaming of others, an attitude based on the unconscious logic that the best defense is a good offense: the problem is in *you* and not *me*. More commonly, however, we will try to get reassurances from our environment that our self-criticisms are wrong. We might do so by achieving success at work, acquiring the trappings of wealth and status, and projecting a lifestyle of luxury and material success. External riches compensate for an internal poverty of self-esteem.

Esther's solution, however, was even more common. Her strategy was to get other people, particularly men, to desire her. Stimulating and gratifying the sexual desire of others are the perfect, if a short-lived, antidote to private feelings of shame. Esther's youthful promiscuity buoyed her up and temporarily banished the effects of her father's rejection. As a contemporary lampoon of this tendency decrees: "It's better to look good than to feel good."

The problem with solutions like Esther's is obvious. They do not address the real problem. After all, our bodies change. They age. They get fatter, weaker, and more brittle over time. If self-esteem is derived from sex appeal, and if sex appeal is based on having a certain kind of body, then what happens when that body begins to see the ravages of time? Esther was horrified by the changes in her body because, without the armor of her sexual charisma and the

nourishment of male validation, she unconsciously experienced herself, again, as the child of a rejecting father. Her past came back to
haunt her. Only her fantasy life "saved" her.

Esther's attempt to deal with her painful past did not, of course,
simply have to do with her father. Her relationship with her mother
entered into her fantasy as well, although in a much more disguised
way. Again, the details of the sexual fantasy contained the clues. I
was struck with the image of the Mardi Gras in her daydream. "It
has to be a festive, happy occasion for some reason," Esther told
me. "I always imagined that Mardi Gras was one big sexy party
where everyone was ecstatic and uninhibited." "A little bit different
than your family was growing up," I offered. Esther laughed, but
then said in serious tones, "It was my mother. She was the anti-
Mardi Gras." She went on to offer this poignant description of her
mother:

> My mother is a martyr, and there isn't anything that I can do
> about it. She is very insecure and also depressed. She's been
> overweight most of her adult life and seems to hate her body.
> She's always commenting on my figure, whether I've gained
> or lost a few pounds, how my clothes fit. She queries me about
> my various diets as if they are the key to happiness or some-
> thing. She grew up poor. She has a deprivation mentality. One
> time I bought her a beautiful antique lamp that I knew she
> would love. She did love it, but all she could say, and keep
> saying, was, "This must have been very expensive. . . . You
> shouldn't have spent so much!"

Esther winced with recognition when I pointed out how much
she shared her mother's insecurity about her own body. In her unconscious mind, Esther had an image of a mother who didn't like
her body and who couldn't enjoy herself. It was an image that

haunted and, to some extent, possessed her. "But it's my own body I hate," she argued, "not my mother's! I left my mother long ago." "Perhaps you left her physically, but she didn't leave you psychologically," I suggested.

Identification is a subtle process. On the one hand, Esther's objection was correct. Her self-hatred was hers alone. On the other hand, Esther had inferred, through her observations of her mother, her primary role model, that this was the way women were *supposed* to feel about themselves. Shame and low self-esteem were unconsciously handed down from mother to daughter. Esther's self-devaluation was an undesired inheritance.

In fact, the influence of her mother's unhappiness went beyond Esther's identification with her. What would be the psychological consequences if she were to reject her mother's unspoken sense of inferiority and instead proudly assert her own beauty and value as a woman? Can we really imagine a child growing up immune to a mother's example? Not likely. According to Esther's unconscious logic, that would represent a symbolic betrayal of her mother. Like any child in her situation, Esther had grown up worried about her mother and felt guilty about doing better than her and leaving her behind. She had to struggle hard to differentiate herself from her mother, and even though her rational mind could accept the fact that she had an objectively happier life than her mother, her unconscious mind was vulnerable to feeling guilty about it. The tension between being *like* her mother and different from her was always present. When she herself finally became a mother, the pull to identify with her own mother increased, and the mother with whom she identified was a mother who was ashamed of her own femininity and did not enjoy motherhood. Esther's sexual ennui and depression represented an attempt to stay connected with her mother and alleviate her survivor guilt. Her mother's shame became Esther's shame.

After we investigated this relationship, we could now see that Esther's fantasy was doing double duty. It was not only negating her father's rejection but was also temporarily overcoming her guilty identification with her mother. The fantasy relieved Esther's guilt because even though she was the star of the show on stage, it was not she who was running it, but a master of ceremonies. More importantly, she and everyone are ecstatic. It's Mardi Gras, pure hedonistic abandon. It is a scene that is the opposite of the grim, worried, and self-critical energy of her mother's home. In the fantasy, Esther is proud of her body and happy to invite the world's inspection of it. Esther makes sure that there isn't an inhibited, ashamed, or self-abasing mother to be found anywhere in her fantasy.

Armed with these insights, Esther's self-esteem slowly improved. It wasn't as if she suddenly felt that she could put her sexuality on display as she did in her fantasy, but she stopped discounting her husband's sexual interest in her, opened herself up again to the possibility that she was desirable, and began to feel more relaxed about sexually teasing her husband. Esther was still drawn primarily to exhibitionistic fantasies in her masturbation and still struggled at times with feelings of depression, but overall her mood—as well as her sex life—improved.

IDENTIFICATION AND THE PROBLEMS OF SEXUAL AROUSAL

Esther's fantasy illustrates a simple but important truth about human emotions, namely that they are intrinsically infectious. If people around us are happy, it's easier for us to be happy. If people around us are unhappy, it is easier for us to be unhappy. Human beings are extremely sensitive to one another's moods; we're wired to be so. In fact, our ability to understand one another is based in part on an ability to empathize with one another's inner states. This is part of being social animals. As John Donne said, referring to our inescapable interdependence, "No man is an island."

This interdependence is most visible in childhood. A patient of mine reported that he always felt blue in the late afternoon and didn't know why. Eventually, he remembered that he had felt this way as a child and that it was associated with coming home after school or after an afternoon of playing outside with his friends. His mother was often depressed and preoccupied, and the mood of the house was dark. My patient resonated with this depression and carried this experience around as a memory that was almost physical in nature. He had never thought of it as a memory, but in fact he was experiencing its repetition each afternoon. He "remembered" with his body and his mood.

In addition to this kind of general process of osmosis, a child will often identify with a parent's moods in an effort to preserve some kind of attachment to that parent. Sharing depression is better than sharing nothing at all. Moreover, the child will feel guilty about being happier than the parent because of a belief that the parent will be hurt or feel betrayed by the child's good fortune. Survivor and separation guilt make it difficult to feel better off than, or different from, others for whom we care.

We also regularly identify with the traits that we most abhor in our parents. If our mothers were martyrs, self-sacrifice will tend to become our default position. If our fathers lost their tempers and bullied us, we'll tend to do so to our own children. We can and do often work hard to overcome and transcend these identifications. My professional life as a psychotherapist is devoted to helping people do just that. But doing so is difficult. As children, we not only lacked an alternative model with which to identify, but we invariably felt that being part of a bad family was better than having no family at all.

When a child of depressed parents grows up, he or she will tend to especially identify with the sadness of other people and have a hard time maintaining an upbeat mood in the absence of external reinforcement. This is why so many sexual fantasies are populated by carefree people or, at least, by excited and aroused people. If the people in the fantasy are not weighed down emotionally, it lends permission to the person who is fantasizing not to be weighed down either. In general, we all feel uplifted when we're around people who are happy, but this is particularly important for people whose emotional default mode tends to be depressive.

In the sexual sphere, this dynamic is especially relevant because unhappiness is usually an erotic turnoff. Since we all intuitively know that sexual excitement is incompatible with depression, when pleasure makes its appearance in a fantasy, it almost always functions as a marker of the other person's well-being. The most bizarre, violent, kinky, degrading, and twisted sexual activity may be taking place in someone's daydreams or sexual practices, but the actors involved are usually all turned on. Our minds unconsciously infer that if everyone is aroused, then no one is really sad or hurt. Everyone had a good time in Esther's Mardi Gras.

THE MAN ON THE BOTTOM: THE CASE OF GLENN

Glenn sought out therapy in order to help him achieve his goal of developing a long-term romantic relationship. Twenty-eight years old and gay, Glenn had had a series of short-term relationships that always foundered in one of two ways: he either felt rejected and unimportant and so left, or else he got bored with his partner's dependence and got rid of him. Glenn had begun to make a name for himself as a medical researcher and felt increasingly secure in the work arena, but he wanted help with his difficulties in love.

I liked Glenn immediately. He was charming, funny, and self-effacing. He was quick to smile and appeared to consider my suggestions thoughtfully. After a while, however, I also began to sense that Glenn's smooth exterior hid more than it revealed. His surface charm was not entirely believable. In fact, there were moments when I had the feeling that I didn't really know Glenn at all, that I wasn't sure if there was a "there" there, and if there was, it might be a lot more troubled than was apparent from the surface. Because he seemed to be working seriously on understanding his problems, however, I initially kept these intuitions to myself, deciding to wait until I felt I had more solid ground on which to explore them.

The opportunity to do so arose one day when Glenn was describing a stressful encounter with his boss. His boss had unfairly criticized him, Glenn said, about faulty statistics that Glenn had included in a research report. He felt ashamed and anxious during and after this encounter, he said, but quickly went into a long dissertation with me about how criticism was helpful, how he shouldn't take it personally. He told me that he had tried to be "mature" in his meeting with his boss and had even thanked him for the helpful feedback. I asked him how it felt to be sitting with his boss thanking him for his own humiliation.

Glenn laughed nervously, paused, and then slowly said, "I actually felt like I wasn't in my body, that I wasn't real . . . I was watching myself act like a 'mature' adult, but wasn't connected to what I was saying." I asked him if this sense of not being real, of "acting" like someone he thought he *should* be, was a common experience. He said it was and that sometimes, when alone in his laboratory, he would briefly get a strange sensation that he was playacting the role of scientist, and he imagined that one day it would become obvious to others that he didn't belong there. I mentioned to him then that I had the sense that he was often disconnected from what he really felt and wondered if he worried that there wasn't anything really there. He laughed a bit and told me that when he'd seen the Woody

Allen movie *Zelig,* he felt that it was the story of his own life. He worried that, like Zelig, he had no core self and, instead, went through life changing identities like clothes.

This insight was extremely important to our work. We quickly saw that Glenn's difficulties in his personal romantic life had to be related to this same sense of disconnectedness and fraudulence. How could he develop real intimacy with a partner when he felt so detached from himself and others? It was at this point that Glenn told me about his sexual cruising and intense involvement in casual sex. Glenn's practice was to go to his office in the evening, under the guise of working, and sit by his window, which overlooked a bar frequented primarily by gay men. He would sometimes sit in an almost trancelike state for hours, just looking and waiting. Sooner or later he'd make a special type of eye contact with someone passing by. The someone would come up to his office for quick sex.

Glenn felt that he was addicted to this kind of stationary cruising. He felt that he could lose himself in it for hours. "It's somehow about connection. I'm waiting." Glenn would usually feel momentarily better after the encounter, but it wouldn't last for long. Why did his connections have to be so dehumanized, brief, and non-emotional? Why did he have to wait and watch rather than go after what he wanted?

Glenn's practice of voyeuristic cruising contained the same dynamics as a sexual fantasy. The entire scenario was similar to a daydream. In fact, Glenn's experience of it *was* dreamlike. He wasn't fully present, except as a body. If sexual fantasies, with their corresponding sexual preferences, are a door into the unconscious mind, what would we be able to infer about Glenn's psyche from his cruising? Because sexual fantasies and preferences are significantly about safety, the details of their choreography are intended to create the conditions of psychological safety so that the person can get aroused. Casual sex with strangers, then, must have unconsciously reassured

Glenn that his worst fears wouldn't be realized. But what *were* his fears?

Because Glenn required anonymity, the dangers had to involve being known, being intimate. We eventually discovered that Glenn had a deep pathogenic belief that he was an insignificant and defective person with whom anyone of value would not be associated. He felt that beneath his attractive exterior lay a damaged self that would at best bore and, at worst, repel people. Glenn, therefore, kept his shameful self hidden behind charm and intelligence. He also hid it behind various forms of conspicuous consumption and behind occasional drug use. The price he paid was, not only a sense of fraudulence, but a feeling of great loneliness. Glenn sat at his window longing for connection but terrified of it. He felt that the best he could have was a quick and emotionally superficial sexual encounter. At least then, he imagined, the other person wouldn't expect anything of him, couldn't possibly be disappointed or repelled, and would leave the encounter satisfied. In addition, he set things up so that potential sex partners chose *him*. All Glenn had to do was sit at his window, on display, and look inviting. The other man did the choosing, thus mitigating Glenn's fear of reaching out and being rejected.

Glenn's sense of insignificance and defectiveness made a lot of sense in the context of what we had come to understand about his family. His parents were, for different reasons, utterly oblivious to their son's needs. His mother was severely depressed, and his father, an investment banker, was completely obsessed with work and money. Glenn told me story after story in which the themes of neglect and invisibility were prominent. He remembered frequent occasions in which his mother "forgot" to pick him up from school, leaving him standing outside, often in inclement weather, while his peers were picked up and taken home. Glenn described childhood injuries and illnesses that were never noticed, homework that was never supervised, and a social life that was nonexistent. His parents fought bitterly and would then make up by going away together on a vacation, leaving the children in the care of a housekeeper. Glenn, furthermore, was obese as a child and ruthlessly mocked and bullied at school, so much so that he would spend his school day anxiously planning his escape routes. His most powerful memory from childhood was sitting alone in his room for hours, reading comic books, drinking root beer, and eating potato chips. It was a grim and lonely environment. No wonder he had trouble with intimacy.

The centrality of shame and rejection in Glenn's psyche was clarified further when he eventually described the sexual details of his one-night stands. He always assumed the submissive or receptive position during sexual intercourse. He was known as a "bottom" in the gay community. "I like to be fucked," Glenn told me. "I'm never the 'fucker.'" I inquired about the unvarying nature of his sexual activity. Did he *ever* want to be on top doing the penetrating? Glenn said that, yes, he did sometimes want to experiment with being a top, but he knew that he never could, though he didn't know why.

I suggested to Glenn that perhaps it was safer being the bottom, being the more passive one. Glenn acknowledged that the thought of being a "top" was anxiety provoking. I pressed him: "What is the danger?" Glenn said that he didn't want the responsibility, "the responsibility of being a good top, of doing it right, of staying hard and satisfying my partner. It's too much responsibility." "But why would you fail?" I asked. "Why would this be a risk?" Glenn didn't know. He just knew that it was safer being a bottom. "Then, at least, you know that the guy is happy, that he's doing what he wants. He's getting off."

At first, this sounded a lot like a familiar story of guilt and worry. However, it seemed to me that Glenn wasn't primarily worrying about hurting his partner by being too selfish. He was more worried about boring or irritating other people as a result of his view of himself as defective. I ventured the interpretation that at least, in his casual sexual encounters, when he was a bottom he was sure that he had something that his partner wanted. He could guarantee that the other person was satisfied because he let that person call the sexual shots and take complete charge of the situation. In this way, Glenn's worry about his insufficiency and inferiority could be counteracted, in practice and in fantasy, making it safe enough for Glenn to get aroused. Glenn agreed with this interpretation and immediately told me that when he did get into relationships, he would often choose men who were poor and whom he would shower with expensive gifts. He thus had something else that the other person would need and want.

Glenn made slow but steady progress in his therapy. His work with me did not primarily revolve around his sexual peccadillos or fantasies but, instead, around issues of his self-esteem. He struggled to acquire the belief that he was unconditionally deserving of love and attention. We gradually entertained this possibility, and a number of changes occurred. First, Glenn's performance at work improved because he began speaking up for himself and asserting his own interests. Second, he met and fell in love with a man who actually seemed to want Glenn to be happy. In the context of this relationship, Glenn still preferred to be a bottom but could begin to experiment with being a top for the first time in his life. As is so often the case when a sexual fantasy or preference is thoroughly understood, his sexual repertoire widened, even though his basic preferences remained the same.

Glenn's case illustrates an important point about sexual fantasy, namely that we need to know its meaning to understand it completely. The superficial story line of a fantasy or the choreography of a sexual preference can point us in a useful direction, but since the same story or behavior can be produced by more than one conflict, it is necessary to know more about the person. Glenn's need to be a bottom in order to get aroused looked on the surface to be a solution to his problems with guilt, much as the submissive position of the sexual masochist functions to reassure him or her that the partner is not being hurt. To Glenn, however, being a bottom solved a different problem, that of his feelings of inferiority and worthlessness. Same preference, different problem.

In order to understand someone's sexual fantasy life, it is necessary to integrate an understanding of general principles with the specific details of that person's background and psyche. For instance, our theory tells us that Glenn's need to be sexually passive has to meet the general criterion of ensuring psychological safety. This automatically limits the number of its possible meanings. It gives us the map, but doesn't tell us the specific route to take. We can reasonably generalize that something about being an active penetrator is likely experienced by Glenn as dangerous, while being a submissive recipient is safe. On the other hand, Glenn's particular history of feeling inferior and inadequate generates the specific meaning that he attaches to being "fucked" and not to being a "fucker"— namely, that only under these circumstances can Glenn be reassured that he's adequately satisfying his partner. Without a general theory, the details of Glenn's sexual life form no pattern at all. In fact, this is precisely why so many people experience their sexual preferences and fantasies as accidental, biological, or otherwise mysterious. But without understanding Glenn's unique life story, a theory about the meaning of his sexual predilections becomes a mechanical and abstract generalization and can easily lead us astray.

OTTO AND HIS FIXATION ON YOUTH

Otto tried hard to please everyone. In his early fifties, he worked as a nurse in a skilled nursing facility and was so devoted to his patients that he would sometimes spend extra time, unpaid, with them if they seemed to need companionship. He was married to a divorce attorney and described their relationship as a caretaking one. Otto would cook and clean and often console his wife, who was frequently overwrought from the stresses of her job. Otto had several long-time friendships, although he admitted that they, too, were one-sided. He would function as a sounding board to his friends, but never vice versa.

Otto began therapy with a psychology intern who consulted me about the case. In his initial sessions Otto talked at length about his dissatisfaction with his marriage. He felt that his wife was excessively needy and insecure and felt burdened by her demands that he take care of her. He was aware that he often felt cheated and deprived, but he was too guilty to talk to his wife about it. Otto knew enough about therapy and psychology to know that this pattern of self-sacrifice cut across relationships and situations, and that the origins of his frustration must lie in his childhood.

Otto's family configuration was unusual. Both parents had grown up in extremely poor and abusive families. In addition, Otto's mother had been born blind. She later married her teacher, Otto's father, whom she had met when she was a student in a special school for the blind. Her husband, himself sighted, had a serious drinking problem. The combination of her disability and childhood hardship had made Otto's mother into a bitter woman, who became progressively housebound. His father, while a respected teacher, was usually depressed at home, occasionally erupting into drunken rages during which he would often hit Otto's mother. Otto told his therapist that he never saw either parent laugh; as far as he knew, they had never enjoyed a single moment of their marriage. The primary mood in the family was one of bitter victimization. When Otto complained about anything, his parents would tell him that he had it better than they, and would go about their business as if Otto didn't exist. I had never heard a description of a family that was as gray and grim as Otto's.

Understanding Otto's childhood configuration helped him and his therapist better formulate some of his central dynamics. Otto was a prime example of survivor guilt. He unconsciously believed that he wasn't supposed to have a better life than his parents. He felt that he was supposed to take care of others and not to expect much for himself. Otto was tremendously guilty about feeling selfish in any way, and he became frequently involved in relationships in which he gave more than he received. In therapy, he soon made use of these interpretations to feel a bit better and to begin to talk to his wife about what he needed from her. Initially, she felt accused, and Otto retreated, but with the help of his therapist, he was able to get his point across to her and encourage her to give more to him.

Happy ending? Not quite yet. Otto began to feel better in every area of his marriage except one: the bedroom. Otto told his therapist that his wife was quite inhibited in bed. After intercourse, she would immediately leap out of bed to douche and return to the bedroom with a towel she would use to clean up any "mess," sometimes going so far as to change the sheets. Only then could she relax and cuddle in his arms. She liked only one position—the straight missionary. Because of his sense that his wife wasn't thrilled about him sexually, Otto began to feel bored in the bedroom. At the same time, he began to notice and fixate on his wife's physical flaws: her hips were too wide, her breasts too saggy, her derriere too flabby, her face too old, her energy level too low. He felt terribly guilty about his critical attitude and to compensate frequently told his wife how beautiful and sexy she was.

Otto and his therapist worked on this problem during the first year of therapy and developed some important insights. Otto felt guilty about his selfish wishes to focus on his own pleasures. It was as if he was unconsciously reacting to his wife as if she were his mother. Like his mother, Otto's wife appeared to him to require a high degree of attention and hard work to be satisfied, and yet, in the end, she rarely was. Otto and his therapist came to understand that his wife's physical flaws represented, in his mind, her damaged self-esteem and emotional neediness. He had unconsciously equated her emotional "problem" with a physical one. She was damaged, and he was supposed to fix her, as he had always tried to do with his mother. As Otto came to understand his guilt better, he was able to be a bit more aggressive, taking charge more in the bedroom, and was surprised and delighted to find out that his wife enjoyed it. While it was a good beginning, however, both Otto and his therapist felt that his guilt and worry about his wife, while important, weren't the whole story.

More of it emerged when Otto felt safe enough to talk to his therapist about his sexual fantasy life. The subject came up during a session in which Otto was again talking about his guilty fixation on his wife's physical flaws. His therapist suggested that perhaps he and Otto had been overlooking something obvious. Perhaps Otto focused on his wife's flaws because it helped him feel more separate from his wife. Just as children often avoid someone with "cooties," Otto responded to his wife's physical flaws as if they were contagious. By selectively reacting to things he didn't like about her body, he created an experience of her as a damaged object *over there* that repelled him, rather than as someone he was close to who might "rub off on him." Devaluing his wife enforced his sense of separateness and put an emotional distance between them. Otto reported that he did have a strong impulse to get away from his wife when he noticed her imperfections. He then admitted that sometimes in the middle of the night, he'd sneak off to the bathroom, where he'd masturbate to pornographic pictures of nubile teenage girls.

"I sometimes even imagine that I'm with such a girl," Otto confessed with great embarrassment, "when I'm having trouble keeping it up with my wife." With the therapist's encouragement, Otto gradually revealed more of the details of his fantasies:

> My lover is extremely happy and loves what I'm doing to her because it all is new to her. Her skin is smooth, almost like it's new. Everything is fresh and exciting and full of wonder. I'm introducing her to incredible sensations in her body that she's never felt before. I'm sucking her tits, and she's amazed at how big her nipples get. I teach her about my cock, and she's squealing with delight at how it feels. . . . She comes repeatedly, over and over.

Otto was extremely ashamed of these fantasies, not only because they seemed disloyal to his wife, but also because they made him feel like a dirty old man. Despite the fact that Otto, like the rest of us, had been drenched with erotic images of teenage girls—whether they took the form of fashion ads or characters on TV—he still felt that his fantasies were deviant. He worried that even his own therapist would be judgmental and moralistic and thus had not revealed these thoughts until he felt safe enough to do so. Still, Otto repeatedly reassured his therapist that he would never remotely dream of acting on his fantasies, although he admitted that he felt addicted to the images.

"The girl is perfectly designed to get you excited," his therapist responded. "She's the opposite of your wife, who is flawed. It's OK to be close to her because you can identify with her newness, her enthusiasm, her sense that her life is all ahead of her. It picks you up, like plugging into an energy source, rather than pulling you down." Otto agreed and added, "It's also that I can do no wrong."

Otto could get turned on by his fantasy nymphet because it was safe to do so. The psychological danger with his wife stemmed, not only from his guilt, but from his identification with her. He loved his wife and felt emotionally connected to her. This made him enormously sensitive to anything negative, troubled, or emotionally out of balance in her. This process, common in couples, was tremendously exaggerated because Otto had been so impaled by his parents' misery and bitterness. He was exquisitely aware of, and reactive to, a woman's displeasure. He couldn't easily separate himself from his wife and maintain his own positive feelings without then feeling totally disconnected from her. His therapist and I came to understand that Otto struggled to maintain his boundaries in whatever way he could even if that meant exaggerating his wife's physical flaws and unconsciously using his feelings of disgust to rationalize his turning away from her.

The image of youthful, spontaneous sexuality solved Otto's problem of identification. In fantasy, Otto could share the girl's upbeat sense of wonder and excitement rather than her human frailty. The nubile teenage girl precisely counteracted the image of a grim and stressed mother or wife—a woman beaten down by the world—images that were symbolically represented by the small physical changes in his wife that Otto chose to focus on and be repelled by. In the pornographic images he created, Otto found the following unconscious equation: youthfulness=unblemished=unspoiled= spontaneous=optimistic=excited. With such a partner, Otto's own Lolita, he could borrow from her energy bank and overcome the danger of identifying with a grim wife or mother.

So what happened to Otto and his fixation on youth? The answer is that Otto never relinquished this particular fascination. He still masturbated to images of young women and admitted that he used such images sometimes when he was having sex with his wife. What did occur, however, was that Otto became more accepting of his wife. He found ways to get around his instinctive critical response to her physical flaws so that their sex life improved. As he understood more of the reasons behind his fetish of youthful femininity, he was able to let himself get emotionally closer to his wife, to become more accepting and tolerant of her "flaws."

Otto's case illustrates the way social and cultural pressures burrow into the deepest levels of our psyches, as well as the way that these deep psychological dynamics make use of cultural symbols to express themselves. The appeal of Lolita images, however, derives not only from our socialization but from the efforts of our unconscious minds to solve highly personal and idiosyncratic problems of self-esteem. Such efforts to counteract our insecurities make use of what the media machine provides us, while at the same time this machine stimulates these same insecurities.

SEDUCING THE POWERFUL:
THE CASE OF AMANDA

In the late 1960s there were a group of women who called themselves "plaster casters." These women were not just rock 'n' roll groupies, sleeping with as many male musicians as they could. At some point in their sexual escapades, the women made plastic molds of the penises of the rock stars with whom they'd slept. The casts were sexual trophies. This phenomenon captures a powerful sexual fantasy found in many people, though more often in women than men, that by seducing a powerful other, we can come to feel special and powerful ourselves.

The fantasy has several facets and is particularly meaningful in a culture like ours in which men have greater power and privilege than women do. First, it contains the idea that a man's power can be psychologically incorporated in the same way that his penis is physically incorporated. His glitter and privilege "rub off" on—and into—her. Second, the woman feels special because a special man has chosen *her* for sex. Something about *her* has drawn his attention. Seducing the powerful is a common strategy for overcoming, not guilt, but shame.

The fantasy of arousing a powerful man, embodied in the image of "plaster casters," is a very close cousin to a common fantasy among women of seducing a man away from his obligations, social role, or sense of personal boundaries. The fantasy tends to involve a dramatic plot in which the fantasizer is so sexually appealing that the object of desire—the teacher, doctor, married man, boss, police officer, priest, or politician—crosses a line, transgresses a boundary, or otherwise violates a code, often at great risk, to pursue her sexually. The fact that such a man seems so driven by desire for the woman is precisely what the woman finds exciting. It means that she's worth it. It was clear, for example, from Monica Lewinsky's interviews, tapes, and writings, that getting the sexual attention of the president of the United States was intensely exciting *because* he combined all the key ingredients of such a fantasy figure. He was powerful, married, and officially off-limits.

This type of sexual fantasy and scenario is more common among women because social power and authority in our society are more often located in men and their roles, and thus women more often find themselves seeking to achieve a vicarious sense of specialness, power, and status through an attachment to and identification with a powerful man. Men too, however, often entertain a sexual fantasy similar to the groupie fantasy in women. In the man's fantasy he seduces a woman who appears to be inaccessible, or such a woman is so attracted to him that she seduces him. The woman may be a teacher, a doctor, a judge, or a police officer. Or she may simply be married. The man imagines being so sexually magnetic that the woman casts aside her role, boundaries, and responsibilities in order to have sex with him. The most common variant on this fantasy involves a scenario in which a woman who is manifestly asexual—

either prim and proper or uptight and officious—gets broken down or loosened up and becomes a lusty creature, sexually driven to connect with the male fantasizer. The glasses come off, the hair comes down, and the woman goes into "heat" because of the man's sexual magnetism. We can see the workings of the same dynamics found in the fantasies of women who seek to seduce a man who is off-limits. While there are obviously differences between getting the president sexually aroused and seducing one's homeroom teacher, the common ingredient is that *the fantasizer's erotic appeal is so special and great that the other person gives up everything in order to connect sexually.*

Amanda was twenty-five years old when she came into therapy with a psychology intern whom I was supervising. She sought treatment for a depression that had been triggered by the recent loss of a job and the ending of an affair with a married man. Unfortunately for Amanda, the two events were related. She had worked for two years as the personal secretary and assistant to a well-known and charismatic Silicon Valley entrepreneur. Soon after getting the job, Amanda learned that her boss, while married, was a notorious womanizer. Nevertheless, when he started showing an interest in her, Amanda felt flattered and interested. They began an affair that Amanda described as incredibly exciting. As she spoke about the power of her attraction to her boss, her therapist found herself thinking of Monica Lewinsky's descriptions of the thrill of knowing that the leader of the free world was "in love" with her. Here was Amanda's version:

Gregory was often on TV. The press sought him out for reactions to almost every new merger or technology. It was weird, but incredibly exciting, to think that the man that CNN was interviewing on that screen had just come from my apartment, where he had been sucking my cunt and begging me to put my finger up his ass! We'd walk into a board meeting, and everyone would be extremely deferential to Gregory, and he'd just take charge; but occasionally we'd make eye contact, and he'd smile every so slightly. That little smile would give me such a thrill. It was like there was this other side of him, and it was mine, all mine; and when we were in bed, he wasn't this famous billionaire, but someone who couldn't get enough of me.

Unfortunately for Amanda, her boss eventually tired of her, and, as a consequence of their breakup, she also felt a pressure to leave her job. These losses precipitated the depression that had brought Amanda into treatment.

Just as Monica Lewinsky had had a history of seducing—or being seduced by—figures in authority, Amanda had had a similar history. She had always slept with her male bosses, and these liaisons had almost always ended in rejections and betrayals, precipitating severe depressions in Amanda and at least one suicide attempt. She knew hers was a self-destructive pattern, but her "good sense" never seemed to be able to stop her from the next poor choice. She and her therapist agreed that the problem must have something to do with an underlying sense of low self-esteem. She intuitively understood that her actions seemed to suggest that she didn't deserve a good relationship with a normal and available man, but as she complained, "Normal men bore me. And yet these big shots end up being such jerks. I must not think that I'm supposed to have a relationship that's both stable and exciting."

How did Amanda develop the pathogenic belief—a not uncommon one—that she wasn't supposed to have a relationship both emotionally and sexually satisfying? The story began in her childhood. Amanda's mother was an anxious woman who used to get up at 4:00 A.M. to make lists about what housework needed doing that day. Amanda felt that her mother didn't think much of her and described once giving a piano recital for her parents, after which her mother's only comment was, "You know, Arthur Rubinstein recorded a beautiful rendition of that piece." Her mother would regularly compliment Amanda's friends in her presence, commenting on how beautiful they looked or dressed. Amanda always felt ugly and, in fact, developed a severe eating disorder when she was sixteen, precipitating a brief psychiatric hospitalization. Her father was a quiet man who was given to sudden outbursts of temper. He would frequently get provoked by something that Amanda did or said and hit her. He never raised his hand to her three brothers, only to Amanda. She remembered incidents when she angered her father, who then chased her around the house until he caught her and hit her. By the time she was three years old, she not only felt rejected by her father, but frightened of him as well.

Amanda was able to see that she chose the men she did in order to fill an emotional vacuum. Her default position was to feel unworthy and disgusting. A "normal" man's attention wasn't enough to disprove these beliefs. His attraction to her wasn't special enough to counteract her self-condemnation. Self-hatred, as we've learned, is inimical to sexual excitement, and Amanda's unconscious belief was that only if someone in authority, someone who was esteemed and special, loved her, could she temporarily feel okay. Once her pathogenic beliefs about her defectiveness were negated by such a man's attention, Amanda felt safe enough to become sexually aroused. She repeatedly, though unconsciously, arranged to be "rescued" from her depressive self-loathing by these affairs. Not only were the men powerful, but they were all married and, therefore, ostensibly unavailable. Yet each time Amanda convinced herself she was so sexually magnetic that these men would be willing to end their marriages for her—an idea that excited her tremendously. Of course, when these men rejected her, she became intolerably depressed because such a rejection confirmed her underlying belief that she was disgusting and unlovable.

A crucial aspect of Amanda's experience of her sexual liaisons was her sense that she wielded power over the men. She saw them as losing control when they lusted after her and perceived them as somewhat helpless. Amanda felt that while they had the upper hand in their public lives, she had it in the bedroom. She reported the thrill of watching one of the giants of Silicon Valley get aroused:

Watching Gregory get turned on turns me on. He gets this look in his eyes when he's worshiping my body and then when he's touching it. It's almost a glazed look, like he's possessed. Sometimes he'll tell me that he wants me to suck his cock, and his voice has such a sense of urgency that it's like if I don't do it at that moment he'll explode or go crazy. When he's turned on like that, I sometimes have this thought that he'd do *anything* for me at that moment as long as I agreed to suck him. That's a real turn-on for me.

Amanda's feeling of power is, of course, not unusual. Our popular culture is riddled with stories and images of men willing to do anything for sex. To say that women get a sense of control, power, and esteem from turning men on and "making" them desire and worship them trivializes the complexity of this dynamic. The costs and benefits of such a strategy, and the social pressures and realities that necessitate it, have been discussed at length by others. My point is not to comment on the obvious fact that women often derive power through being the object of desire, while men derive it from being the one doing the desiring, but to explore the psychological reasons why such power can be sexually arousing to women.

It was arousing to Amanda because it counteracted her feelings of helplessness. She felt, for a moment at least, that she was calling the shots. This feeling represented a reversal of her experience in her family, as well as her experience much of the time in her current life when she felt subject to the whims of others, buffeted by their moods, never sure of where she stood. In her moment of sexual triumph, looking into the eyes of a powerful man consumed by longing, Amanda was symbolically turning the tables on her reject- ing mother and her violently volatile father because she was com- pletely safe at that moment from being a helpless victim. Power and control were hers.

What about highly exciting sexual fantasies and situations in which one of the participants is *supposed* to be helpless, for example, bound, restrained, or extremely submissive? That is different. In such formalized rituals of dominance and submission, helplessness is always more symbolic than it is real. The helpless partner is vol- untarily agreeing to the role. True helplessness in which our emo- tional or physical well-being is completely dependent on another person is actually debilitating and frightening and therefore com- pletely incompatible with sexual excitement. Amanda's fear of her father's frightening outbursts was not voluntary. Not only did she develop the pathological belief that she *deserved* his punishments, but she came to feel enfeebled, quick to defer, and fearful of con- frontation of any kind. In this state Amanda couldn't possibly feel the freedom to get excited. For her to feel safe enough to get sexually uninhibited and aroused, she needed to create situations in which she did *not* feel helpless. Getting a powerful, potentially scary pa- ternal figure to be swept away with lust for her fit this bill exactly.

Given the destructive outcome of her affairs, it is appropriate to question the real extent of Amanda's "control." Ultimately, in terms of her real life, the man held all the cards. He mattered more to her than she did to him. He was economically powerful, and she was economically marginal. The actual power balance obviously favored him. However, when it comes to the subjective experience of sexual excitement, the only relevant issue is what power meant to *her*. It was irrelevant to Amanda's unconscious mind whether she was really in control of her man. Amanda's unconscious mind was trying to solve a problem that didn't have to do with the "real" outside world but with her internal world. Her mind was trying creatively to arrange a scenario in which she could feel psychically safe, a state of mind in which the psychological dangers of childhood were momentarily banished.

With the help of her therapy, Amanda was able to confront some of her childhood traumas. Over a period of time she developed a more sympathetic attitude toward herself and toward her predicament as a child. She developed greater self-compassion, eventually understanding that she had indeed been helpless as a child, that it wasn't her fault, and that she no longer had to feel as endangered in relationship to men. When she finally left therapy, she was experimenting with the possibility that she could enjoy sex with an "ordinary" man and still feel good about herself.

The larger question of why Amanda could get involved only with unavailable and narcissistic men was crucial to her therapy, although not necessarily identical to the issues underlying her sexual preferences. It has long been my observation that women who tend to be "groupies" or who gravitate to situations in which they seduce and get involved with unavailable men are women who unconsciously believe that they don't deserve to have relationships based on mutuality. Such beliefs usually turn out to be the result of some type of survivor or separation guilt, a deep and irrational conviction that they are not supposed to have more of the good things in life than their parents. Romantic success would mean a symbolic act of disloyalty to and rejection of their families, no matter how destructive these families are.

Women who act out in this way are still working to make the best of a bad situation. They are certainly motivated to experience sexual pleasure and intimate connection, and unconsciously arrange to do so through the use of the various scenarios such as those we saw played out in Amanda's case. We should never make the mistake of assuming that psychologically healthy people have the most intensely exciting sex. Amanda's sexual pleasure was intense, even though her overall level of emotional maturity was low. The issue isn't whether her excitement in seducing powerful men was objectively healthy, but how it came to work at all.

SAFETY AND THE SEXUALIZATION OF ABUSE

Helplessness often plays other important roles in the genesis of sexual fantasies. It is quite common that children who were abused grow up and develop sexual fantasies loosely based on their abuse. Girls who were sexually molested often develop fantasies in which they are sexually abused, degraded, or otherwise enact a masochistic role. Other girls from similar backgrounds replay elements of their sexual victimization as adults by turning the tables on men and enacting roles in which they act sexually cruel and dominant—the classic dominatrix. Children who were terrorized or beaten in nonsexual ways also incorporate aspects of their helplessness into their sexual daydreams and preferences. Someone who was beaten as a child might enact or imagine sexual situations in which he or she is beaten or, on the other hand, is doing the beating. All of these reenactments reflect attempts to master intolerable and traumatic feelings of helplessness by means of a sexual fantasy.

It makes sense that sexual fantasies of domination that feature being in control could provide reassurance for the pain of helplessness and childhood abuse. When a patient of mine who was sexually abused as a child grew up and became a dominatrix, telling me that she liked the feeling of power that she had over men and enjoyed the men's humiliation, I could easily see how she was turning the tables on her abusive father and seeking refuge in power. But how can masochistic scenarios or fantasies of sexual self-abasement provide a sense of safety or mastery to a person who has been actually physically hurt or sexually terrorized?

The answer is complex. One essential aspect of a sexually masochistic fantasy is that the pain and helplessness are voluntarily created and experienced. The helplessness is not real. The masochist is always in control of the type, duration, and degree of pain that she or he endures. The adult indulging in a fantasy of sexual surrender or abasement is actually saying to her or himself: "I'm recreating a terrifying and traumatic scene, but this time I'm in control because I'm scripting the scene as much as my partner is." The "victim" in the adult sadomasochistic scenario is not really a victim. She or he is constructing a situation in which the pathogenic beliefs that stemmed from childhood abuse are being momentarily disproved, thereby creating the conditions of safety necessary to become aroused. Trauma is turned on its head. The slave turns out to be the master, and the master is sexually dependent on the slave. A game is set up in which the victim of childhood abuse finally gets to win. This is the context of safety that allows sexual excitement to emerge.

Not only in sex do people repeat traumatic situations in order to master them. After the San Francisco earthquake of 1989, a new game appeared in child-care centers all across the city. It was called "earthquake," and it involved an endless repetition of the traumatic and terrifying events of that October day. These children were mastering their fear by repeating the frightening event over and over, reexperiencing bite-sized portions of their original terror, and each time arranging a reassuring outcome by being safe at the game's end. They were the directors of the scene, not the victims of it. Human beings cannot tolerate helplessness for very long. They either shut down, fight back, or find some way to pretend it doesn't exist. This is what victims of sexual and physical abuse often do in their sexual lives.

It is easier to understand that sex creates shame than that it overcomes it. It is easier to experience sex as a loss of control than as an attempt to regain it. Nevertheless, sexual fantasies and preference negate feelings of shame and reverse feelings of helplessness. Bringing tremendous unconscious creativity to the effort, they represent the mind's constant striving for mastery and transcendence on the road to pleasure.

4

From the Conventional to the Bizarre:
Interpreting Sexual Fantasies

O happy horse, to bear the weight of Antony! . . .
—Cleopatra, William Shakespeare, *Antony and Cleopatra*

*I've tried several varieties of sex. The conventional position makes
me claustrophobic and the others give me a stiff neck or lock-jaw.*
—Sophie Tucker

When I first began writing this book, several people asked me if I
was going to include some kind of glossary in which people could
look up their sexual fantasies and find out what they meant. I imagined that such a glossary would resemble the old-fashioned "dream
books," popular in the early days of psychoanalysis, in which the
symbolic meanings of various elements of a dream were indexed and
interpreted. If someone wanted to know why he or she dreamt of
snakes, that person could look up "snakes" and perhaps learn something like "snakes are phallic symbols." I initially cringed at the
suggestion that I include a similar type of index because I believe
that such a cookbook of interpretations, whether it involves elements of a dream or a fantasy, is fundamentally misleading. One of
the main principles that guides my work is that the meaning of
something "depends on the patient." The meaning of a thought,
feeling, or behavior is intrinsically subjective and idiosyncratic, and

it is the job of the therapist to understand the world from the patient's point of view, not according to some objective formula. A snake never *always* means any one thing. Nor can a sexual fantasy of domination be assumed always to mean the same thing. It might be intended to overcome guilt in one patient's psyche, be a way of feeling special in another's, and be a method of overcoming helplessness in the mind of yet another person. When I am sitting with a patient in my consulting room, there are few universal explanations of anything. It almost always "depends on the patient."

On the other hand, a theory is no good if it can't generate generalizations. I have proposed a theory of sexual excitement that I think can be applied to everyone's fantasies and preferences. As a result of applying this theory to the fantasies of a great many patients, my own and those of other therapists, some broad patterns have emerged. Some fantasies regularly seem to be attempts to deal with guilt, some with shame, rejection, and helplessness, and some with problems of identification. It is possible to make certain broad correlations between a fantasy and its likely meaning. An erotic fantasy of being humiliated, for example, is usually created as an attempt to master unconscious feelings of guilt. Knowing this gives us a start in understanding the meaning of such a fantasy when we encounter it.

Bearing in mind that we cannot determine the precise meaning of a fantasy without knowing a lot about the fantasizer, I am going to briefly describe a wide range of fantasies and offer an explanation of what they probably mean, educated guesses based both on my clinical experience and theory. Most of these fantasies, however, did not arise in clinical situations, but were gathered from the Internet or from various collections of erotic stories. They are not presented as "cases" in which relevant family background was available or in which a therapist had the chance to conduct a serious inquiry into their meaning. Instead of an in-depth analysis of a small number of cases my intent here is to present the barest outlines of a large number of fantasies gathered from nonclinical sources, snapshots that sample some of the amazing range of creative scenarios that the human mind produces and employs in the interest of achieving pleasure.

How is it that a woman can get sexually aroused by the fantasy or reality of being slowly asphyxiated, or a man by wearing panties, or a woman by being led around by a leash? How can someone imagine or enact a situation of being urinated or defecated on and be sexually excited and not repulsed? What could it possibly be about being diapered or having one's wife be raped in one's presence that turns some people on?

The fact that these scenes could produce sexual excitement seems bizarre and incomprehensible at first glance, and yet, armed with the particular theory of sexual arousal offered in this book, we can make some good educated guesses as to their meaning. Therefore, the following list of fantasies and their possible explanations are not only intended to be a useful starting place in understanding such fantasies in the real world, but also will demonstrate the versatility, power, and efficiency of this special approach to sexual arousal.

Sadomasochistic Fantasies
MASOCHISM AND SEXUAL AROUSAL

Sexual sadomasochism is a state of mind in which scenarios—in fantasy or in reality—of pain, devaluation, humiliation, or helplessness cause arousal. We will first examine the experience of sadomasochistic excitement from the point of view of the masochist.

In order to convey the almost infinite range of masochistic fantasies that the human mind can create, I want to list and discuss a sample of postings I recently found on an Internet bulletin board, a place where people can offer opinions on a particular subject by typing and then "posting" them and inviting other visitors to the site to respond to these postings. A peculiar type of conversation gradually emerges. This particular bulletin board is dedicated to sexual fantasies. Each posting has a title, limited to a few words, that suggests the broader fantasy that will follow if the viewer clicks on and opens it. Each title is then followed by the pseudonym of the person doing the posting.

The following titles and pseudonyms were listed exactly as they recently appeared on this web site:

My Hot Wife, by Cuckold
Fuck My Ass with Your Huge Cock, by Chris
Looking for Girls to Take a Walk on My Body, by Doormat-Girl
See Me Obey? by Ass Man
Human Toilet for Women, by maleslave
Looking to Be Used, by Tina
Diapers a Turn-On, by Son
Women Kicking Men in the Balls, by John
I Want to Kiss My Lady's Ass, by Per
Bent over a Chair, by Jenni
I Need Some Blow, by Dope Fucked Slut
Sniffing Butts, by Brian
Humiliation, by Sara
I Want to Be a Slave to a Woman's Cunt, by Aaron
Situation Wanted: Houseboy, by Terri
Need a Rough Guy, by Anonymous
Public Pussy Shaving, by Ellen
Searching for a Spanking, by Chris
Hypnotize Me, by Simone
I Like to Smell Girl's Bicycle Seats, by Dingleberry David
Girls—Have You Ever Pinned Someone Down and . . . ? by Greg
Forced Feminization, by Matt

Each of these titles represents a different fantasy, a different scenario that the writer finds arousing, and yet they all share the theme of pain, submission, or degradation. Some of them are shocking, others bizarre, and still others amusing. But they all function in exactly the same way, by counteracting certain beliefs or feelings that would otherwise make sexual arousal difficult.

Without knowing the life histories of the contributors to this bulletin board, I would nevertheless guess that their fantasies are attempts to deal with unconscious feelings of guilt. The mechanism is simple: by empowering someone else to hurt or degrade them, the writers reassure themselves that they are not the ones doing the hurting or degrading. The unconscious logic is a kind of perversion of the Golden Rule: *Have others do unto you what you feel guilty about doing unto others.* Since guilt inhibits sexual arousal, its diminution produces excitement. If someone is guilty about feeling superior to others, then a fantasy about being inferior is arousing because it eliminates any trace of the crime. If someone feels guilty about being strong, then a fantasy about being weak and helpless might appease the conscience enough to allow sexual excitement to emerge.

Let's apply this general principle to the list of fantasies above. If a woman feels guilty about being stronger than men, the fantasies suggested by such titles as "Need a Rough Guy," "Looking to Be Used," "Searching for a Spanking," or "Hypnotize Me" would negate that guilt. In these fantasies, the woman is used, roughed up, or rendered helpless, and therefore she is unconsciously reassured that she poses no threat to men about whom she could feel guilty. Since these fantasied situations eliminate her guilt, she can let herself fully express her powerful sexual feelings. If a man feels guilty about feeling superior to or critical of women, then fantasies of being degraded by a woman, such as "Human Toilet for Women," "Women Kicking Men in the Balls," "Girls—Have You Ever Pinned Someone Down and . . . ?" or "I Want to Be a Slave to a

Woman's Cunt," would probably be perfectly suited to easing his conscience. In these scenarios the man has unconsciously arranged to be the victim and not the victimizer, the degraded one and not the one feeling disdain. Since women are now safe from his scorn and criticism, he can let himself get aroused by them. The details of the fantasy sometimes offer clues as to which sin is being absolved. If the fantasy is about being humiliated, it may be that the person's guilt is about feeling proud or superior. If the fantasy is about being rendered helpless, then the guilt might be about being too powerful.

Masochistic fantasies of all kinds tend to rest on psychological dynamics involving guilt. If a patient reported any of the fantasies listed above, I would be instantly alerted to the possibility that he or she was struggling with feelings of omnipotence, guilt, and worry. I would like now to examine, in more detail, several other variants of sexual masochism that we have not encountered thus far and that illustrate the workings of guilt in interesting ways.

GOLDEN OR BROWN SHOWERS

A small number of people, usually men, get aroused by the fantasy or actuality of someone, usually a woman, urinating or defecating on them. These scenarios are referred to as "golden showers" or "brown showers." Since this activity is repulsive to most people, and its power to cause pleasure probably incomprehensible, it offers us a good example of how a theory of sexual excitement based on the concept of safety can easily explain the seemingly inexplicable. As with most masochistic fantasies, the central issue here is guilt. The manifest humiliation unconsciously expiates a deeper guilt. A boy who grows up feeling guilty about feeling contempt for or shame about his mother reverses this painful situation and makes himself the object of contempt and shameful degradation. Our language offers us a powerful way to represent symbolically the act of degrading another person—we say that we were "pissing" or "shitting" on that person. In the sexual fantasy or enactment, the man is pissed or shit on, rather than vice versa. Urine and feces become the symbolic representations of the feelings of hostility that were once directed *at* a woman but are now being received *from* one.

MEN WEARING WOMEN'S PANTIES

There are men who get sexually aroused, in reality or fantasy, by wearing women's panties. The pattern often is that these men, in fantasy or reality, wear women's panties underneath their traditional masculine clothes. The "secret" presence of the panties is sexually arousing. Consider some of these postings on the aforementioned sexual fantasy web site:

Stroking in Mom's Silk Panties, by Ben
Hard in Panties, by Chris
Looking for Panty Play, by Jerking in Panties
Girls—Make Me Your Panty Slave, by Panty Guy
In Mom's Panties and Bras, by Johnnie

Why are some men aroused by wearing panties? There is a high probability that the answer is that, instead of feeling guilty about their strength or selfishness, these men are attempting to overcome guilt about their masculinity. Sometimes this guilt resulted from growing up with a father who was weak and ineffectual or a mother who was unhappy and envied men. As boys such men might have had difficulty feeling proud of their masculinity, unconsciously worrying that such pride would hurt their parents. For example, if these mothers appeared burdened and downtrodden, their sons might grow up not only feeling guilty about being too separate but about feeling superior to them and, later, to women in general.

How does wearing women's panties solve this particular problem of guilt? The mechanism is simple, but the logic is unconscious: by identifying with the very beings—women—about whom they feel guilty, these men are unconsciously absolved of their imagined sin of belonging to a different and (in their minds) preferable gender. Psychoanalysts call this mechanism "identification with the victim." Since masculinity itself has become somehow equated with hurting women, men's psyches come up with a creative solution: wearing panties. The panties function as an unconscious symbolic reassurance to women, originally their mothers, that these particular men are *not* different or superior. Wearing panties beneath masculine clothing becomes a creative compromise for such men, symbolically reassuring their mothers that the boy is their secret ally. "It's all right, Mom," the boy is unconsciously saying, "I'm only *pretending* to be a real man." With their guilt alleviated, however, these men can get sexually aroused in a masculine way by getting an erection.

DIAPERED AND TREATED LIKE A BABY

Why would a grown man or woman want to be treated like a baby, humiliated by being diapered and treated as if he or she were utterly helpless? Yet sexual bulletin boards are littered with fantasies with such titles as "Baby-fied and Humiliated" and "Want to Breast-Feed." I myself have seen two men in therapy who became aroused by the fantasy of being diapered and breast-fed. The key to these fantasies was the man's imagined lack of responsibility. Like other masochistic fantasies, these scenarios of being treated like a baby by a strong and sexy mother unconsciously relieved the fantasizer of the responsibility of making the woman happy, a responsibility that he experienced as burdensome and enervating. A baby is *supposed* to be selfish and cared for, something that these men were too guilty to allow themselves to feel as children or adults.

Additionally, the fantasy of breast-feeding was arousing because it disconfirmed the man's pathogenic belief that women didn't—and couldn't—want to give to him, but instead required *his* care and feeding. Being breast-fed symbolized a psychological situation in which the man allowed himself to take from and be given to by a woman without guilt or shame. This dynamic would be the same for women who enjoyed a similar fantasy of being infantilized. In its essence, it is not gender specific.

ASPHYXIATION FANTASIES

A very small number of people get aroused by the fantasy or enactment of a scenario in which they are being choked or in which their air supply is being cut off in some other way, as for instance, by having a plastic bag around their heads. This particular fantasy is seen more often in women than in men. Usually, the woman is being asphyxiated by a male partner who has the role of bringing the women right up to the edge of losing consciousness. Notwithstanding the fact that asphyxiation can produce sexual arousal on a purely physiological basis, in reading about these fantasies, the theme of helplessness is repeatedly mentioned. The women being choked, like the masochist being tied up, have relinquished control to another person.

Asphyxiation is an activity that is realistically dangerous but paradoxically functions on an unconscious level to establish the conditions of safety necessary for sexual arousal. While the conscious intent may be to endure and survive a dangerous state of helplessness, the unconscious intent is to overcome feelings of guilt and worry. In typically masochistic fashion, such people are likely giving omnipotent power over their lives to another person as a way of reversing and counteracting an internal tendency to feel omnipotent toward others. These people probably grew up struggling with guilty feelings of responsibility for others, feelings that made them feel too powerful and as a result overly worried about others. By reversing the situation and rendering themselves helpless and in the complete control of someone else, they can stop worrying and get excited.

DOMINANCE AND SEXUAL AROUSAL

For every masochistic fantasy or behavior, there is a real or imaginary sadist lurking in the wings. For every fantasy in which one person is aroused by being degraded, hurt, or made helpless, there is someone in a complementary role doing the degrading, hurting, or dominating. When Simone titles her fantasy "Hypnotize Me," she needs a hypnotist to make it work. When Chris asks someone to "Fuck Me in the Butt with Your Hard Cock," the complementary role is obvious. If Aaron wants to be "A Slave to a Woman's Cunt" or John to be "Kicked in the Balls by a Woman," they require women who get turned on by slaves or who like to kick men where they are most vulnerable. When people post a masochistic fantasy, they are fishing for someone with a complementary fantasy. When they find one, a conversation results, a fantasy is created or enacted, and sexual pleasure results.

Interestingly, the same bulletin board from which I culled the prior list of masochistic fantasies did not contain quite as many overtly sadistic or domination fantasies. There were a few:

Wife as My Slave, by Joe
At the Slave Auction, by Merlin
I Can Control Any Man, by Caitlin
Spank, by Punisher

Punishing My Slut Daughter, by Big John
Slave for Sale, by Boss

I think that one of the reasons visitors to this site were less likely to state explicitly wishes to dominate than to respond to the explicit invitations of masochists is that one of the key ingredients of a successful domination fantasy is that the person being dominated or enslaved is aroused by the process. The overwhelming majority of sexually sadistic fantasies, scenarios involving forcing others to submit, hurting, humiliating, or even torturing them, require the real or imagined pleasure of the victim in order to be arousing. Therefore, it is psychologically safer to *respond* to a masochistic overture than it is publicly to *demand* one. The man who enjoys a rape fantasy, or enacts one with his partner, needs to feel that the other person is aroused and therefore not really injured. The master rules only with the consent of the slave, and this consent is most powerfully conveyed by the slave's sexual excitement.

Thus, when I hear about a sadomasochistic fantasy from the point of view of the dominant party, I think that there is a high probability that the person is struggling, just like the masochist, to overcome problems with guilt. The key to understanding this process is to remember that the sadist, master, or "top" is inflicting pain and abuse on a victim who, in reality, doesn't actually feel victimized—who instead is sexually aroused. Since there is no true victim, there is no crime. Domination fantasies in which the victim is not only *not* hurt but sexually aroused powerfully disconfirm our guilty beliefs and as a result free up our sexual excitement. Let us analyze several variations on this theme.

RAPE FANTASIES

Common among men, and infrequent among women, these fantasies involve raping or sexually overpowering a partner, usually a woman. The woman objects at first, but then comes to like it. By the end, she is sexually ecstatic and a full participant in the sex. The meaning of this fantasy is that the person doing the raping is attempting to master feelings of guilt about hurting others, usually women, and so creates a fantasy in which he *appears* to be hurting her but really isn't. The woman welcomes his aggression and isn't hurt by it.

There is, however, another type of rape fantasy among men that does not depend at all on the woman's arousal. In these fantasies the erotic charge is connected to actually hurting the woman. They are arousing not because they overcome guilt, but because the man has the power to hurt and frighten a woman. This may well be the fantasy that most frequently accompanies actual rape. It is easy to see how the idea of female arousal during a rape fantasy can counteract a man's guilt about hurting women. But how can our theory account for those cases in which her real pain and fear are required for actual arousal?

One important psychological issue in these situations usually involves what psychoanalysts call an "identification with the aggressor." The rapist, in fantasy or reality, is doing to the woman what he has experienced on some level being done to him. She is getting hurt, not he. She is helpless, not he. If a man grows up having experienced himself as the helpless victim of the ruthless and frightening attacks of a more powerful person—for example, a parent—then that man will grow up with a powerful obstacle to being sexually connected to another person. Helplessness and fear, as we know, are inimical to sexual arousal. By turning the psychological tables, by being the one who is violently frightening and violating rather than frightened and violated, such a man can feel momentarily relieved of this obstacle and feel safe enough to get aroused. A man who enjoys a woman's actual pain without any fantasy that the woman is secretly enjoying it is likely a man who has somehow been, in his most intimate relationships growing up, victimized, humiliated, or wounded.

The second dynamic often seen in these types of fantasies is survivor or separation guilt. The perpetrator identifies with a sadistic parent because of an unconscious belief that he is not supposed to be healthier, i.e., less cruel, than that parent. For such a man, loving instead of hurting, symbolically represents a condemnation of and triumph over the parent. In these cases violence is a distorted form of loyalty.

MASTER/SLAVE RELATIONSHIPS

Similar to a rape fantasy, a master/slave relationship is just what it says. The person enacting the role of "master" has total control and power over his or her slave. This fantasy can be acted out in elaborate rituals in the real world or simply imagined. The psychological dynamics, though, are similar to those behind the type of rape fantasy in which the victim gets aroused, namely that the master is acting in an entirely selfish and ruthless manner without any real negative consequences. The slaves ask for a master, seek one out, and enjoy it. The master gets to be aggressively self-serving without a pang of conscience. Guilt is overcome, and sexual pleasure is the reward.

However, master/slave relationships contain another dynamic as well, one that is crucial to many sexual fantasies. *The master and slave provide each other with a special kind of attention and recognition that counteracts an internal sense of being unimportant, invisible, and without value.* For the master, the slave's devotion is evidence that he or she is important, the center of the slave's world. For the slave, the master's attention—even if this attention involves figuring out the precise manner in which pain and degradation are to be inflicted—makes the slave feel that he or she is important enough for the master to want to control or hurt. People prefer to be the object of negative attention rather than be invisible. In the master/slave relationship, in whatever form it is constructed, an intense bond between the two parties counteracts feelings of insignificance and loneliness.

INCEST FANTASIES

Incest fantasies are common. To the extent that they are acted out in the real world, they are invariably destructive to the child. In real life, childhood victims of incest grow up feeling responsible for their own violation, "bad" for having "provoked" it, worthless because they weren't protected, confused about personal boundaries, and often prone to reenact such abuse with their own children. Incest *fantasies,* however, are not necessarily so destructive. They are usually never acted out and may simply be attempts to overcome conflicts involving guilt and recognition, just as we saw in domination/submission fantasies.

It is crucial here to differentiate between a fantasy that is directly destructive to another person because it is enacted—for example, incest—and a similar fantasy that may very well reflect the fantasizer's psychopathology that is kept private. Obviously, such psychopathology may hurt other people in various ways, but in the present instance I'm distinguishing between a fantasy that is directly harmful when acted on and one that is only privately entertained. In both cases, sexual excitement results from the negation of pathogenic beliefs. I will take up in more detail the issue of private verses enacted fantasies—what accounts for the difference and its moral and psychological ramifications—in chapter 7 and the "Conclusion."

Incest fantasies take many forms. Sometimes they involve a step-parent or stepchild, enabling the fantasies to circumvent prohibitions against "real" incest. In father/daughter fantasies, whether constructed from the point of view of the father or the daughter, there are often themes of punishment. The daughter has been "bad" and needs to be punished. Sometimes the daughter is replaced by a baby-sitter. The plots vary. Often, either the parent or child is "accidentally" discovered naked, or masturbating, or in some other lewd or lascivious state. Similarly, with mother/son incest there are many variations. The mom may be a neighbor's mother or the son a neighbor's son. The son may be a delivery boy or the "mom" figure a much older sister. Sometimes the mother surprises the boy and finds him masturbating or reading pornography. Other times the boy surprises the mother in the bathroom or sunbathing. The following fantasies appeared on an Internet bulletin board of sexual fantasies:

Daughter's Slumber Party, by Mr J
Honey! I Know That You Sleep in the Nude, by Stepdad
Baby-Sitter Fantasy, by Single Father
Neighbor's Kinky Daughter, by Mr. Smitts
Mom in a Thong, by Geoff
Mom, Are You Almost Ready? by Kevin
Mrs. Robinson, by Benjamin
Mom's Boyfriend, by Angie
I Would Love to Rip My Mom's . . . by Son
Daddyluv, by Kitty
Young Lady Ditching School, by Horny Neighbor

The content of most of these fantasies is self-evident. But what are their meanings? In many cases the meaning involves a complicated attempt to overcome not only guilt but feelings of rejection. A man's incest fantasy of a sexy, seductive mother or mother figure may, on the one hand, counteract his real or imagined experience of a grim and depressed mother around whom the man, as a boy, felt worried, guilty, and responsible. He creates a fantasy of a mother who is sexy and alive. We can see, however, that the incest fantasy simultaneously disproves feelings of neglect and rejection in the man because the fantasy mother is getting aroused in a *special* way by her son, responding intensely to him, and only him, in a way that the real mother never did. The maternal incest fantasy takes care of two feeling states that normally dampen sexual desire—guilt and neglect. As a result, the fantasy enables the man to get excited.

For the mother expressing incestuous wishes toward her son, or a son-substitute, such as a neighbor boy, the function of her fantasy is similarly twofold. On the one hand, the son—inexperienced, full of hormonal pressures, and under the sway of the mother's authority—reassures the mother against fears of rejection. The son is enthralled and seduced by the mother's womanly sexuality and isn't in a position to be "choosy." On the other hand, the son's youth conveys a sexual vitality and inexhaustible carnal desire that counteracts the woman's worries and guilt about draining a man her own age. The boy is full of sexual vigor, and as a result, she is too.

Similarly, fathers' incest fantasies about their daughters or daughter-figures carry similar mixed meanings. The girls are nubile and inexperienced, open to whatever the father, or father figure, can teach them. The men are therefore unconsciously reassured against the dangers of failure, of disappointing their partners in the same way that they might feel with their wives or that they might have felt with their mothers. The daughter looks up to him and is eager to take whatever he gives her. At the same time, just as the boy's fantasy about a sexy mother counteracts the effects of having a grim one in the real world, so, too, the father's fantasy of a sexy daughter counteracts the same kind of debilitating experience of worry and guilt for unhappy mothers and women in real life. Sexy women, whether in the role of mothers *or* daughters, enable the man to disconfirm his pathogenic beliefs about women, beliefs that hold his sexuality in check. The result is the flowering of sexual pleasure.

Finally, for the woman imagining herself having sex with a father figure, either in the present or through her identification with a young and sexy daughter figure, the issues are familiar ones. In these fantasies the father is filled with desire for the daughter, providing in the process a powerful current of reassurance to the girl that she is special and valuable. This counteracts real or imagined experiences of rejection, experiences that would have given rise to feelings of worthlessness. In addition, because the father figure is portrayed as so powerful, the girl—and woman—can let go of her guilt-based sexual constraints and freely express her excitement without worrying about hurting the man.

Homosexual incest fantasies can be understood in similar terms. Male sexual fantasies involving a father or father figure can provide unconscious reassurances on a number of levels. The sexual attention of a powerful man reassures the fantasizer that he is special. It is a connection that helps protect him from an anxiety-provoking or otherwise uncomfortable closeness with the mother, thus providing a sense of psychological safety that makes sexual arousal possible. Such a man might feel endangered by worry or guilty in relation to women and feel relieved by his special connection with an older, stronger man. Similarly, a woman who imagines sex with an older woman/mother figure may be looking for someone who is strong and sexual in order to counteract experiences with a real mother who is weak and grim. The sexy mother in fantasy replaces the repressed one in reality and, as a result, makes sexual arousal possible.

MULTIPLE PARTNERS

Three is not a crowd when it comes to sexual fantasy. Some variation of group sex is a common fantasy, particularly among men. The ménage à trois has been enshrined in popular culture as an expression par excellence of sexual hedonism. But when we really study these fantasies, we realize there are many variations possible on the theme of group sex, and each may have a slightly different meaning. Among the possible variations with which people play in their imaginations are:

1. A man imagining having sex with two women.
2. A man imagining having sex with another man and a woman.
3. A woman imagining having sex with two men.
4. A woman imagining having sex with another woman and a man.
5. A man watching two women have sex.
6. A man watching a man and a woman have sex.
7. A man watching two men have sex.
8. A woman watching two women have sex.
9. A woman watching a man and woman have sex.
10. A woman watching two men have sex.

The predominantly heterosexual sexual fantasy bulletin board that I've been quoting from to illustrate the wide variety of sexual daydreams found in the general population contains several variations on the ménage à trois:

I Want to Suck Your Hubby's Load from Your Pussy, by Jim
Would You Fuck My Wife? by Husband
Watching Hubby's Cock Slide into Your Pussy, by Denise

My Husband Wants Me to Fuck Dan. Anyone Game? by Anna
I Come Home Early and See My Wife . . . , by B
Two Friends Stripping My Wife, by Monty

Thus, there are many permutations of the theme of group sex that appear in sexual fantasies, and while there are significant overlaps, there are often subtly different meanings connected to each one. Jim's thrill comes from interacting at least as much with another man as with a woman. "Husband" and "B" want to watch their wives being "fucked" by another man (Monty even imagines that there are two of them) rather than participate in it. Denise seems to be primarily focused on watching another woman be penetrated by her husband, while Anna's sexual aim is to have sex with another man in her husband's presence. Sometimes the scene is embroidered by various important plot devices. The man getting aroused by watching a man and woman have sex might specifically prefer that the woman be his wife, or that she be raped, or even that there be more than one man. A woman who is aroused by the fantasy of being with two men might construct a scenario in which her husband is "asleep," and she has sex with another man in her husband's presence.

What are the meanings of group sex fantasies? In my experience there are usually one or more of the following unconscious aims behind these scenarios.

First, the presence of more than one partner may simply mean that one is getting at least double the attention. As the focus of the sexual ministrations and energy of multiple partners, the fantasizer powerfully disconfirms the pathogenic belief that he or she doesn't deserve to be admired, catered to, or loved. Fantasies of group sex are reassuring and, therefore, momentarily liberating.

Second, the presence of more than one partner can mitigate the guilt that some people feel about burdening their partners with their sexual appetites. A woman who feels guilty about the strength of her own desire can let go of her sexual constraints if there is more than one partner to "handle" her. A man who worries about hurting a woman with his sexual ruthlessness can reassure his conscience if the power of his sexual energy is absorbed by multiple partners.

Third, when a heterosexual man imagines being with another man and a woman in bed, he may be attempting to master burdensome feelings of responsibility for women, guilty beliefs that he's supposed to satisfy women and make them happy. If another man joins him in bed, he doesn't have to shoulder the burden by himself—the weight of responsibility is shared with someone else. Similarly, if such a man gets aroused by simply *watching* a couple have sex, I think that he is dealing with the same issue, but once removed. In this case, the voyeur can *imagine* that he's the man having sex. Since he's actually not, he is free from the responsibility that he imagines goes along with sexually satisfying a woman. He gets to have sex without worry or guilt. The same dynamic can apply to a heterosexual woman imagining having sex with another woman and a man or watching this other couple have sex.

Fourth, given that one's responsibility for sexually pleasing others is diminished, the danger of rejection is correspondingly lessened. If ensuring the other person's satisfaction is a team effort, then one's own contribution is less likely to be singled out and criticized. Diffusing responsibility diffuses not only blame, but the danger of being rejected.

Fifth, many men get aroused by the depiction of two women having sex. Most heterosexual pornography has at least one obligatory lesbian sex scene. Although some analysts argue that this scenario invites and evokes the feminine or even homosexual longings in many heterosexual men—the male voyeur is identifying with one of the women in the scenario—I believe that the role of guilt and worry might be even more important here in several ways.

Just as in the case of a man getting aroused by watching a heterosexual couple have sex, the man who gets aroused by the sight of a lesbian couple can identify with each of the parties but without the guilty burden and obligation of pleasing anyone. He's not directly involved and so can't fail. Further, the fact that there is no man to be found in the scene makes it safer for the male voyeur to identify with one or both of the women because many men unconsciously believe that women feel ambivalent about men to begin with. When a man is watching two women have sex, he can enjoy a pleasurable fantasy of having sex with a woman without having to worry about any untoward effects of his own masculinity. The women can't be provoked by masculinity because it is absent.

Sixth, if a man or woman has homosexual desires but feels guilty about them, watching or participating in group sex can be a way to circumvent this guilt. Watching a heterosexual couple have sex or imagining participating in sex with them opens up multiple opportunities for identification. A man might identify with the woman having sex with a man, a woman with the man having sex with a woman. However, because the scene is scripted as explicitly heterosexual, the fantasizer can trick his or her conscience into overlooking the real homosexual longings that are being gratified.

GANG RAPE

Heterosexual gang rape is as underreported as rape for the same reasons as rape in general—the victims feel ashamed, and the justice system discourages reporting. The fantasy of gang rape, however, is much more common than its enactment. Pornography fuels the fantasy. So do movies, from Stanley Kubrick's *Clockwork Orange*, or Vittorio De Sica's *Two Women*, with Sophia Loren, to *The Accused*, starring Jodie Foster. *The Accused*, in particular, delves, not only into the devastating effects on the victim, but the interpersonal dynamics among the men who participated and covered it up. The power of the male "group" to permit the expression of sexual violence and to brand as "traitors" any man who objects is based on the same psychological mechanisms we have been using to explain other sexual fantasies, namely the centrality of safety in sexual arousal. Responsibility is shifted from the individual to the group. It is not *I* who am doing something aggressive and sexually ruthless—*we* are responsible. Guilt is reduced, and excitement can then flourish. In the *fantasy*, as opposed to the enactment, of a gang rape, the woman is usually not even hurt. The rape becomes more like a consensual act between a promiscuous woman and several men. These plot devices enable the individual man to counteract his worries about hurting women with his sexual desires and, thus, to get aroused.

VOYEURISM: THE PEEPING TOM

We've already touched on the voyeuristic potential in some people, exploring the excitement that may accompany watching other people have sex. Sexual voyeurism takes other forms as well, most notably that of the Peeping Tom, a man who spies on girls and women hoping to see them in some state of undress or lascivious activity. One variation on the Peeping Tom theme involves men who enjoy the fantasy of looking under a woman's skirt. In fact, there are a number of sexual fantasies listed on the sexual fantasy bulletin board that involve a title like "I Love to Peek Under Women's Skirts." Harkening back to childhood experiences of "accidentally" dropping something on the floor in order to look up girls' skirts, these fantasies—usually proffered by men—involve the excitement of piercing the mystery of the female body. There are Internet web sites devoted to nothing other than the posting of still photographs and videos of unsuspecting women caught in some stage of undress or inadvertently revealing their underwear to the camera. There are even men who position a hidden camera on the ground in order to record a brief glimpse of whatever lies hidden beneath a woman's dress. What is going on here?

The excitement connected to "sneaking a peek" under a woman's skirt lies first in the fact that it is forbidden. In the man's mind, the woman is involuntarily giving up her "secret." The guilt that the voyeur feels about his interest in the female body, a guilt based on his perception that women will be offended by such interest, is neatly circumvented by the fact that the object of his curiosity isn't aware of it and so can't object. The pathogenic belief that women will regard a man's prurient interest in her as demeaning is disproved by the fact that she doesn't know anything about it. In addition, some men grew up feeling that their mothers wouldn't let their sons get close to them, and the sons felt rejected and excluded. In voyeuristic "peeping," the man dramatically reverses this rejection by sneaking under it, so to speak, and enjoying a moment of stolen intimacy denied to him. With his guilt mitigated and his sense of rejection reversed, the man can then get excited.

EXHIBITIONISM: PHOTOGRAPHING AND VIDEOTAPING SEX

In the popular film from the 1980s *Sex, Lies, and Videotape*, various women become aroused by the interest of a man who has recently arrived in their town and who has the "hobby" of videotaping women recounting their sexual life histories. The interviewer appears to lack any obvious prurient interest in the women but seems to be driven by a wish to draw them out and get them to reveal the most intimate details of their lives. The women are invariably sexually aroused by this process, often leading to actual sex, which may also be videotaped. What is arousing about being seen in this way? Why is it that some people like to be "on camera," even if that camera doesn't always have a flattering lens? And taking this process to its logical sexual extreme, why do some people like to take pictures of themselves having sex or even make movies of it?

While uncommon, this fantasy or behavior is not rare. The excitement comes from the awareness that one is being photographed during sex. The actual psychological meaning and purpose of such exhibitionism, as revealed in *Sex, Lies, and Videotape,* are that the person being recorded is gratified primarily by the attention, the fact that he or she is important and the object of a special focus. The movie makes this explicit because it sets the women's experience of being interviewed in a context of their overall loneliness and isolation. The stranger with his video camera is the only man in their lives who seems to regard their experience as worthy of attention.

On a broader level, exhibitionism of this sort is often motivated by an attempt to master feelings of rejection and neglect. If we did not feel that we were on our parents' emotional radar screen growing up, being watched by a camera is a powerful antidote, counteracting the feelings that we aren't deserving of special attention. Having negated these feelings, exhibitionism allows sexual excitement to flourish.

Flashers—men who expose themselves to women—are a special case of exhibitionism. The man's excitement comes in large part from the shock and fear he evokes in women by exposing his penis to them. What's the thrill for the man here? Since we know that the fantasy being enacted reverses the chilling effects of particular unconscious beliefs and feelings, then what are those beliefs and feelings? There are two problems that flashers are probably attempting to solve—shame and neglect. Sometimes people who are afraid of heights make themselves jump out of planes, or people who are afraid of rejection force themselves to be sociable. In a similar vein, a man ashamed of himself, particularly his masculinity, may briefly triumph over his shame by showing off the source of it. Doing the very thing we fear can be an attempt to master it.

The second problem that flashing attempts to solve is feelings of neglect. Someone who traumatically experienced growing up as being rejected or invisible inevitably feels himself to be deserving of such disregard. Such a man momentarily feels freed from the burden of such feelings, however, when he manages to evoke shock, disgust, and fear from women by exposing himself to them. Whatever else he is, he is not invisible and overlooked. Neglected no longer, such a man feels unconsciously reassured and safe enough to get sexually aroused.

BODY TYPES AND SEXUAL AROUSAL

Most people tend to be initially attracted to a particular body type. Some people take this to an extreme and fetishize particular parts of the body, making their presence a requirement for sexual arousal. Some women find themselves attracted only to tall men, while some men will only be able to get aroused fully by women who have large breasts. While we've discussed many of the dynamics of fetishism, let me suggest, based on my clinical experience and general theoretical approach, some possible meanings of various fetishistic preoccupations about the size and shape of the human body:

Tall men might symbolize strength to a woman or, for that matter, to another man. A tall man represents someone you can depend on and someone whom you can't easily hurt. For someone struggling with worries about overwhelming a man, such an attribute would be reassuring and permit excitement to emerge more readily.

Heavy women might symbolize plenty and abundance. Some people are sexually attracted to a big women because her size unconsciously suggests that she has a lot to give, that she is a bountiful vessel of maternal supplies, someone who will help counteract feelings of being deprived. She might seem like someone who is so substantial that you can't hurt her, thus mitigating feelings of guilt. Finally, a person might develop a sexual fantasy or preference involving a heavy woman because, since our culture values thinness, a heavy woman is imagined to feel lucky to have *any* partner and won't be dissatisfied or critical.

Big breasts might similarly symbolize a woman who has a lot to give, therefore counteracting feelings of disconnectedness and deprivation and permitting the flowering of sexual pleasure. The opposite may also be true. Men who have a secret disdain for women— but feel guilty about it and hide it—may unconsciously exaggerate their admiration for the most obvious marker of femininity, breasts.

Big penises have multiple meanings in our culture. One of these meanings is that they signify strength. Therefore, someone who psychologically requires that a man be strong in order to counteract his or her guilt might fixate on the size of a man's penis. In addition, some people will talk about how a big penis "fills them up." In this sense, a big penis signifies being well fed and taken care of, a sensation that would reassure against feelings of deprivation.

Crippled or injured body parts are arousing to some men and women. Some men have a fetish about crippled women, and some women are drawn to men who have a physical handicap. For men, a crippled woman can lessen feelings of unconscious guilt because, since she is already injured, she can't be injured any further in fantasy. Additionally, as was true in the case of heavy women, deformed or handicapped women can't, in the man's mind, be "choosy," and thus his fears of rejection can be allayed, and his excitement can safely emerge. For women drawn to men with injuries or handicaps, the same dynamics may apply. In addition, in the woman's unconscious mind, a crippled or injured man can't hurt her. Some women are physically afraid of men, and with this danger reduced, they can get aroused more safely.

GAY MEN AND SEXUAL AROUSAL IN
HETEROSEXUAL WOMEN

Some women are aroused by gay men and may become sexually expressive with such men in a more confident and spontaneous way than they can with straight men. The issue here is clearly one of safety. Gay men make it safe for these women to become sexually aggressive because the women know that their overtures won't be reciprocated. These are women who have anxieties about being sexual with straight men because they're afraid of being overpowered or rejected, on the one hand, or of hurting the man with their sexual power, on the other. In either case, the fact that the gay man won't cross the line between playful flirting and real sexual behavior is intensely reassuring to such women. A variation on this particular attraction may be found in cases in which the challenge of "turning" a gay man straight offers the woman a reassurance that she is *especially* attractive.

This list of sexual fantasies and practices does not begin to exhaust the possibilities. The human mind is continually creating the conditions under which sexual excitement can occur, weaving images from popular culture with the idiosyncratic twists and turns of its unconscious. But as widely varied as these fantasies might appear, the underlying mechanisms are the same. Beliefs and feelings that inhibit sexual arousal are counteracted by the images and stories of which fantasies and sexual preferences are constructed. Whether it is an elaborate, highly stylized sexual ritual or simply a picture in our minds, psychological safety is necessary for our sexual desire to flourish.

5

Sexual Pleasure and Boredom in Relationships

Marriage must incessantly contend with a monster that devours everything: familiarity.—Honoré de Balzac

When turkeys mate, they think of swans.—Johnny Carson

A comedian always got big laughs when he lamented, "I was making love to my wife the other night, and it wasn't working; so I asked her, 'What? You can't think of anyone else either?' " The joke hides the serious issue that sometimes sex doesn't "work" in a relationship. In fact, sexual dissatisfaction is a national epidemic. Based on interviews with more than three thousand Americans, a recent study in the *Journal of the American Medical Association* found that 25 percent of women were unable to achieve orgasm, 30 percent lacked interest in sex, more than 30 percent of men suffered from premature ejaculation or other sexual dysfunction, and a high percentage of respondents of both sexes complained that they didn't have sex often enough. Why are so many people unhappy in the bedroom? And how can understanding the dynamics of sexual arousal help us answer this question?

To understand sexual ennui and misunderstanding, we have to identify the forces that create and sustain sexual excitement as well as those that diminish it. It seems apparent that there are "natural" or universal tendencies for sexual intensity to decline over time in a long-term relationship. The unconscious processes underlying these tendencies are found in everyone. There are also, however, specific conflicts that create boredom. These conflicts are grist for the mill of therapy when the problems they generate are bad enough to bring the person or couple in to ask for help. The sexual history of a couple reflects the interaction of these two factors, the universal and the particular.

When a couple's sex life declines in frequency and intensity, the question arises, "Is this decline normal or abnormal?" Is the couple merely going through what everyone goes through, or is there something wrong that needs to be addressed? Normal, however, is difficult to define. After all, everyone brings his or her own conflicts into the bedroom. There is not a couple alive who embodies either pure psychological health or pathology. To make matters worse, an intimate relationship always opens the mind to its greatest fears and vulnerabilities. We go to bed naked in more ways than one. Therefore, even in the best of circumstances, how can intimacy and familiarity *not* trigger highly idiosyncratic issues in both of the partners in a couple, and how can these issues not inevitably affect their sex life? If there is an unresolved issue or conflict in someone's life, it will invariably appear in the bedroom.

Furthermore, the social expectation and standard of a "good" sex life greatly complicates our ability to identify a bad one, to tell where normal ennui ends and pathological boredom begins. Americans tend to have unrealistic expectations about the "normal" frequency and intensity of sex in a relationship. Our culture promotes an ideal of sexual bliss, a high-octane libidinal longing that is supposed to be present regardless of the length of time that a couple has been together, the physiological effects of aging, the availability of romantic time, and the presence of fatigue, work stress, or children.

A healthy sex life is supposed to be frequent, creative, and intense. Therefore the inevitable fact that real people in real long-term relationships cannot and do not act as though they are in the heat of passion all the time causes many people to feel a sense of shame, disappointment, and failure. Never mind that millions of people are in the same boat, and that everyone tends to temper his or her sexual enthusiasm over time in a long-term relationship. Many patients have confessed to me a private disappointment or guilt that they're having sex with their partners only two or three times per week; others, that it's only once a month. Whatever the frequency, it comes to feel to the people involved like a "problem." They worry about their or their partners' lack of desire. Having defined themselves as sexual underachievers, they can't talk to anyone else about it because they're ashamed, or if it comes up, they lie about it. The topic of sexual frequency is shrouded in a cloud of unrealistic expectation and embarrassment.

In order to counteract this irrational performance anxiety, it is important to understand the factors that maintain and erode sexual intensity in relationships. If some degree of sexual boredom is universal, perhaps it needn't be so shameful. In addition, it is equally important to explore and explain the myriad ways that these universal factors can interact with special psychological problems that afflict many people in the bedroom. Such an explanation of sexual chemistry and boredom will, at every step, be grounded in exactly the same model of the mind that we used to decipher the meaning of private sexual fantasies—namely, that sexual excitement is inevitably entwined in the issue of psychological safety.

THE NATURAL DECLINE OF SEXUAL INTEREST

Familiarity tends to breed sexual boredom. Notwithstanding our cultural idealization of eternal romantic intensity, most people intuitively understand that sexual intensity wanes with time, familiarity, and intimacy. This process of "waning," however, may be quite slow and is rarely linear. Sexual attraction and desire can and do ebb and flow in an intimate relationship, usually diminishing under stress, and always mirroring the mood states and the general ups and downs of the relationship. In addition, while the overall sexual intensity of a relationship may begin to fade, with ennui often replacing ardor, the quality of sex for some couples may improve as they become more intimate. Familiarity with our partner's body and sexual interests can obviously enhance our ability to arouse and please that partner—and vice versa. The increased safety that mature love can provide may counteract sexual inhibitions as much as the novelty and idealization of a new infatuation.

There are clearly great variations among couples in the quantity and quality of sexual changes that occur through the years. But even in relationships in which intimacy improves sexual communication, the overall level of activity and desire eventually tends to decline. It is harder to stay constantly aroused by someone whom you've seen in sickness as well as in health, at his or her worst as well as best, when he or she is feeling and acting grumpy, depressed, tired, and anxious, as well as sunny, charming, funny, empathic, and strong. True intimacy, of course, involves encountering and tolerating just such complexity, even as that complexity is lessening the perfection of the initial and blissful idealization. Intimacy and sexual desire can make uncomfortable bedfellows. Let us examine why.

When couples initially get together, their sexual attraction for each other is usually very strong. The intensity of their desire and the thrilling newness of each other's bodies combine to make the connection exciting. A powerful current of idealization courses through each person's experience of the other. By idealization, I mean that the other's virtues are exaggerated and liabilities minimized. Your partner can do no wrong. His or her body is intensely stimulating, sexual technique masterful, and passion exhilarating. As H. L. Mencken once wrote: "To be in love is merely to be in a state of perceptual anesthesia—to mistake an ordinary young man for a Greek god or an ordinary young woman for a goddess." In the throes of a new sexual relationship, one person's arousal brings the other's to a higher level and vice versa. An open channel of lust and desire between the partners is uncontaminated by worry, guilt, shame, self-doubt, or helplessness.

Idealization is ubiquitous in human relationships. Children idealize their parents, parents idealize their children, and we all tend to idealize people in authority. We endow those we idealize with special powers and virtues and cannot seem to see them as complex, flawed, and multidimensional people like us. This process is most exaggerated when two people fall in love. The other's beauty, sexiness, capacity for passion, intelligence, wit, empathy, strength, altruism, or courage is exaggerated and taken to be the whole of who he or she is, while weaknesses of any kind are overlooked, diminished in importance, or rationalized away.

Sexual idealization is facilitated by a lack of familiarity between the partners in a new couple. They may think that they know each other's innermost souls, but realistically they don't. This relative lack of knowledge promotes the process of idealization because there aren't any inconvenient emotional blemishes to get in the way. Tendencies toward depression, anger, or withdrawal are muted by the soft glow of idealization. Familiarity may not necessarily breed contempt, but a lack of familiarity can bring out the best in anyone.

Lack of familiarity also promotes psychological distance. New lovers are both merged and highly separate. They feel merged because of the intense identifications that accompany falling in love and separate because their real lives are not yet interdependent. The sense of fusion that often accompanies intense sexual excitement is possible precisely because, in the beginning of relationships, each person is more anchored in his or her separate reality than at any other time. The partners' emotional and practical lives are not nearly as intermingled as they will be. *Because of the actual psychological distance that must underlie even the most intensely love-struck couple, each person can safely throw him or herself into the other's experience, including the other's sexual experience, without the risk of losing him or herself in the process.*

The feeling of intense connectedness is grounded in the reality of psychological distance. The subjectively intense *feeling* of union is with an idealized version of the other person, not with the whole person. The sense that new couples have of discovery and of delightful surprise is more intense than it will likely ever be as they get to know each other better and more objectively.

INTIMACY AND SEXUAL RUTHLESSNESS

One consequence of the greater sense of psychological distance in the beginning of a relationship is the enhanced capacity for sexual ruthlessness. As discussed in an earlier chapter, sexual ruthlessness involves that dimension of sexual excitement in which we are entirely selfish and *not* concerned about the excitement or well-being of our partner. Ruthlessness describes the quality of desire that enables a person to surrender to the full force of his or her own rhythms of pleasure and excitement without guilt, worry, or shame of any kind. Without sexual ruthlessness, we become enslaved to the feelings of the other person and can't get maximally, or sometimes even minimally, excited. Because the early stage of a sexual relationship is one in which the partners in the couple idealize each other but feel a certain psychological distance as well, there is less of an occasion to worry or feel guilty about each other, to encounter each other's raw nerves, vulnerable egos, or real or imagined flaws. By connecting with a "perfect" partner, our own value is automatically enhanced. In addition, the greater the psychological distance, the greater the feeling of "otherness" that we have toward our partner, the safer it is to treat that partner as a sexual object. Distance and separation promote sexual ruthlessness because the target is, in some sense, farther away.

Over time, however, certain idealizations become difficult to maintain and psychological distance begins to yield to the experience of intimate familiarity. It seems to be a universal experience. Couples become familiar with each other's bodies, and they encounter these bodies in less than perfect condition and in less than sexy situations. Bodies get sick, expand or contract, become firmer or looser, and have all sorts of other functions that are anything but romantic and arousing. As physical familiarity increases, so does emotional familiarity. Each person learns more and more about his or her partner. Over time, couples begin to anticipate what each other will feel, say, and do. This means they also know each other's preferences, fears, and vulnerabilities. They know exactly how to hurt each other and make up to each other. They know which topics to avoid and which are safe. The intimate familiarity of a couple always involves a loosening of personal boundaries and a certain degree of merger and mutual identification. This is a more real intimacy and merger than the temporary experience of ecstatic oneness seen in the early phase of a sexual relationship. Each person feels he or she really *knows* the other, for better or, perhaps increasingly, for worse.

Often, of course, this presumption of understanding turns out to be false. Couples hide things from each other all the time. They misread each other constantly and make false assumptions, project feelings onto each other that are really their own, blame each other when they themselves feel guilty, and are ignorant of blind spots derived from their gender, culture, or personality. Nevertheless, couples usually develop at least the subjective experience that they know exactly what each other is feeling in a given situation. Familiarity breeds the presumption of understanding and becomes increasingly laced with powerful processes of identification. The point at which one person stops and the other starts is not altogether clear.

This kind of deep immersion in and empathy with one's partner's experience is a double-edged sword, even in the healthiest of couples. On the one hand, understanding creates the foundation for intimacy. On the other hand, knowing your partner's faults can create worry, dissatisfaction, guilt, and problematic identifications. Consider the familiar situation of the following couple. Partner A tends to be a bit depressive, while partner B tends to take on the caretaking role, always sensitive to signs of unhappiness in his or her loved one. This couple might be generally happy and high-functioning, blending together complementary character traits into a stable partnership. The caretaker partner, partner B, might have a tendency, as caretakers do, to feel a bit more than the average amount of guilt about being selfish, and the depressive partner, partner A, might have a bit more of a tendency to be self-preoccupied. Early on in this relationship, however, partner A's underlying temperament might not have been visible or might have been made invisible by the rose-colored glasses of idealization. Perhaps such a partner might have been experienced as only "low-keyed" or "serious," traits that paled in comparison to all of his or her endearing and sexy qualities. As a result of their growing intimacy, however, the caretaker, partner B, becomes increasingly aware of the depressive tendencies of partner A, and as this awareness grows, so does his or her worry, sense of responsibility, resentment, and guilt. These feelings, no matter how mild or subtle they may be, are inimical to sexual excitement because they inhibit the sexual ruthlessness necessary for arousal. The relationship may even be healthy and open enough for them to talk about these issues but, unless the fundamental character structure of the two people completely changes, these feelings and their effects on sexual passion will always be at least latent. Familiarity, then, has contributed to a dampening of sexual excitement in an otherwise high-functioning couple.

Or consider a couple in which one or both partners are basically modest about exhibiting their bodies or displaying their sexuality. Modesty often develops in people as a normal attempt to deal with feelings of shame and rejection. Let's suppose that in this hypothetical couple, their vulnerability to feeling shame is only a whisper, hovering in the background, and not significantly detracting from what otherwise might be a healthy relationship. Such a couple might even be reasonably sexually active. In the beginning their mutual idealization may help them overcome feelings of sexual embarrassment by exaggerating each other's confidence, spontaneity, and exuberance. As they become more intimate and attuned to each other's psyches, however, each partner may more readily and clearly sense the vulnerability to shame and self-criticism in the other. One person's need to turn the lights off during sex, while initially seen as a charming shyness, now feels more like a neurotic insecurity. The other person's preference to give rather than receive oral sex, initially seen as generosity, now seems suggestive of shame. Such increased attunement works *against* passion in this case, because the feelings of insecurity and shame that are being sensed, however subtle, may elicit worry and feelings of responsibility—a sexual wet blanket.

In addition, powerful currents of identification inevitably come into play in the intimate realms of a long-term relationship. Partners not only sense each other's feelings, they identify and empathically resonate with them. It may not be consciously apparent to either one that this is what's happening. People sense, often unconsciously, the vulnerabilities and weaknesses of loved ones, feel them almost as if they are their own, and never become aware that this process is occurring.

So one partner's shame becomes the other partner's shame as

well. Embarrassment becomes contagious, and both partners begin to feel a bit self-conscious. The partner who might like to have sex with the lights on unconsciously resonates with the partner who is embarrassed about it and therefore becomes more restrained. The partner who might want to give oral sex unconsciously identifies with the one who's ashamed of his or her genitals and, consequently, begins to feel embarrassed and inhibited, too.

It may seem as if many of these dynamics would be more evident early on in a relationship when the partners are unfamiliar with each other; but more often, the intensity of sexual desire early in a sexual relationship often overrides feelings of embarrassment and self-doubt. As couples get to know each other, their deeper awareness of each other's vulnerabilities can become their undoing. The other's inhibitions and the shame upon which they rest begin to wear down spontaneity and passion. We are just too close, too identified with our inhibited partner, to escape the experience.

Sexual enervation doesn't necessarily imply that something is wrong. These are descriptions of the normal dynamics of identification and emotional attunement. The familiarity and connectedness that long-term couples generally experience not only promote these dynamics but would be impossible without them. Everyone, after all, wants to be understood. We admire couples who know each other so well that they finish each other's thoughts, and the experience of "growing old together" is a comforting and gratifying prospect for most people. The problem here is that the price of such comfort usually involves a certain degree of sexual apathy.

Identification is not the only ingredient of normal long-term intimacy that affects sexual desire. The closer we are to our partners, the more they begin to wear the mantles of the primary caretakers from our past. Freud called this process *transference* because we transfer the psychodynamics of our childhood onto our present relationships. The more emotionally significant the other becomes, the more likely we are to experience him or her according to templates laid down in our families.

Nowhere are adults more dependent than in the relationship they have with their partners, and at no other time was this dependency as strong as it was in childhood. Therefore, the normal emotional dependency in long-term relationships inevitably contains echoes of these earlier attachments. There is an old joke that says that when two people have sex, there are six people in bed: the two lovers and the parents of each of them. The truth behind the humor is that intimate sexual relationships necessarily open the psychic doors to the repetition of our own original parent-child relationship.

Transference constantly occurs in relationships. If our mother was unhappy, we will become selectively sensitive to unhappiness in our partner. Sometimes this makes us more empathically supportive, but at other times, it stirs up burdensome feelings of guilt and responsibility, with a corresponding impulse to get away. If our father tended to bully his family, we will either tend to be especially intimidated by conflict with a partner or become overly defensive in the face of it. If our father was weak, we will tend to react selectively to signs of weakness in a lover. An example of this situation occurred with a woman who had a weak father and who sought my help for a troubled marriage. Her primary complaint was that she could not tolerate her husband becoming even mildly depressed or ill. She found herself feeling contempt rather than concern and consequently often felt guilty. Unconsciously, she had transferred her feelings about her father onto her husband.

Another patient of mine, a relatively healthy young man, could not bear to hear his wife complain. His mother had been something of a martyr, and he'd grown up feeling responsible for the impossible task of making her happy. He felt that he was supposed to fix everything; and when he couldn't, he felt helpless and guilty. The normal frustration that anyone might feel in response to the complaints of a loved one was enhanced in the mind of this patient because of transference. What might have been only a minor annoyance to another man became an intolerable accusation for which this patient felt responsible. We don't have to be neurotic in order to relive the past in the present. It comes with being human.

Another patient, a successful attorney known for being aggressive in court, had a tendency to become inordinately sensitive to slights in her intimate relationships. If her partner was distracted for even a moment, she'd take it as rejection. Our work revealed that her mother was also easily emotionally wounded, often feeling neglected and rejected by her husband and children. The patient, to her chagrin, realized that her hypersensitivity to rejection was an identification with her mother and that she lived out this identification in intimate relationships. In this form of transference, however, the patient wasn't transferring her experience of a parent onto a partner; instead, she had assumed the role of one parent, her mother, and treated her partner as if he were the other parent or even herself as a child.

As complicated as this sounds, it is really quite simple. In our original relationships with our parents, we develop an emotionally charged picture of who they are and an emotionally charged image of who we are as children—images that we internalize. In the case of the attorney, she found that she was living out her picture of her mother's life and transferring her picture of her father and herself onto her partner. As a child she had felt like a bad and selfish girl who frequently hurt her mother. As an adult she frequently felt like her injured mother and experienced her boyfriend as a bad and selfish person who was hurting her. As a child she saw her father as someone who hurt her mother. As an adult she felt like her mother and easily saw her partners as hurtful, exactly like her father. This dynamic of identifying with our parents and treating others as we were treated by them is referred to by psychoanalysts as *turning passive into active.* It is another unconscious distortion of the golden rule: *Do unto others as you would have others do unto you* becomes *Do unto others as others once did unto you.* In order to protect oneself from reexperiencing the helpless vulnerability that can often be evoked in intimate relationships, an experience that one suffered passively as a child is unconsciously turned around and actively done to another.

The relevance of transference to sexual boredom is obvious. To the extent that we unconsciously experience our partner or ourselves as similar to a parent, and to the extent that earlier parental relationships contained elements of worry, guilt, and shame (which most of our childhoods did), those feelings will enter our love life even more than they would most other aspects of our lives. Transference can, and often does, intensify the normal processes of sexual boredom by importing into the bedroom those aspects of our childhood that would tend to inhibit the free, spontaneous, and ruthless pursuit of pleasure. Because all of us have had at least some problematic experiences with our parents, the pressure to reexperience them in the context of our adult relationships is bound to interfere with sexual desire.

THE GOOD, THE BAD, AND THE UGLY: PATHOGENIC BELIEFS AND SEXUAL COMPATIBILITY

If the processes of identification and transference that accompany normal healthy intimacy can mute the intensity of sexual passion, it is not difficult to imagine the effect that these processes can have on the libidos of sexual partners who already have significant psychological problems. And yet, while it is probably the case that all of us have emotional problems of some kind, it is also the case that some couples maintain a feeling of sexual compatibility, however muted it may become over time, while other couples' ardor fizzles completely. What accounts for these individual differences? What determines whether there is a good sexual fit? Interestingly, the sexual chemistry in a couple isn't reliably correlated with the psychological health of the individuals involved. So-called sick people can have healthy sex. Why can some relationships work sexually even though the individuals involved seem quite psychologically troubled in other parts of their lives?

Just as sexual fantasies arouse us because they counteract our pathogenic beliefs, so, too, do good sexual relationships. *Sexual compatibility is determined by the extent to which our pathogenic beliefs negate or reinforce those of our partner—and vice versa.* And it is in intimate sexual relationships that our pathogenic beliefs about ourselves and others have the most direct opportunity to be confirmed or disproved. If we're prone to feeling guilty about overwhelming people we love—a prime example of a pathogenic belief—that guilt will surface most forcefully in our sexual relationships. If we're vulnerable to feeling shame, the choreography of our sexual relationships will either evoke or overcome that shame more directly than in other areas of our lives. If we're anxious about intimacy in any way, or conflicted at all about pleasure (and who of us isn't?), our sexual relationships will be the first arena in which these conflicts appear. In the naked world of sexuality, we often lack our usual defenses, the armor of language, wealth, and social role. Sex becomes a high-stakes game, a referendum on our self-esteem, exposing our pretensions, mirroring our narcissism, and assuaging our anxieties. Sexual desire is an extremely sensitive barometer of the ups and downs of our psychological lives.

Our sexual partners, therefore, have to perform the same function as sexual fantasies, namely, to establish the conditions of safety necessary to allow sexual excitement to emerge. After all, when it comes to the choreography of a real live sexual relationship, fantasies and preferences have to be enacted with another person. A good sexual connection in a couple requires that each partner's predispositions to the emotions and beliefs that dampen excitement be counteracted by the other person.

Sexual attraction, however, happens in a flash. It doesn't usually seem to wait until we've rationally figured out if the other person can make it safe for us get aroused. The process is not a conscious one. People tend to be romantically drawn, at least initially, to exactly the right person who can help them disprove certain irrational beliefs. It seems mysterious, almost magical, to the people involved, but in my clinical experience, the initial attraction is based on a great deal of nonconscious perception and information processing. If we are worried about hurting a partner with the intensity of our sexual desire, but find ourselves with a partner who seems to particularly enjoy aggressive intensity, that partner is making it safe for us to get turned on. We don't have to do a battery of psychological tests to find such a person.

Sometimes we can sense this quality in a potential partner. One woman I treated claimed she knew instantly that her current boyfriend would be great in bed because of a certain "look" about him. Upon reflection, she realized that this "look" was one of arrogance, and it was to this arrogance that she was attracted precisely because it reassured her that she couldn't push him around. Another example of this dynamic is the "love at first sight" that a male patient of mine recently experienced. This man had left a marriage to a woman who was quite depressed and with whom he had no sexual spark whatsoever primarily because of his chronic worrying about her. One night, when he was out at a tavern he frequented, he felt an intense physical and emotional attraction to the new bartender who had recently been hired. He realized later that the key to his attraction, to feeling as if this were love at first sight, was his perception of her as happy, outgoing, exuberant, and robust. He had grown up feeling guilty and worried about a mother who was frequently emotionally unavailable and often bedridden. It is no wonder he responded viscerally and powerfully to the image of a strong and happy woman.

A final example of the power of unconscious perception and chemistry involved a man who grew up in a strict fundamentalist home and felt ashamed of his body and sexuality. He found himself drawn to women who were somewhat exhibitionistic. He unconsciously sensed that their comfort with their own bodies, with their own sexuality, would rub off on him—that he would be able to identify with a woman who was uninhibited. He liked women who seemed comfortable being bawdy and flirtatious, who liked to dress in a sexy way, and who seemed to like sexual verbal repartee. He felt that he could sense all of this in the first moment of meeting a woman.

In all these cases, to the extent that each partner is able deliberately or inadvertently to disprove or counteract the other partner's pathogenic beliefs, prospects for a good sexual chemistry will improve. To the extent that each partner confirms or reinforces the other partner's pathogenic beliefs, the likelihood of sexual inhibition or dysfunction increases.

"THE GOOD": THE CASE OF MARK AND BETSY

A good sexual relationship is like a good sexual fantasy. It is exciting because it is unconsciously safe. Let us first examine a relationship in which, like a successful fantasy, each person's worst fears get successfully assuaged. Mark and Betsy consulted me for a short time about problems that their five-year-old son was having making friends in school. They had each been in their own individual therapy and were, as a result, highly psychologically minded people who wanted to be sure that nothing in their own relationship was contributing to their son's problems. We met over a period of about four months, during which time their son seemed to do better. During this period, however, I had a good opportunity to get to know Mark and Betsy, and supplemented my observations with information garnered from their prior therapists. As it turned out, their relationship provided a window into the workings of a healthy sexual relationship. The key to this success lay, not only in their capacities for love and empathy, but in the fact that their pathogenic beliefs seemed to line up in ways that helped, rather than hurt, their sexual chemistry.

Both Mark and Betsy had been previously married to partners with whom they eventually had great sexual difficulty. Betsy told me that she had always felt relatively secure about her physical appearance and her sexuality, but she was insecure about her intellectual capacity. Her first husband was a brilliant man who initially seemed to respect Betsy's intellect. This in itself was an aphrodisiac to Betsy because the promise of a "mutual admiration society" of the mind represented a powerful antidote to her own sense of unworthiness and shame. After a short time, however, her husband began to criticize her intelligence and to reject her. Where he had previously thought her witty, he now implied that she was boring. She came to experience him as cold and withholding. Betsy shut down completely.

Betsy had the irrational belief that she did not deserve to have a kind man love her, that she was somehow intrinsically defective in a man's eyes. Her marriage had gone from counteracting to reinforcing this belief, one that had arisen in her childhood. Her father had been quite cold and had periodically beaten Betsy. One time, Betsy recalled, her father had overturned the dinner table and chased her around the house in an attempt to catch her and hit her for some minor offense. She locked herself in the bathroom and stayed there all night in fear.

Her mother, on the other hand, not only failed to protect her from her father's violence, but tended toward obsessive worrying and seemed to take it out on Betsy in the form of frequent criticisms about her appearance and intellect. One time, Betsy recalled, her mother was having lunch with Betsy and her friend Amy. Betsy was reporting, with some excitement, how she had been approached by a modeling agency to do some work for them. Betsy's mother suddenly said, "Look at how beautiful Amy's hair is. . . . Don't you wish you had lovely curls like her?" Over the course of her growing up, Betsy had internalized her parents' criticisms and secretly saw herself as both unattractive and stupid. She had always tried to cover up this insecurity by at least becoming physically pleasing to men, something she became quite good at doing. Betsy's first marriage had initially offered her a taste of redemption and the promise of disproving her pathogenic beliefs precisely because her husband seemed different from her parents. He was not only attracted to her physically, but he seemed to validate her intellectual competence as well. Eventually, of course, he repeated her parents' devaluation of her and reconfirmed these same beliefs.

Mark's experience had much in common with Betsy's. He had been married to a woman whom he described as shrewish and emotionally brittle. She frequently belittled him and responded to his protests by withdrawing into hostile silences that would go on for days. She would criticize Mark if he wanted to play poker with his friends or if he bought and wore clothes that he thought looked particularly sexy. Unfortunately, Mark was familiar with such treatment, as it repeated key aspects of his relationship with his mother, a passive and hypochondriacal woman who had frequently made him feel guilty for wanting to be independent of her. Whenever Mark and his mother had a disagreement, she would act hurt and not speak to Mark until he caved in and apologized. Once, when Mark was about fourteen, he and his high school girlfriend, Sue, went to Mark's house after school to study. As it turned out, Mark's mother wasn't home, and he and Sue were in the house alone. It was common practice in Mark's family not to lock the front door, and so none of the family members ever carried keys. That afternoon, however, out of nervousness about being alone with Sue, out of not wanting to be disturbed—to this day Mark can't remember why—when he and Sue came home to the empty house, he locked the front door behind them.

The studying lasted about the time it took to open their backpacks, and then Mark and Sue went up to Mark's room to "fog up our glasses," as Mark put it. Some time later, Mark's mother came home, and to her surprise and great irritation found the front door locked. Because she didn't have a key, she had to ring the doorbell to be let in. She was enraged to find Mark alone with Sue, who quickly gathered her books and left. Mark's mother was so upset that he had been with a girl "under her roof" that she refused to speak to him for five days. Mark remembered that he was eventually reduced to weeping and begging for his mother's forgiveness.

Interestingly, when Mark initially met his first wife, he was immediately attracted to her precisely because he perceived her as strong, the polar opposite of his mother. She was an outspoken feminist, and her public persona was that of an independent and assertive woman. This turned Mark on because it counteracted his expectation and belief that he was always supposed to be a "good guy," responsible for weak and unhappy women. Soon after they got married, however, he saw that her strength was superficial, barely concealing how brittle and controlling she was, and his sexual attraction decreased accordingly.

When Mark and Betsy got together, each brought his or her own psychological baggage to the relationship. Mark had the guilty and irrational belief that he was a selfish guy and that he was supposed to worry about and take care of needy women. He was good at being sensitive to others' needs but bad at taking care of his own. Betsy had the irrational belief that though she might be sexy on the outside, she wasn't any good on the inside, that she was stupid and unlovable. She was relatively confident sexually but insecure in every other way.

Mark and Betsy's marriage turned out to be a match made in heaven, partly because they had complementary pathogenic beliefs. Their strengths and their weaknesses lined up in such a way as to sustain a passionate connection. Good chemistry, in other words, doesn't depend only on the similarity between two people, but also on the precise way that their differences line up. The psychologies of Mark and Betsy meshed in a way that made it safe for both of them to feel tremendously excited. Betsy, unlike Mark's first wife, had no problem admiring men and Mark in particular. She enjoyed sex and liked to show off her body and turn her partner on because she took her partner's arousal to mean that he was pleased and satisfied with her, and his arousal turned her on. Betsy's psychology was an aphrodisiac to Mark. He could let go of his customary caretaking vigilance and indulge his own needs because his self-indulgence made Betsy feel happy, not hurt. Betsy even wanted Mark to be sexually selfish because only then could she be sure that he was completely fulfilled. A woman who was thrilled by his selfishness rather than offended by it negated Mark's guilt and enabled him to get aroused. If Betsy had had less of an exaggerated need to please men, Mark might not have been able to convince himself that it was safe to be selfish and thus might not have felt secure enough to get maximally excited.

Mark, unlike Betsy's first husband, had no problem being sensitive and caring. Betsy didn't expect much in the way of caretaking—in fact, she struggled with a belief that she didn't deserve any at all. As a result, Betsy responded intensely to Mark's kindness and felt sexually liberated by it. She felt understood and accepted when he was attuned to her, something easy for Mark to be. Thus, Mark powerfully disproved Betsy's irrational self-denigrating belief that she was defective and repulsive, making it safe for her to become sexually exuberant. If Mark had had less of an exaggerated need to take care of women, Betsy might not have felt reassured enough to let go and enjoy herself.

Chemistry comes about when it is easy for each person to disprove the other person's pathogenic beliefs. The ease with which one partner reassures the other flows from who they are as people, not from a deliberate plan. Chemistry comes from being and not doing; it seems natural. It was natural for Betsy to admire Mark and to make his pleasure a top priority. If examined on its own, Betsy's temperamental need to please men might even appear exaggerated or self-abnegating. But if viewed in the context of her background and current relationship with her husband, Betsy's way of loving and adoring men was actually one of the pillars that supported this very healthy and happy relationship. This was balanced by Mark's sensitivity to women, which he had spent his life perfecting. Even though Betsy didn't require, as had his first wife, its constant exercise, he was by far the most understanding and caring man that she had ever met. Their personality quirks lined up in such a way that they naturally provided the reassurances that they each needed to free up their capacities for pleasure and excitement.

Betsy and Mark did have a basically healthy relationship and sex life, but the fact that they each had their own psychological baggage certainly created periodic frictions. This was real love, after all, not the storybook variety. There were tensions that arose from the very traits that had brought Mark and Betsy together. Betsy's belief that she was unlovable didn't go away simply because Mark loved her. Mark's guilt didn't just go away because Betsy never blamed him. These were feelings and beliefs that went back a long way and, while modified, were still operative in each person and thus were bound to cause problems, but they could be worked through in a relatively straightforward way because underneath there was a strong connection and sense of complementarity.

What if such a complementarity isn't there? What happens if each partner's pathogenic beliefs reinforce the other's? What happens is bad chemistry and a sexual impasse. Sexual problems in a couple often stem from a system in which the very thing that one person needs to reduce feelings of guilt, rejection, or shame enough to get aroused is the very thing that the other person would feel too guilty, rejected, or ashamed to provide—and vice versa. To illustrate this painful, but common, dynamic, let's consider the case of Jim and Laurie.

"THE BAD": THE CASE OF JIM AND LAURIE

As she sat in my office during our first session, Laurie nervously and repeatedly looked at her husband, Jim. Jim seemed remote and had positioned his chair so that it pointed about forty-five degrees away from Laurie. As is so often true with couples, these physical postures turned out to be symbols of the underlying tension in their relationship, namely that Laurie was anxious about their attachment and Jim was burdened by it. Laurie and Jim had been sent to me by their individual therapists for couples counseling because of a complete breakdown in their sexual relationship. Their presenting complaint seemed simple enough: Laurie had developed a medical condition that, even with treatment, resulted in decreased vaginal lubrication. In order to have sex without pain, she needed the help of an artificial lubricant of some kind and had suggested to her husband that they incorporate its application into their foreplay. Jim, however, found himself feeling terribly upset about this idea because of his belief that if Laurie's vagina was being lubricated artificially, he could never be sure if she was genuinely excited. He told her that he could tolerate it—barely—if she applied the lubricant herself, as long as he wasn't around to see it or didn't have to do it himself. He found himself repelled by the notion because of what he felt it communicated—or failed to communicate—about Laurie's sexual desire. Laurie felt hurt by Jim's attitude, interpreting it as a rejection of her. She wanted Jim to desire her so much that he would *want* to do whatever it took to make sex enjoyable and easy. As Laurie's anxiety about Jim's interest level mounted, Jim was not only unable to reassure her but seemed to become somewhat defiant in his insistence that their sex life wasn't so great to begin with. Eventually, they stopped having sex altogether.

The most striking thing about this situation was the extent to which Jim and Laurie completely misunderstood each other. Each person's subjective experience seemed so compellingly true that she or he was unable to grasp, much less validate, any competing version of the truth. Each had a need for reassurance that felt totally obvious, reasonable, and valid. It felt to both Jim and Laurie that to concede the other's point of view, to put themselves in each other's shoes, would be to relinquish their right to have their own emotional needs validated and met. This is a common psychological predicament in couples. Understanding yields to an emotional zero-sum game—if one person is right, the other person has to be wrong.

The deeper truth was that while Jim and Laurie's needs for reassurance were legitimate from their subjective points of view, each of them was also in the grip of tormenting feelings and fears that, at their heart, did not have a rational basis at all, feelings and fears that derived instead from their own backgrounds and that had been imported into their relationship. Their subjective experiences not only were vastly different, but each was partially based in distortions born of childhood trauma. Each of them was driven by unconscious demons that masqueraded as reasonable, conscious concerns. Ultimately, this was the reason that they couldn't communicate well about sex. They couldn't yet face, much less speak, the deepest truth about what they felt.

What didn't Jim and Laurie adequately understand? First of all, Jim was more worried than he admitted that he couldn't satisfy Laurie. In fact, his ability to satisfy a woman was at the core of his self-image. It was as if a woman's dissatisfaction completely impaled him; he felt that he had no choice but to take it to heart. Jim's father, who had a history of job failures and two previous marriages, had abandoned the family when Jim was about four years old, leaving him to be raised by a mother who was openly hostile toward men. Soon after her husband left her, Jim's mother came out as a lesbian and began publishing a radical feminist magazine that often pilloried men. According to Jim, his mother's view was that men were usually disappointments if not outright misogynists. He remembers that his mother hung a poster over their toilet that read: "Men: Can't Live with 'Em. Can't Just Kill 'Em." He said, with just a note of irony, "I had to look at this every time I peed. . . . No wonder I was confused about what it meant to be a man!" Given this environment, it was inevitable that Jim would develop the irrational belief that women weren't ever happy with men. At the same time, however, he came to feel that if he didn't make them happy, he was, in the words of his mother, a "pig" like his father.

For Jim to lubricate Laurie artificially would be to leave unanswered the question of whether she was *really* happy with him. In his unconscious mind, he was guilty until irrefutably proven innocent. It didn't matter that Laurie reassured him otherwise. In Jim's mind, physiology spoke louder than words. Jim was in the grip of what might have been called a "maternal transference" to Laurie in the sense that he experienced her needs as accusations, just as he had with his mother. For Jim to plunge ahead and *not* worry about Laurie's "true" feelings of arousal, to have sex with her because he simply wanted to, was to risk being experienced as a selfish pig of a man. The more anxious Laurie became about his interest, or lack thereof, the more difficulty Jim had feeling desire because her complaints and anxiety unwittingly raised the specter again in his mind of an unhappy and unsatisfied woman for whose unhappiness he was responsible. Burdened by the "impossible" task of making Laurie happy, Jim went on "strike," gave up, or simply turned away. And as most people who are in the grips of a sexual problem are wont to do, he then blamed his partner, maintaining the flimsy rationalization that Laurie wasn't *really* into sex, despite her protests (and medical evidence) to the contrary.

Laurie, on the other hand, was unknowingly in the grips of her own pathogenic childhood beliefs. She had grown up with a mother who systematically belittled her and made her feel inadequate. Laurie was developmentally delayed when it came to her motor skills. She stood and moved awkwardly and had poor coordination. Her mother used to call her names like "ducky" because her toes pointed inward, and made jokes at her expense when she tripped or had trouble balancing things that she was carrying. Laurie complied with her mother's disparagement and felt disgusting and deficient as a person and particularly as a woman. Her problem with vaginal lubrication threatened to reinforce her feeling of being defective as a woman. For Laurie, the only way to counteract this pathogenic belief about her femininity was for Jim not only to *not mind* if she used artificial lubrication, but for him to get turned on by applying it himself during their foreplay. She interpreted his unwillingness to do so as a confirmation that her worries about herself were justified, that she was disgusting to men and inadequate as a woman. Laurie was not aware of what was really at stake for her. She hid her own intense insecurity about her femininity behind her "reasonable" expectations that Jim stop holding an unavoidable medical condition against her. She couldn't communicate the deeper levels of her self-loathing and anxiety because she didn't understand them herself.

What, then, was the core problem here? To oversimplify somewhat, Jim experienced Laurie as an unhappy mother, and Laurie experienced Jim as a critical and rejecting one. Neither of them understood this because each one experienced him or herself as having legitimate needs and grievances that were being ignored. Laurie couldn't understand Jim's worry, not only because he didn't understand it himself, but because she was seeing him through the distorting lens of her own idiosyncratic anxieties. Jim didn't understand that Laurie felt that when he gave up on trying to please her, she took this as a sign of his disgust for her femininity, a disgust that she secretly felt was well deserved. He couldn't understand this, not only because Laurie didn't fully understand it herself, but because this wasn't at all Jim's experience of her problem with lubrication. Neither one of them could understand the other's point of view. Each of them was in the grips of the reemergence of a childhood theme that was distorting their own and each other's reactions.

Sexual interest is an extremely sensitive barometer of conflicts in a relationship. Sexual problems can be the earliest sign of a covert fight or hidden sense of injury and misrecognition in a couple. It is often a tip-off to the secret workings of guilt and anxiety, even when the surface manifestations of such feelings might be missing. It is in the intimacy of our sexual lives that the fault lines of our psyches are most obvious. Jim couldn't understand Laurie's feelings of rejection because, in his mind, he wasn't rejecting her—he was simply defending himself against his worry that he wasn't making her happy. Laurie couldn't understand Jim's feelings of guilt and inadequacy because she didn't actually think he was selfish or inadequate but felt inadequate herself.

As we worked to clarify these issues, Jim and Laurie became more sympathetic to each other and began to make compromises. Laurie gave up on some of her insistence that Jim lubricate her each time they had sex, and Jim began to experiment with lubricating Laurie as part of their foreplay.

". . . AND THE UGLY": THE CASE OF ROB AND NICOLE

My patient Rob was inordinately worried about pleasing his wife, Nicole. He had grown up with a mother whom he experienced as often unhappy and self-abnegating. His father was absent most of the time. Rob felt responsible for his mother and very guilty about being too selfish, hedonistic, ambitious, or aggressively assertive. He developed the irrational belief that if a woman saw him as too ruthless or selfish in taking sexual pleasure, she would feel left out and hurt. Therefore, Rob was tentative in bed with his wife and ultra-sensitive to clues about Nicole's mental state, particularly her level of sexual readiness and excitement. He was cautious, gentle, and slow in his lovemaking, rarely initiating it unless he was sure she was interested. He refrained from staring too intently at her breasts or genitals, talking "dirty," or being rough or coarse with her. As we discovered, Rob, of course, secretly wanted to do all these forbidden things but felt enormously guilty about it. He privately fantasized about being a voyeur but couldn't put it into practice. As a result, his general sexual motivation became muted.

Rob's considerate style of lovemaking, however, was anathema to Nicole. Her most exciting sexual fantasy was to be thrown on the bed and ravished. She wanted Rob to take over and not worry about her pleasure. She was turned off by Rob's deference because she felt that she was being made to feel responsible for everything. Tender regard turned her off. In fact, when Rob demonstrated this kind of deference, Nicole would get irritated and complain that he wasn't doing it "right." When Rob tried to be a "nice guy," Nicole would shut down and feel critical.

The irony was that they were more alike than they knew. Nicole had grown up with a great sense of guilt of her own toward both parents. She felt guilty about being stronger than her mother, a woman she described as depressed and often bedridden. She had surpassed her mother in almost every area of her life, from school to sports, and felt guilty about having done so. Nicole then developed a need to put herself down and developed the pathogenic belief that she wasn't supposed to have a better and more exciting sex life than her mother as well. In addition, Nicole was often worried about her father, whom she saw as weak and unreliable. Her father was an alcoholic who consistently brought the family to the edge of economic chaos.

So why couldn't Nicole simply tell Rob the truth, that she actually wanted him to be rough and ruthless with her, that it wouldn't hurt her, and that the last thing she wanted was for him to worry about her? To the extent that she did tell him, why couldn't Rob simply change course and act as the aggressive lover that he secretly wanted to be?

The problem, at one level, seemed clear. Both Rob and Nicole were unconsciously guilty about hurting each other. Both were burdened by exaggerated feelings of responsibility. Both felt that they had to worry about the other's inner state and well-being to the exclusion of their own selfish pleasure. Because these beliefs were so ingrained, because they had originated in the cauldrons of their family lives, they simply didn't and wouldn't believe the other's claims to the contrary. Rob didn't really believe Nicole when she said that she wanted him to sexually dominate her. She might *say* that she wanted Rob to stop worrying about pleasing her, but the fact remained that she seemed displeased a lot of the time in bed.

Nicole, on the other hand, didn't really believe Rob when he said that he urgently wanted to be more aggressive in bed, but that he held himself back out of a fear that he'd hurt her. She didn't believe him when he eventually admitted that he was turned on by objectifying women's bodies. After all, Rob did act tentatively in bed and seemed to be overly anxious about his performance. His actions spoke louder than his words because they confirmed her unconscious belief that men were basically weak and that she had to take care of them. Ironically, Nicole would have liked more of this kind of sexual admiration and voyeurism in her sex life with Rob but couldn't take Rob at his word that this was what he also wanted.

When Rob told her that she did not have to feel responsible for him, that as far as he was concerned, she should even feel free to throw *him* on the bed and have her way with him, she couldn't believe this sentiment either. Nicole was stuck in the belief that the only way she could really let go was if she had a partner who was bigger, stronger, and sturdier than she. She obviously felt too guilty to gratify her own sexual desires and impulses with impunity. Rob might be saying that he was holding himself back and that he wanted her to be more sexually assertive, but the power of her transference obligated her to discount his explanation.

Misunderstandings like this can go on for years. Both Rob and Nicole were afraid that if they took control of the situation and aggressively went after what they wanted, they would hurt each other. In addition, they both had the unconscious belief that, in light of their parents' grim experience of the world, they weren't supposed to have a fantastic sex life. Guilt was the glue that held this sexual stalemate in place.

Rob's sexual fantasies clearly functioned as an antidote to the feelings and fears that were holding him back in bed. In his fantasies he was the lustful voyeur, and the object of his desire was none the worse for wear. Nicole's sexual fantasies were similarly indicative of her underlying conflicts. Nicole would fantasize about being raped by a powerful man who treated her with utter indifference. It turned out that both of them used these fantasies, not only to masturbate, but to get and stay turned on with each other on the rare occasions when they had sex. If they had been able to talk about and understand each other's sexual fantasies, they would have had further evidence that neither of them was as fragile and uninhibited as they both secretly feared.

Clinically, we see this type of situation all of the time. If each member of a couple is overly responsible and self-effacing, their sexual chemistry usually suffers. And such pairings are common, mainly because the underlying personality traits of guilt and responsibility are common. If you put two people with these types of issues together in a relationship, the intimacy can often threaten sexual desire. In the beginning of such a relationship, the presence of mutual idealization remedies each person's tendency to feel overly guilty and responsible. As idealizations yield to the sober exigencies of everyday life, however, trouble starts to brew. Still under the sway of their childhood feelings and beliefs about the fragility of others and the danger of hurting them, each person reacts to a growing perception of his or her partner's vulnerabilities by becoming more tentative, less aggressive, more restrained, and less aroused. Sexual ruthlessness and sexual desire itself become inhibited. The ongoing irony—or tragedy, depending on how severe the inhibitions are— is that each partner actually wants nothing more than for the other to be ruthless, to assert, and to take what he or she wants without worrying so much about the other's well-being.

THE PROBLEM OF "THE GOOD WIFE"

Sexual misunderstandings often seem part of our culture. Consider the common situation in which a woman suppresses her own sexual longings in order to be the "good" wife and mother that she assumes her husband expects. Her guilty conviction is that she can't be—and shouldn't want to be—both a lustful woman and a responsible wife and mother. Her husband, however, experiences his "good" wife as asexual, innocent, and fragile, and therefore feels highly responsible for her. He worries about hurting or degrading such a "good" woman with his "dirty" interests, and consequently he feels somewhat sexually turned off at home. The man's worries are usually heavily exaggerated by transferences from his childhood, a past in which he probably felt unduly responsible for his mother. In addition, men in our culture are steeped, whether they know it or not, in what is called the "mother/whore" split—the split image of women as either asexually maternal and on a pedestal, or degraded and sexually "loose." The man is, therefore, further driven to transfer his sense of obligation to and responsibility for his mother onto his wife. Under the sway of these transferences, he inevitably suppresses his excitement because his unconscious mind assumes that his wife needs protection and *not* uninhibited sexuality. In fact, the reason that many men put their partners on pedestals in the first place is because of their unconscious need, motivated by guilt, to reassure the "fairer sex" that they won't be sullied or contaminated by selfish, aggressive, and prurient male impulses.

What does the man, then, do with his "prurient" sexual interests and needs? He becomes prurient elsewhere. He splits off his sexual preferences and projects them onto other women—strangers, models, porno actresses, or the sexually wild and uninhibited women who populate his fantasy life. The key for the man is simply this: *In his imagination, these "other" women love sex.* They love to have it in every position, place, or manner that he can imagine. He doesn't have to worry about hurting these women with his lust because he imagines that they're lustful themselves.

The tragedy is, of course, that this man's wife would usually like to have sex more wildly and more frequently. Why can't she? The surface answer is that her life as a wife, mother, and, often, wage earner, simply wears her out. But if we probe beneath her physical and social burdens, we can often find very particular psychological ones. Often, for instance, we find that the woman has suppressed her sexual longings under the illusion that that's what her husband wanted or because of a guilty, unconscious belief that she isn't *supposed* to feel wild or ruthless sexual desire in her role as good wife and mother. Her own fantasy life may, in fact, be filled with sexual escapades in which she's much more out of control of her excitement. They may even be "dirty," aggressive, fetishistic, and wild— precisely the kind of qualities and proclivities that her husband would like to have in a sexual partner. But she has often had to relegate these to her fantasy life, perhaps only occasionally acting them out, not only because of social sanctions against this sort of sexuality in women, but because of her deep conviction that her husband couldn't handle these desires and would either become hurt or reject her if he knew about them. The wife unconsciously protects her husband's ego by taming her own passion. The irony is clear: both the husband and wife want the same thing—a looser, wilder, more passionate sex life—but are prevented from having one because of the unspoken, and often unconscious assumptions that the other person cannot or will not participate.

Many couples, both gay and straight, desexualize each other. In traditional heterosexual relationships, it is common for women to desexualize themselves and their male partners. Despite the ethos of sexual liberation, many women feel that once they've gotten into a committed primary relationship, particularly when this commitment leads to marriage and children, they are supposed to give up the wilder sexual intensity that might have marked their single years. A patient of mine, complaining of a lack of sexual interest on her part after her marriage, made light of the problem in the following quip: *"How do you get a Jewish girl to stop having sex? Marry her!"*

This joke speaks to more than anti-Semitic stereotypes. It is an attempt to capture the (often) dramatic change in their feelings about sex that many women and men, Jewish and non-Jewish, experience when they "settle down."

One of the most important things that the joke leaves out is the degree to which society expects women to lose their sexual passion and intensity when they become mothers. This broad social expectation that women suppress their sexuality often resonates with conflicts in their childhoods. The key to this desexualization lies in how much guilt these women feel about having more sexual pleasure in their lives than their own mothers did. This belief is usually unconscious, developing as it did in early childhood and adolescence when a daughter is vulnerable to any communication from her mother about the importance of sexual fulfillment in her own as well as in her daughter's life. This communication may be explicit—I've heard many stories from women who grew up consciously knowing that their mothers were sexually unhappy because these mothers frankly told them so—or it may be conveyed through the way that a mother lives her life. In the end, the result is the same. These daughters grow up with the unconscious belief that if their mother's marriage, sex life, and life in general wasn't a good one, the daughters shouldn't lay claim to much excitement either.

A colleague of mine told me about a patient of his who seemed to represent an extreme example of the degree to which a woman can feel driven to suppress, and then redirect in fantasy, her own sexuality out of an unconscious sense of guilt. His patient was engaged to be married. She had grown up with a strong injunction from her mother to not be "promiscuous" but to get married early and raise a family. Her mother was an unhappy housewife who had carefully supervised her daughter's social life and kept asking the daughter when she was going to "make her happy" by getting married. The daughter eventually became engaged to a man who seemed responsible and kind but with whom she felt sexually inhibited. She knew that her fiancé wanted to have a wilder and more frequent sex life, but her unconscious need to be "good" made her act as if she was supposed to be constrained in the bedroom.

This patient, however, had an active fantasy life that belied this sexually proper image. She used to surf the Internet and visit sexual chat rooms in which those present would, under the cover of anonymity, indulge her sexual fantasies. Her favorite fantasy was one she called the "slutty bride" fantasy. In the fantasy she was having sex with her husband's best man and groomsmen on her wedding day, all the while wearing her formal, white lace wedding dress. She was being defiled, treated like a whore, and felt just like one on this, the most important and virginal day of her life. The fantasy had to be "dirty," rough, and crude. The psychological point of it was to rebel radically against her compliance with her mother and dismantle the image of herself as a "good girl." To the extent that she was ostensibly degraded in her fantasy, it only further diminished her guilt—she was, after all, a secret harlot underneath the trappings of a virginal bride. Her guilty compliance and identification with her repressed and repressive mother inhibited her, while fantasies of being a harlot freed her up to get aroused.

At times the manifestations of sexual problems in the bedroom seem to be so stereotypical that they seem like part of a Hollywood movie—older man leaves wife for younger woman, sex dies out after the birth of the first child, economic strain leaves little time or energy for sex, power struggles on the emotional level breed hostile rejection in the sexual arena, alcoholism or drug use suppresses all senses, including sexual ones. Even though these patterns of sexual dysfunction are common and strongly impacted by social influences, they all involve highly personal, and often unconscious, processes that are not immediately apparent.

Consider, for instance, the many ways in which hostility between partners regularly interferes with sexual arousal and performance. It's probably universal that when our partner is hostile, we feel rejected and vice versa. Intimate relationships sensitize people to rejection, and rejections regularly occur in most intimate relationships. "Not tonight, dear . . . I have a headache" has entered our vernacular as the classic form that sexual rejection takes. She or he may really have a headache or may be, as this remark usually implies, covertly rejecting the other's sexual advances. And rejection, as we've seen, is incompatible with sexual arousal.

There are many other ways for hostility and rejection to be conveyed in a relationship—various forms of chronic fighting, "tit for tat" rejections, covert power struggles, or competitions that are, or become, sexual. Examples of these dynamics are legion. On the simplest level, people often withhold sex as a classic weapon in both the cold and hot wars that they engage in with their partners. It seems to be a common pattern that a woman won't "give" her man sex because he won't take care of her emotionally. Or a man is so angry at his partner that he ejaculates immediately after penetrating her, leaving her dissatisfied. Or either partner might be feeling devalued by the other and may subtly criticize his or her sexual performance.

These kinds of bedroom wars can go on for years, with sexual passion their primary victim. Some people are more disposed to feeling rejected than others, more sensitive to slights than others. The difference usually involves the extent to which people felt rejected by one or both parents while growing up. Some are so highly sensitive to rejection they are prepared to read it into situations that might, in fact, be ambiguous or even benign. I have had patients who will infer from a look, a gesture, or a tone of voice that his or her partner isn't sexually interested, and this will immediately be read as a rejection and turn the patient off. Sometimes this sensitive person's inferences are correct. At other times they're not. In a situation where there isn't, in fact, a rejection—when, for instance, one's partner is simply tired or distracted and *not* offering a sexual rebuff—the prophecy can and does become self-fulfilling. The person reeling from an imaginary rebuke sexually shuts down and thereby rebukes his or her partner.

Often, however, fights between couples can be *resolved* by sex. I have heard many patients, as well as friends, report that some of their most exciting sex has occurred in just such situations. Using sex to make up after a fight is a scenario so enshrined in our culture that it seems natural. But if fighting usually turns people off, what is it about certain types of fighting that enhances sexual passion? Why is it that, for some couples, the emotional reconciliation is accomplished in bed?

The answer lies not in the inherent erotism of anger or conflict, but in the way sexual arousal functions as a solution to the problem of emotional distance, loss, and pain. Couples often, in fact, unconsciously *arrange* to have arguments to begin with in order to create emotional distance. Sexual excitement can then safely emerge and help the couple reestablish a connection. This is a complicated but important process, one that most people have experienced at some point in their relationships. It's worth a closer examination.

The real psychological threat to sexual passion in such situations is not the fighting—it is what the fighting is intended to counteract. Fighting is an effective way of establishing psychological separation. When people are fighting, their opponent—in this case, their partner—is "over there," outside and apart. Arguments build a fence between people. Sometimes these fences are intended to hurt the other person. Other times their unconscious purpose is to resist forces in a relationship that promote identification and merger. Intimacy promotes this type of psychological closeness, which, while comforting on one level, can be threatening on another. It collapses the differences between people, and therefore makes an individual's sense of self and of sexual ruthlessness difficult to maintain. Sexual excitement is imperiled because there isn't enough differentiation to allow for it. Arguing, therefore, can be first and foremost an attempt to free ourselves from the threatening and sexually inhibiting effect of intimacy and merger.

As a result of the differentiation created by the argument, sexual excitement again becomes possible. Now the partners are facing each other as two individuated people. The threat of merger reduced, sexual ruthlessness is possible. It becomes safe to get excited again. Moreover, the couple becomes motivated to get excited because fighting threatens each of them with the dangers of loss and rejection. Merger and identification produce the need to fight that produces the need to have sex. Depending on the personalities involved, this cycle can be repeated endlessly.

Patterns of fighting and sexual reconciliation are not heterosexual phenomena. They are human phenomena born of the inherent tensions between intimacy and sexuality, between psychological closeness and separation. In fact, the dynamic—and often vicious—circle of merger-fighting-separation-sexual excitement-intimacy-merger is often reported in lesbian couples. There is a phenomenon known as "lesbian bed death." The issue seems to be that lesbian relationships often promote, and are grounded in, strong currents of identification and bear the stamp of powerful maternal transferences. These processes can, on the one hand, be one of the pillars of an unusually deep and satisfying intimacy. On the other hand, the kinds of identification upon which this closeness is grounded can lead to a collapse of the separation and psychological distance required to sustain erotic excitement, causing the relationship to become tilted too much toward nurturing and not enough toward ruthlessness. The fighting/reconciliation cycle, then, easily gets activated.

On one level, a couple's emotional and sexual life can seem

strangely unrelated. Couples who are emotionally close may be sexually inhibited, while estranged or acrimonious ones may only have a good sex life keeping them together. Some couples describe their initial sexual connection as similar to being struck by lightning; others feel as though they've grown into it. Still others never do ignite any sexual fire. All couples are burdened by being exposed to a vast array of social conditioning concerning what they should feel sexually, how they should feel it, and what they should do about it. But complicating these external pressures on our sexuality are the vast array of very particular psychological issues with which we each grew up. Our beliefs and feelings about them are, ultimately, what will determine sexual compatibility.

Of course, couples are rarely aware of these dynamics. People tend to feel that their sexual responses, or lack thereof, are mysterious and somehow biological. Couples will say, "The spark has just gone out of our relationship," as if the "spark" is a fact of nature. On the other hand, sexual attraction and intensity are equally experienced as "natural" or biochemical in nature. "We just have good chemistry," couples will say, as if chemistry has no psychological explanation. But, as I have shown, sexual chemistry—or its absence—arises from meaningful psychological sources. Awareness of these sources can only benefit couples trying to understand and communicate what is going on in their relationships.

6

The Role of Sexual Fantasies in Psychotherapy

The noblest pleasure is the joy of understanding.

—Leonardo da Vinci

Not everything that is faced can be changed; but nothing can be changed until it is faced.—James Baldwin

In the course of investigating the twists and turns of a patient's life, I inevitably encounter sex. In this chapter I want to describe how I work with sexual fantasies in psychotherapy. How does sex emerge as a topic? How do I approach its investigation? If the dynamics of sexual arousal involve someone's most important psychological conflicts, how do I work with the many bridges between sexual and nonsexual issues? If, as I've argued, fantasies negate certain pathogenic beliefs that inhibit us, and if some of our basic problems in life stem from these same beliefs, then how do I use fantasies as a tool in understanding what really ails my patients? To answer these questions, it is important to describe in much more detail than I have so far exactly how I work as a psychotherapist.

The manner in which I practice psychotherapy is well suited to uncovering the hidden meanings of sexual fantasy because it is based on a theory of the mind that is especially sensitive to these meanings. When a patient and I discover the unconscious logic behind a particular sexual preference or daydream, we open a door to understanding the causes of the psychological problems that brought the patient into therapy to begin with. In my practice, these problems usually are not explicitly sexual in nature. In contrast to a sex therapist, who specializes in treating sexual dysfunction, I treat people seeking help with more general life problems, from marital strife, to work inhibitions, to severe states of depression and anxiety. As a result, my approach to sexual fantasies and sexual preferences, when they do emerge in therapy, is not to change or "fix" them unless this is something the patient explicitly wants. My clinical strategy involves making use of patients' sexual fantasies and preferences to illuminate the innermost workings of their minds, which as a result helps us solve their other, nonsexual, problems.

Most of us are unaware of the deeper meanings of our sexual fantasies or preferences and lack the motivation to discover them. We go through our lives having sexual thoughts and daydreams every day, getting aroused now and then, and never feel the need to understand the exact chain of mental events that precede and cause our experience. Except if we're in therapy. In therapy people not only have the opportunity, but often the motivation, to explore their sexual wishes and fears. The opportunity arises because the therapy relationship creates conditions that are safe enough for people to talk about private and embarrassing subjects like sex. The motivation comes from a number of sources, depending on the patient. Some people obviously *want* to talk about their sexual thoughts and feelings when sex is a problem of some kind. My patient Rob, for example, consulted me because of his inability to get, and stay, sexually excited with his wife, Nicole. Our psychotherapeutic work began with an exploration of Rob's feelings about sex and focused on the conditions under which he could get aroused—including in his fantasies—and those under which he would become sexually inhibited.

Sometimes patients enter therapy with sex the furthest thing from their minds, only to find it surfacing as the therapy proceeds. Jim and Laurie, for example, didn't come to see me because of sexual difficulties but because of their concern that stresses in their relationship were contributing to their son's psychological difficulties. It emerged during our consultation that one of their stresses was, in fact, a significant sexual problem involving Laurie's need for a special kind of stimulation and Jim's discomfort in providing it. Esther, of the Mardi Gras fantasy, sought treatment for depression not sexual difficulties. It was only in the course of exploring her low self-esteem that the importance of her sexual inhibitions and exhibitionistic fantasies emerged.

In my experience, the more common clinical situations in which the causes of sexual excitement are discussed are ones in which the focus isn't on sex at all. Instead, in the course of dealing with such problems as low self-esteem, anxiety, marital discord, or work inhibitions, patients discover that their sexual fantasies shine an especially bright light on the nonsexual problem with which they're struggling. This was the case with my patient Matt, who came to see me because he was having panic attacks in response to competition and conflict at work. In the course of exploring his fears of confrontation and his guilt about self-assertion, Matt eventually revealed the details of his addictive use of phone sex. Neither he nor I viewed phone sex as his central problem, but we were able to use it to get to the heart of the issue that lay behind Matt's difficulties at work, namely his irrational guilt about burdening and draining others with his needs. The presence of guilt was not surprising to either of us. Rather, Matt's phone-sex fantasy threw into sharper relief the origins and meaning of this guilt. Based on this understanding of Matt's sexual fantasy, we better understood the difficulty he had at work in aggressively asserting his own interests. Matt unconsciously believed that if he demanded what he needed at work, his coworkers and bosses would feel burdened and drained just as his mother had.

Thus, some people seek therapy for help with sex, and others use sex to help with their therapy. However, despite their potential therapeutic utility, sexual details are difficult for many people to talk about. Often patients only hint at their fantasies; and when they do reveal them, they're couched in generalities. This reticence isn't necessarily problematic. Sex isn't all there is to life and, therefore, to the process of changing one's life. While sexuality is an important channel to and from the core of our psyches, it is not the only one. I have had people in therapy for many years, plumbed the depths of their feelings about themselves, their families, and their partners, and helped them resolve core issues in their lives, and never elicited any significant interest on their part in discussing the gritty details of their sexual fantasies or behavior. On the other hand, my clinical experience also tells me that while sometimes the absence of such discussion is due to a lack of clinical relevance, more often it is a function of shame.

SHAME, SELF-ACCEPTANCE, AND SEXUAL FANTASIES IN PSYCHOTHERAPY

Sex is embarrassing to talk about even in the context of a confidential, nonjudgmental therapy relationship. As a result, patients will frequently censor their sexual thoughts and feelings. They will talk about the most private aspects of their work and love lives, recount the most embarrassing situations of their childhood, and reveal their most unflattering thoughts but resist talking about the details of what sexually arouses them or turns them off. At one level this resistance merely reflects the general shame and repression that surround the subject of sex in our culture. Despite the fact that we're all bombarded with sexual images by television, movies, magazines, and billboards, and despite decades of sex education and self-help books promoting sexual honesty and communication, most of us still feel that the details of our sex lives are private and not for public consumption, even by a therapist. There is still a widespread view of the body as shameful and its products and appetites as forbidden.

The sexual shame I see in my patients, however, is not just a function of a repressive culture. Sometimes it involves specific and personal concerns that their thoughts and preferences are pathological, shamefully deviating from their personal ideals and self-image. My patient Jan, for example, was a feminist who was ashamed about her rape fantasies. However, after she understood the true meaning of her fantasy—that it was intended to overcome her guilt about being stronger, not weaker, than men—she felt much less ashamed and more self-accepting. One of the goals and benefits of psychotherapy involves lessening patients' shame about their sexual fantasies and desires by understanding their underlying motivations. Patients often feel embarrassed about their sexual thoughts because they assume that their thoughts define who they *really* are. But Jan didn't really want to surrender her power in real life to a man or be actually raped. Psychotherapy can help people distinguish between who they fantasize themselves to be and who they really are. Insight always enhances self-acceptance.

In the real world, however, fantasies are not always completely private. Sue, a woman in therapy with a colleague of mine, preferred real sexual practices that were rough and based on heterosexual sadomasochistic roles, involving behaviors ranging from light bondage or enactments of rape to actual physical pain and humiliation. Sue also believed, with some embarrassment, that her sexual behavior expressed her innermost longing for a man to overpower her. She couldn't let herself off the hook by reminders that her fantasies didn't reflect what she really wanted; her actions apparently spoke louder than mere fantasies. The question, then, arises: since Sue is acting out, and not just fantasizing about, her desires, doesn't the difference between fantasy and reality become blurred? In my clinical experience, Jan and Sue are more similar than different, and the clinical distinction between fantasy and reality is still crucial. The manifest behavior that Sue prefers in the bedroom is no more a transparent expression of her "true" self than is Jan's private daydream. Neither Jan nor Sue wants to be weak or raped in reality; both insist that the actual sex that is occurring is consensual, and both ultimately are getting excited by the *fantasy* of being helplessly overpowered while remaining, in reality, in control. Jan's control is obvious since she is the sole author of her fantasy, while Sue's control is hidden but just as real. Sadomasochistic scenarios, like the ones that Sue enjoys enacting, always give the masochist the power to say no at every moment, to regulate the exact amount of helplessness, humiliation, or pain that she or he endures. Sue is in charge of her own domination.

Neither woman is actually overpowered. Sue, the practicing masochist, is engaged in the same fantasy as Jan, the imaginary masochist, and for the same reasons. It is irrelevant, in terms of the psychological meaning and function of the fantasy, whether the theater in which it is staged is public or private. Sue may be obliged to modify her fantasy in order to accommodate her partner, while Jan is not, but the underlying issues are the same. Both women are attempting to overcome feelings of guilt and pathogenic beliefs about hurting their partners by arranging to be dominated and "forced" to have sex. Domination is the imaginary means to a pleasurable end, not the end in itself.

Whether we act out our fantasy in a consensual way or keep it as a private daydream, we are writing a script, performing a role, and the result is theater, not reality. When patients like Jan and Sue come to realize this in therapy, they feel less shame and, as a result, improve their self-esteem.

The clinical importance of the distinction between fantasy and reality was equally important—and complicated—in the case of Otto, the patient who admitted that he masturbated to porno-graphic images of teenage girls. The main issue in Otto's therapy wasn't sex at all, but his struggle to feel more separate from his wife and to decrease his reactivity to her perceived imperfections, which, to Otto, included both her tendencies toward depression and the physical signs of her aging. In the course of trying to treat the prob-lems in his marriage, his use of pornography surfaced, and our anal-ysis of its true meaning helped his overall treatment enormously. Otto's primary impulse was not to go out into the real world and have sex with teenage girls but instead to achieve sexual pleasure through a fantasy scenario that felt safe. Once he understood that teenage girls unconsciously represented happy women for whom he didn't have to feel responsible and by whose moods he wouldn't have to be contaminated, and not real girls whom he wanted to use and exploit, Otto felt more sympathy for himself and less shame. As a result, he and I were able to work productively on the psycho-logical problems of guilt and identification that were creating the need for pornography to begin with. Such use began to decrease, and his relationship with his wife improved.

The cases of Jan, Sue, and Otto illustrate how psychotherapy, by explaining the hidden logic behind sexual fantasies, can reduce pa-tients' shame and even open up the possibility of changing the basis of their sexual arousal. I say "open up the possibility" because un-derstanding our fantasies doesn't necessarily mean that we want, or need, to change them. Instead, we may simply use increased insight into their meaning to feel better about having them to begin with. Many of us feel weird or deviant about the ways that we get aroused, and understanding the secret logic behind our preferences can feel liberating in and of itself without producing any other change whatsoever.

If we do want to change them, however, deciphering their hidden meaning will help us in several ways. Only when we see that our sexuality is a product of the human mind, that it is constructed and not somehow embedded in our chromosomes, can we conceive of changing it. In addition, if we want to alter our sexual fantasies, we have to first eliminate the shame surrounding them. Therefore, reducing shame by analyzing the unconscious origins of our sexual fantasy life is a necessary, although not sufficient, condition for change.

Whether or not we want to transform our sexual natures, it is important to remember that the presence of a fantasy isn't necessarily a psychological problem in and of itself but a way that the human mind manages to create what it perceives as safe conditions under which it can achieve sexual pleasure. There are exceptions to this rule. Sometimes patients explicitly work in therapy to change a fantasy or preference because it is interfering with their lives—disturbing their relationships or putting them at risk in some way. A patient whose treatment I supervised wanted his wife to dress him up in women's clothing as a prelude to sex, a request that horrified and disgusted her and led her to shut down both sexually and emotionally. This patient loved his wife and wanted to restore their intimacy, and so he sought to figure out ways that he could incorporate elements of his fantasy into their lovemaking in ways acceptable to her. The only way he could do this successfully, however, was to understand the inner dynamics of his cross-dressing preference.

We came to understand that his wish for his wife to dress him in women's clothing involved his guilt about secret feelings of superiority to his wife and women in general. Cross-dressing, it turned out, was a way of abasing himself in his wife's eyes in order to magically reassure her that he didn't look down on her or other women. After analyzing these dynamics, he found ways to enjoy forms of sexual submission in which his wife was able to happily participate.

Other times, of course, therapy needs to focus on changing a sexual fantasy regardless of the patient's expressed wish to do so. If Jan were to act out her rape fantasies by picking up strangers, she might well be exposing herself to disease or physical assault; and whether or not she wanted to change her fantasies, I would view them as problems that needed treatment. And whether or not he saw it as a problem, if Otto were to act out his fantasies by attempting to seduce teenage girls, I would view this not only as harmful to the girls but to himself and make the process of analyzing and changing his fantasies an urgent priority. The point here is that therapists should never take their patients' view of their own sexual fantasies at face value, just as therapists would never sit back and passively accept their patients' manifest willingness to solve other problems as the ultimate guide to therapeutic technique. To use an extreme example, if a patient told me that he was thinking about killing himself by jumping off the Golden Gate Bridge and that he didn't view this as a problem in need of treatment, I would disagree and actively attempt to change his thinking and stop him. (In fact, the therapist is not only ethically obliged to prevent suicide, stop child abuse, and warn potential victims of a patient's intent to harm them, but in most states he or she is legally obliged to do so.)

My general therapeutic stance toward a patient's sexual fantasy life, then, straddles the fence between following the patient's lead and following my own. Unless a patient gives me reason to believe otherwise, I don't automatically think that his or her daydreams or preferences are clinical "problems" to be solved. On the other hand, I am cognizant of the fact that patients don't always know what's best for them and may need the benefit of my protection and authority in order to avoid harming themselves. Having said this, the fact remains that most of the time my approach to eliciting and understanding my patients' erotic imaginations is entirely guided by them. My role is to attempt to understand patients' fantasies from their point of view, to listen carefully for what these fantasies mean to them. Except when my patients' fantasies or preferences threaten to hurt themselves or others, I attempt to leave my own values, politics, and sexual predilections at the consulting room door.

THE ROLE OF PATHOGENIC BELIEFS IN PSYCHOTHERAPY

I approach the subject of sex in exactly the same way I approach every other topic in therapy, namely by attempting to decipher its deepest level of psychological meaning from the patient's subjective point of view. Like most therapists, I try to use empathy to see the world as my patient does. I understand the essence of psychological meaning, however, in a slightly different way than many other therapists. Influenced by the groundbreaking psychoanalytic research of Joseph Weiss and Harold Sampson, I believe that people in therapy are always struggling against their pathogenic beliefs, unconsciously looking for ways to disprove and transcend them. Some therapists, particularly some psychoanalysts, view their patients as caught between their wish to grow and their wish to remain sick. The clinical approach of these therapists emphasizes the importance of dealing with their patients' "resistance" to change, that is, their attempts to thwart and sabotage the therapists' efforts to help them in the service of holding on to their symptoms. In contrast, my approach is based on the belief that people not only come into therapy with a wish to change and master their pathogenic beliefs but even have an unconscious strategy about how to do so.

Of course, most people don't come into therapy complaining

about their pathogenic beliefs. They don't usually say such things as, "I feel like I don't deserve the good things in life," or, "I have a fundamental sense that the world is scary because that's the way my family felt." They come into therapy with such problems as insomnia, marital conflict, depression, or fears of flying. Their pathogenic beliefs lie just below the psychic surface, organizing their experience of the world, and yet the patients themselves are not usually conscious of these dynamics. In my experience, while patients can't usually tell me about their pathogenic beliefs, they subliminally know they are there. They can feel them at work. One of my main goals as a psychotherapist is to help patients discover, describe, and thoroughly understand their pathogenic beliefs.

Joe, a patient of mine, complained bitterly about the fact that his wife was selfish and that he felt he was constantly giving her more than he was getting. He felt the problem lay primarily in his choice of a partner not in his pathogenic beliefs. As we talked about his family background, however, Joe revealed, in moving terms, similar feelings of sacrifice and self-abnegation that he'd felt as a child. His father had been disabled by a stroke when Joe was seven years old, and his mother had had to work to support Joe and his three younger sisters. He was given the responsibility of caring for his sisters much of the time and felt that he was forced to give up his own childhood in order to fill in the gaps left by his parents' physical and emotional absence. Joe developed a series of pathogenic beliefs as a result. He wasn't supposed to want anything for himself, he wasn't supposed to complain, and he should always take care of people less fortunate than himself. He grew up feeling guilty about wishes to put himself first or to be taken care of.

Joe married a woman who was somewhat needy and with whom he felt drawn to replicate the painful childhood situation in which he was forced to be a caretaker, a pattern that confirmed his pathogenic beliefs about relationships. Given these beliefs, Joe could never ask his wife for anything and had difficulty refusing her requests. After he and I came to see how understandable, albeit painful, it was that he had grown up feeling that he was supposed to give up his own life for others, and how he was reenacting this situation with his wife, Joe began to experiment with saying no to her and with articulating his own needs more clearly. To his delight and surprise, his wife was more resilient than he had thought and became more responsive to his need for caretaking.

Joe's case illustrates a common pattern: people often begin therapy with a false or incomplete theory about what ails them, but respond quickly and positively when their underlying pathogenic beliefs—the real source of their problems—are identified.

Consider the case of George, a thirty-six-year-old physician who consulted me for help with his depression two months after he had separated from his wife of ten years. He and his wife shared custody of their six-year-old son. George was miserable about the damage that his decision to separate might do to the boy. In the first session he told me that even though his wife had herself also been trained as a physician, she had cut back on her medical practice in order to raise their son, leaving George as the primary breadwinner in the family. George described his wife as chronically depressed and passive, highly critical of him, and almost completely uninterested in sex. In his experience, his wife, while a devoted mother and housekeeper, expected George to completely take care of her (she was relieved, he believed, when the birth of their son gave her a good reason to stop working) but rarely did the same for him.

George told me that he thought he was depressed because he was grieving the loss of his marriage and family. He had recently read a book about divorce that explained how people in his position need to go through the same stages of mourning as someone does in response to the death of a loved one. George got choked up when he told me that he felt alone and sad much of the time and needed help experiencing and working through his grief.

I asked George to tell me a bit about his childhood. He told me that his father was a salesman who was rarely home and that his mother was a "survivor."

"Do you mean from the war?" I asked.

"No, from her life," he said. "She always seemed like she was barely surviving being alive, much less being a mother. Everything was hard for her. When I think of my childhood, I think of my mother's strained, unhappy face."

George told me that he learned early on that life really began when he left the house and that it had to be put on hold when he returned. He kept his outside life secret from his mother, he said, because if he showed too much excitement or enthusiasm at home, he sensed that his mother became more depressed and bitter and would find a way to deflate him. George described himself as a bit of a loner, the kind of child who always daydreamed. His primary daydream as a child, he told me, was that he was part of someone else's family. When George met his wife in medical school, he found her attractive and serious. "I didn't hear any bells ring or fireworks explode," he said, "but she felt comfortable to be around and seemed like she could provide a secure home."

As I listened to George, I wondered about his pathogenic beliefs. He presented his grief and loss as his main problem, and yet his wife, like his mother, seemed more like someone you'd feel relieved to get *away* from rather than sad about losing. Sure, I told myself, one can feel a lot of pain losing someone who is familiar, even if problematic, and George's partial loss of his son had to be emotionally significant. Still, the fact that he evinced no relief but only sadness about the separation did not make complete sense, even though he was sitting in front of me crying. My experience, as well as my theory, told me that pathogenic beliefs involving separation and survivor guilt were often operative in troubled marriages like George's, keeping them together too long and making their dissolution especially painful. Given the parallels between his wife and his mother, I wondered if George's real problem might lie as much in his guilt as in his grief.

To test out this speculation, I said to George, "You mentioned that you kept your accomplishments secret from your mother. I wonder if one thing you might be keeping secret from yourself here might be that you actually feel relieved about leaving your wife and feel guilty about it, like you're not supposed to want to have an easier life with someone you can have fun with and who can take care of *you* for a change."

There was a pause, and suddenly George stopped crying and began to laugh. "I'm not sure why I'm laughing," he said, "but somehow what you're saying feels completely right, like a weight is being lifted. Somehow I must feel that this separation process is *supposed* to be really hard, just like everything else in my life."

I suggested that since George felt guilty about leaving and about being glad to get out, he had to make the entire process as painful as possible, filled with grief, loneliness, and torment, rather than acknowledge his hopefulness and joy. George went on to talk about how terrible life had been with his wife, especially over the last few years, and how excited he secretly felt about the possibility of a new life.

George's conscious view of his depression was that it was caused by feelings of loss. The real cause of his depression, however, was his separation guilt, his pathogenic belief that he wasn't supposed to leave an unhappy woman behind in order to "selfishly" pursue his own pleasure. Because of his guilt, George's sadness and feelings of grief were exaggerated in order to conceal from himself his relief and excitement. His case illustrates how patients come into therapy suffering from pathogenic beliefs of which they are unaware but which, when correctly identified and understood, can produce immediate relief and stimulate psychological growth.

One of my main goals, then, is to help my patients become aware of their pathogenic beliefs and change them. This is often a slow and difficult process because these beliefs are not factual ones, such as "the earth is flat," which could be disproved, or opinions like "schools shouldn't teach sex education," which could be altered by a persuasive argument, but instead are often more like sensibilities that feel entirely natural, not even like a belief at all. Pathogenic beliefs are often like breathing—they are taken for granted in much the same way that we take for granted the existence of oxygen when we breathe.

Therefore, my approach to psychotherapy usually involves making my patients aware, metaphorically, of their breathing, conscious that they have these beliefs to begin with, that beliefs are not facts of nature, and that, therefore, they can be altered. Once I am able to do this, my goal is to help patients see that while their conceptions were once a reasonable and adaptive response to their childhood environment, they are no longer either reasonable or adaptive in their adult lives.

I look for evidence of these emotional belief structures in everything that my patients say, feel, and do. One patient I treated tended to feel chronically misunderstood and rejected by other people. He presented plenty of evidence that this was realistically true. He didn't, in other words, think that he was suffering from a "belief" at all, much less a pathogenic one. At one point he broke his leg and couldn't leave his house to shop or do even the simplest errands. We were speaking by phone, and I asked him why he hadn't asked any of his friends for help. He told me that his friends were selfish and that he therefore hadn't asked. I knew from his history that his parents had often acted severely rejecting toward him, and so I suggested that he believed that his friends would resent his dependence, just as his parents had, and that despite his complaints he secretly complied with the view that he was a burden. I told him that he was seeing himself and his friends through the eyes of his cruel and insensitive parents. Because he was desperate, he agreed that he had to at least try to get some help. He called a few of his friends and asked them to bring him some groceries, which to his surprise, they gladly did. At this point he was willing to entertain the possibility that his chronic feeling of neglect was as much belief as it was reality and, to the extent it was the latter, it might be a self-fulfilling prophecy.

I approach sexual fantasies in exactly the same way—that is, I seek to explore the underlying beliefs that give rise to them, beliefs about which the patient is almost always unaware. Carl came to see me because he was depressed and had a tendency to ruminate so much about every important decision in his life that he was effectively immobilized. He couldn't decide if he should move, buy a new car, change jobs, put an ad in the personals section, or even if he should jog in the morning before breakfast to get the day off to a good start or wait until the evening in order to unwind and get a good night's sleep. His descriptions of his childhood were relatively sparse and emotionally flat, even his account of his father's death when he was young. He did relate one powerful memory about his mother that he sensed was significant. He remembered that she would spend about one hour each morning getting dressed, a process that always included her putting on a wig, even though as far as he could remember there was nothing particularly wrong with his mother's natural hair. Nevertheless, as he watched her put on her wig every morning, Carl felt that his mother was donning a disguise, something artificial, and didn't want to hug her because he hated the feel of her synthetic hair. To this day, Carl told me, he can't stand to be close to his mother and feels that there is something inaccessible and cold about her.

In the course of talking about his desires and frustrations in intimate relationships, Carl told me that he was especially attracted to tall and athletic women. He denied that his sexual preference had any particularly deep psychological meaning, claiming that since he himself was athletic, he simply appreciated a woman who kept herself in shape. A few sessions later, however, he told me that one of his earliest sexual fantasies—the one, in fact, that he first used to masturbate to when he was an adolescent—was a daydream in which he and a girl were boxing and in which he frequently ended up wrestling with her in "clinches." Something in the hard, physical contact aroused him.

As Carl was telling me about his sexual preferences and masturbation fantasy, I was wondering about his pathogenic beliefs. What sorts of feelings about himself and others would the fantasy of boxing and wrestling with a strong woman address? What ideas might it correct or fears might it assuage? How would it, in the terms of my theory, make him feel "safe"? Based on his relationship with his mother, Carl had grown up feeling that intimacy with a woman was difficult, if not dangerous, that women weren't very genuine and comfortable with who they were. Given the interpersonal minefield that Carl associated with relationships with women, I surmised that sexual excitement would have a difficult time safely flourishing.

It then seemed clearer how his fantasy and preference momentarily solved this problem and made sexual pleasure possible. First of all, Carl's ideal woman was big and strong and didn't need the kind of cosmetic crutches and tresses that his insecure mother seemed to require. Carl's fantasy woman could take care of herself and didn't require his, or anyone's, help or worry. Second, and more important, boxing and wrestling are intensely physical forms of sustained contact. Two bodies collide forcefully. This fantasy negated Carl's sense that connecting with a woman was difficult and artificial—the connection between him and his female opponent was direct, immediate, and unmistakably real.

I pointed out to Carl the centrality of his feelings of disconnectedness as a child and how, in his sexual daydreams, he unmistakably connected with a woman and did not have to feel that she was faking it. "I guess I can at least be sure that her wig won't fall off," Carl agreed.

We were then able to use this insight to understand better his problem of having difficulty making decisions. He told me that when he was faced with having to make a decision, he suddenly felt weak and alone and, as a result, inordinately worried about his ability to make the "right" decision. He wondered if this feeling of being alone had to do with his sense that he couldn't really lean on his mother or trust that she was really there in his corner. He must have given up expecting help from his mother, he reflected. "If I ever turned around to see if she was really in my corner, I'd probably find that she was fussing with her hair," he said. Inevitably the conflicts interfering with our sexual vitality are the same conflicts causing trouble elsewhere in our lives.

SAFETY, TESTING, AND CHANGE IN PSYCHOTHERAPY

Because our childhood attitudes and expectations can cause us so much suffering, we come into therapy highly motivated, consciously or unconsciously, to change them but are also afraid to do so; they have, in our minds, protected us against various dangers. If I became placating and deferential as a child because of the belief that my self-assertion would hurt my father and provoke his retaliation, then I might be loathe to give up such a belief as an adult because of the risk, however miscalculated, of reexperiencing the very danger that

I'd worked so hard to avoid as a child. The reason people seem to "resist" change is not, as many therapists believe, because they're deriving gratification from being sick, but because they're trying to ensure their own psychological safety. At the same time, however, if they come to therapy for help with the distress that their pathogenic beliefs are causing them, they are going to be looking for ways to make it safe to change. As Weiss and Sampson have shown, patients not only look for safety in their therapy in order to change, but they actively attempt to create it.

Patients actively use therapy to establish the conditions that will make it safe enough for them to confront their painful and irrational beliefs and feelings. On the simplest level, they seek to be understood, and when they succeed, as Carl did, they begin to feel safe.

How does understanding help us feel safe? The answer lies in the process by which raw experience becomes personal experience, how our feelings acquire a unique and personal meaning to us. As children we come to know we are angry, sad, scared, or hurt through the responses of our caretakers. We learn to correctly identify our feelings because our parents have correctly identified them first. The old question "Does a tree make a sound when it falls if there is no one around to hear it?" is especially applicable to the concept of psychological pain. Can people know the extent and meaning of their suffering if there is no one around to hear and empathize with it? The answer, generally, is no. If there is no witness to our experience, it doesn't feel legitimate. Most of us didn't understand the true causes of our suffering as children and couldn't articulate our pathogenic beliefs, not simply because our cognitive capacities to do so were limited, but because our environments were deaf to certain aspects of our experience.

Carl's aversion to his mother's artificiality, for example, was certainly never understood by his mother, and his father wasn't around to empathize with it either. Most of us grow up in situations in which our suffering lacks a witness, someone who really "gets" what we're going through. As a result, we feel tremendously relieved when our therapists finally see, accept, and understand our inner worlds. When we feel seen, we can better see ourselves. We finally have a nonjudgmental witness to help us validate our experience.

Patients acquire a sense of safety in therapy in other ways as well. Weiss and Sampson's research, and my own experience, have shown that patients actively, if unconsciously, *test* the therapist to see if it is safe enough for them to bring forth the most troubling parts of themselves for examination and to try out new and healthier attitudes and behaviors. If the therapist passes the test, the patient feels safer and is able to move forward. If the therapist fails the test, the patient's progress stalls or even regresses. This testing process isn't random or accidental but is part of the patient's overall plan for healing, recovery, and growth. As I sit and listen to patients, I am thinking about whether, and to what degree, they are testing me. And when I can figure out the nature of the test, I try my best to pass it and facilitate their plan for mastery and growth.

Patients test in many different ways that, unless one understands this concept, appear paradoxical and confusing. Patients commonly test by inviting their therapist to confirm their worst fears and expectations, to traumatize them in exactly the same way that their parents did originally. They carefully observe and unconsciously evaluate their therapists' responses as either confirming or disconfirming their pathogenic beliefs, subliminally hoping all the while that the therapist will do the latter.

A patient of mine, Margaret, grew up feeling that her independence threatened her mother, that the mother needed her daughter to remain dependent on her. Margaret's pathogenic belief that she shouldn't be independent lest others feel hurt and rejected interfered with her ability to finish college and support herself. When she came to see me, she began subtly to disagree with my interpretations and to make choices that defied my recommendations. I sensed that she was testing me to see if, like her mother, I would become hurt by her independence. If I defensively attempted to assert my authority and control over her behavior, I would fail Margaret's test, and she would not be able to feel safe enough to face her conflicts about her independence. With this in mind, I took a very accepting and nonchalant attitude toward her contentiousness and tried to remain nondefensive when she disagreed with me, while also attempting to make her aware of what was going on. Eventually, she brought forth a memory that she had previously suppressed: whenever Margaret went to a slumber party as a child, her mother would get a migraine headache. Margaret realized that she had inferred as a child that she was hurting her mother by leaving her. I took this memory to be a confirmation that my understanding of Margaret was correct, and that I had passed her test. As a result, Margaret was able to move forward with the process of understanding her conflicts about independence and changing them.

Patients test in many other ways as well. One patient told me after five sessions that she felt better and wanted to stop. I told her that I didn't think she was ready, that her problems were significant, and that we should continue our work. The patient seemed immediately relieved and told me about incidents in her childhood where she had been in trouble and no one in her family had noticed or seemed particularly concerned. She described how she used to use marijuana or cocaine almost every day during her last two years of high school, and her parents seemed too preoccupied to notice. My understanding of this situation was that she wasn't protected as a child and worried that she didn't deserve protection. By telling me she wanted to stop, she tested to see if I, too, would ignore her difficulties. When I refused and told her that she needed further help, she felt safer and was able to tell me with greater ease about her sense of childhood invisibility and neglect. She couldn't face this painful aspect of her childhood until she felt assured that it wouldn't be repeated with me.

Sexual fantasies can often be involved in testing. Matt, the patient with the phone-sex fantasy, related the precise details of his telephone scenarios only after he felt safe enough to do so. This sense of safety was facilitated by the fact that I successfully passed certain of his tests. At first Matt only mentioned in passing that he had an "interest" in pornography, then that he had occasionally tried phone sex, and eventually that he was heavily involved in playing out a very specific sexual fantasy about breast-feeding almost every day. At each stage I attempted to help reduce Matt's shame about talking about these issues, communicating acceptance and curiosity about what he was describing. I conveyed to him that his sexual interests reflected a perfectly understandable attempt to express certain forbidden longings and to overcome particular inhibitions that he had acquired in childhood. In other words, each step that Matt took in revealing his sexual predilections was a kind of test, inviting me to condemn or pathologize him in some way. When I instead normalized his sexual interests, he felt safe enough to convey their full plot and importance.

Often, patients aim to master their pathogenic beliefs by testing their therapists in quite a different way, a way upon which my own theory and clinical approach place particular importance. I refer to this as "passive-into-active" testing, a concept first described by Weiss and empirically defined and tested by Weiss and Sampson. In passive-into-active testing, patients will often do to the therapist what was done to them, replay a childhood situation in therapy, but reverse the roles and treat the therapist in the same unpleasant ways in which they had felt treated by their parents. The test involves seeing if the therapist will be as daunted and traumatized by this behavior as were the patients themselves as children. They secretly hope that the therapist will be healthier and stronger than they were, and that as a result they will be able to identify with this health and strength, silence the voices of the past, and move forward in their lives.

A patient who was sexually seduced or otherwise abused by a parent might be extremely seductive in therapy, inviting the therapist into all sorts of compromising situations. In this model the patient is turning passive into active, actively repeating her (given the high incidence of sexual abuse among girls, it is usually a woman) experience of seduction, intrusion, and guilt with her therapist, but this time, reversing the roles. The therapist usually passes this type of test by gently refusing the seductive invitations. A patient who had suffered growing up with a parent who was inconsolably unhappy, and who often made the patient feel guilty, might come into therapy and act as if nothing the therapist does is right or can satisfy the patient. The therapist is made to feel guilty about not doing enough for the patient in the same way that the patient felt guilty about not doing enough for the parent. The tables get turned, and the patient carefully—though not always consciously—studies the therapist's reactions in order to discover a better way of relating. If, however, the therapist gets overwhelmed by feelings of helplessness and failure, and reacts defensively, the patient will not be able to move forward.

I saw an extreme example of this type of testing in a patient, Rita, whom I treated when I was just beginning in private practice. Rita was chronically suicidal but refused to go into the hospital. Nothing I said or did seemed to help her. As time went on, I felt increasingly guilty, helpless, and incompetent. Eventually I realized that she was turning passive into active. Rita's mother had been chronically depressed and had killed herself when the patient was fourteen. The father had blamed Rita, telling Rita that her mother had been overwhelmed by the burden of raising her. Rita was traumatized by her guilt over her mother's death, and as a result she had never been able to be happy for very long. She was plagued with the pathogenic belief that she had killed her mother and didn't deserve to have a life, let alone a better one. Rita's suicidal tendencies represented an identification with her mother, and in therapy she tortured me—without conscious intent or malice—with the unspoken accusation that I couldn't help her and, as a result, would be responsible for her death.

Passive-into-active tests are not always easy to pass. In the case of Rita I had to try to demonstrate that I would not let myself feel tormented by feelings of guilt and helpless responsibility in response to her depression and threats of suicide in the same way that she had been in response to her mother's. In addition to trying to help Rita understand and modify her sense of omnipotent responsibility for her mother and the resulting need to punish herself, I tried to convey to Rita that while I cared a lot about what happened to her and would try to prevent her from doing harm to herself if I could, I wasn't ultimately responsible for her living or dying and would not be blackmailed into feeling otherwise. Rita was not only outraged by what she decried as my "meanness" but tested it out by making a suicide gesture on the eve of one of my vacations. She called me at home to tell me that she had just cut herself but would not tell me how much she was bleeding, how deep the cut was, and refused to go to the hospital. She was turning passive into active, putting me into a position of helpless and guilty responsibility. I told her that I was calling the police and was having her involuntarily hospitalized until I returned from vacation. She became enraged, telling me that I was abandoning her when she was in her greatest need. I told her that she was trying to make me feel the same way she had felt when she was a child, as if I had life-and-death responsibility for her, and that my wish to go on vacation—symbolically, to enjoy life—was equivalent to wishing her ill. I told her that while she had been plagued with these ideas as a child, they were as false then as they were now, and that I wasn't going to be victimized by them as she had been. In other words, I was indirectly telling Rita that I was going to protect her and make sure that she was in a place where I didn't have to worry about her while I was on vacation.

The police did indeed pick up Rita, and she was hospitalized while I was away. When I returned, she was much calmer, and she told me that she was secretly relieved when she realized that I was going to protect myself and that she couldn't ruin my life with her various machinations. She was able to reflect on how automatically she feels responsible for every bad thing that happens around her and has always felt this way. The therapy began to take on a new flavor, with much less drama and suicidal preoccupation. My passing her passive-into-active test—by not responding to her suicide gesture as if I were a fourteen-year-old girl who felt that she had killed her mother—enabled Rita to feel safer and less guilty herself.

MECHANISMS OF CHANGE IN PSYCHOTHERAPY

Patients come into therapy wanting to master their problems. The goal of therapy is to help them identify and change the pathogenic beliefs that underlie these problems. Deepening their understanding is one important route to change because once we see how our currently painful and unreasonable view of the adult world originated as a reasonable and adaptive response to our childhood world, we not only reduce our shame and increase our self-compassion, we give ourselves the chance to revise this view in a healthier direction. Understanding alone, however, is not always enough to facilitate change.

In order to effect lasting change, people need new experiences in which their pathogenic beliefs are repeatedly proved to be false in a way that they can believe on a deeper level. This is why I often en-

courage my patients to experiment with new ways of being and acting in order to help provide them with more immediate, visceral,
and experiential evidence that the dangers that they anticipate will
not necessarily occur. Someone who is afraid of being rejected for
being selfish needs to have safe opportunities in which selfishness
does not provoke rejection. Someone who worries that he or she will
make other people feel drained and resentful by their dependence
needs to test out the waters and express their dependency needs.

Often, as in the examples I gave of testing, patients get experiential evidence from their therapist that their pathogenic beliefs are
wrong. Therapists are in a unique position to provide such evidence
because, when they interact with patients, they are not as distracted
by their own conflicts and vulnerabilities as are other important
people in patients' lives. When a patient tests to see if I'll be rejecting, hurt, devalued, envious, or bored, and I manage to convey
that I don't feel any of these things, then that patient has experienced a small dose of an alternative and healthier reality, perhaps
enough of one, if repeated over time, to begin to wear away the
foundations of his or her irrational expectations and default assumptions about the nature of reality. Understanding is one-half of
the equation, and new experience is the other.

When working with patients' sexual fantasies and preferences, I
don't use any special techniques but instead approach their sexuality
as I would any other important aspect of their lives. However, the
question still arises: what do the concepts of pathogenic beliefs,
testing, passive-into-active, and corrective experiences have to do
with sexual fantasy? The answer is that sexual fantasy can function
as a cause and effect in all of these dimensions of the clinical process.
As I've mentioned, patients will often talk about their sexual fantasies only when they feel safe enough to do so. A great deal of
psychotherapeutic work often needs to be done to reach such safety.

Understanding patients' sexual fantasies cannot only deepen understanding of their core problems but can guide therapeutic technique in more direct ways. Sometimes a fantasy tips the therapist off as to how the patient is likely to test, and what the therapist should do when this happens. In these cases, sexual fantasies can function as a kind of operator's manual for the therapist to provide the right interpretations and experiences that will help patients change their underlying belief structures.

Consider, for example, the case of Sue, the patient who enjoyed sexual scenarios in which she was bound and dominated. Once I understood that the function of these scenarios was to reassure her against her guilt about being too powerful and hurting a man, I anticipated that she would somehow test me to see if I could tolerate her being strong without feeling threatened or hurt. I further understood that if I became defensive or otherwise communicated that she was too much for me in some way, she would immediately detect this and would not be able to work through her conflict about being stronger than men. In other words, once I understood the meaning of her sexual preferences, I knew more about what Jan needed from me. She needed not only understanding but a certain demonstration of strength and an ability to appreciate hers. Jan did test in just this way. She began to criticize me and my ideas in an increasingly forceful manner. I agreed with her in an easygoing way when I thought she was right and held my ground—leavening it at times with humor—when I didn't. She visibly relaxed and became more trusting of me over time.

When I understood that Otto's pornography obsession involved his fears about becoming too identified with a depressed and aging woman, I knew that it would probably be important for me to be relatively upbeat so as not inadvertently to create the same problem in his therapy that he had in his life. As opposed to some therapists who emphasize how important it is for the patient to repeat and relive conflicts with the therapist, in my experience it is often easier for a patient to get to the bottom of a problem if it is *not* actively occurring in full force with the therapist. Otto would feel safer looking into his hypersensitivity to the downbeat moods of others if he didn't have reason to experience one in me. Similarly, with George (the patient who finally left his marriage to a very unhappy woman, and who struggled with the guilty belief that separation was supposed to be painful), I also knew that if my manner was too serious or "heavy," this would confirm his belief that he wasn't supposed to leave his marriage unscathed or be lighthearted in any way.

Patients are extremely sensitive to the nuances of their therapist's style and often read into it signs about how they are supposed to feel or act. To help my patients feel safe, the more understanding I have about their pathogenic beliefs—understanding that is often enhanced through knowledge of their sexual fantasies—the better able I am to anticipate certain tests in the therapy and to pass them.

Just as my understanding of sexual fantasies is based on the concept of safety, so, too, is my understanding of the process of psychotherapy. People can face painful memories, feelings, or thoughts, or brave the dangers of making changes in their core attitudes, only if it is safe to do so. Safety is the key to understanding how sex, the mind, and therapy function. It is the concept that unifies what we do in bed with what we do in therapy.

This is often particularly salient in patients who had mothers who acted highly victimized and about whom their children had to worry and feel guilty. Almost inevitably these patients turn passive into active and act like victims in their therapy. The "test" becomes to see if the therapist will, indeed, feel guilty and worried as the patients did when they were children.

A female therapist consulted me about the case of a patient, Rick, who had been in therapy for nine months for treatment of depression when he revealed that when he traveled on business, he often tried to hire a prostitute who would urinate and spit on him. These activities allowed him to become sexually aroused. Despite his therapist's prodding, Rick had provided her with scant information about his childhood, except for describing his father as "impatient" and his mother as "quiet." Based on my understanding of sexual fantasies, I made a series of observations and predictions about Rick and the probable course of his therapy that turned out to be true. I said that I thought that Rick had probably had a weak or masochistic mother who frequently led the patient to believe that he was abusing her, hurting her in some way—in effect, implying that he was "pissing" on her. In his sexual fantasy Rick identified with his mother, the martyr who was pissed and spat on. This role mitigated his guilt and enabled him to get turned on. He was now the victim, not the victimizer. I said that I thought that the fantasy was an antidote to his guilt and that was why it was exciting. His therapist eventually was able to confirm these speculations. The patient's mother, it turned out, had had to give up her career as an actress when she got married and became pregnant with the patient and never let either her husband or son forget how much she had sacrificed.

Additionally, I was able to make certain predictions about this patient's therapy. I said that I thought that either the patient would try to make the therapist feel that she was hurting him, a passive-into-active test, or else would somehow devalue or "piss on" the therapist. In either case, by understanding the underlying dynamics of the case, the therapist would have a pretty good sense of how she was supposed to respond in order to disconfirm the patient's pathogenic beliefs and make him feel safe. If he tried to make her feel worried and guilty, she should be careful not to do so; and if he tried to put her down, she should definitely stand up for herself and not in any way let him infer that she was feeling victimized or martyred. My colleague was able to confirm many of these predictions. The patient was subtly degrading to the therapist, frequently criticizing her office, choice of art, the way she dressed, and her intelligence, and seemed quite relieved when the therapist was robust and confident in her responses.

The case of Glenn represents another example of a therapy that was greatly facilitated by understanding the patient's sexual fantasy. When Glenn, the medical researcher in chapter 3, told me that he liked to sit at the window of his office at night and "cruise" men who came by, inviting them in for anonymous sex, we were able to figure out that this scenario was an attempt to counteract his feelings of disconnectedness in a way that also ensured he wasn't responsible for making the other person happy. Armed with this insight, I was also able to make some educated guesses about how Glenn might use therapy, and how I might best help him. His sexual fantasy reinforced my initial impression that he might have difficulty connecting with me and would worry that he wasn't satisfying me by being a "good enough" patient. As a result, I thought that it would help him feel safer if I counteracted these worries by being particularly active in reaching out to him and by expecting very little in the way of therapeutic "progress." Although I fully planned to analyze these feelings with him, if and when they came up, I also knew that in order to make it safe enough for him to explore them, I should also attempt to counteract them in practice by actively connecting with him in a way that conveyed that whatever he did in therapy was satisfactory.

In this sense, Glenn's sexual fantasies and preferences informed my technique. They provided crucial information about his pathogenic beliefs and about the dangers that he was attempting to overcome, which I could use to provide him with more of what he needed in therapy. Of course, in Glenn's case, as with all of my patients, when I have hunches or make predictions about what I need to do to make a patient feel safe in therapy, I rigorously attempt to keep an open mind, to allow fully for the possibility that I'm wrong and might need to change direction completely. In my discussion of testing, I said that a patient will respond to a passed test by moving forward, and he or she will respond to a failed test by becoming stalled. In my emphasis on how patients respond to my intervention, I was indirectly emphasizing a guiding principle of my work—that I attempt to use the patient's responses to what I say and do as the ultimate arbiter of the value and truth of my theories.

It is enormously useful for therapists to constantly generate hypotheses about what is going on in their patients, inside and outside therapy, because theories, even provisional ones, help us to explain what we're seeing and feeling. In fact, one of our functions as therapists is to help our patients develop better, more accurate, and more useful theories about themselves in order to be able to make healthier choices in their lives. So generating and testing hypotheses and predictions about the patients that I'm treating are essential to my clinical approach. It is equally crucial for therapists to be "empirical" in their work, that is, to use their patients' responses to their interventions as important measures of whether these interventions are right or wrong, and to use patients' therapeutic progress as the ultimate barometer of whether or not the therapist is doing the "right" thing.

SEXUAL FANTASIES ARE DIFFICULT TO CHANGE

My approach to patients' sexual fantasies is identical with my approach to everything else important they tell me. I help them explore the meaning of their daydreams and preferences, the feelings and beliefs they are both expressing and counteracting, and attempt to use these as a window into their deepest levels of psychological functioning. Whether or not sexual fantasies and preferences are used to explain someone's pathogenic beliefs or are themselves explained by such beliefs, their appearance in therapy offers patients a useful tool for understanding and growth. In my clinical experience, however, sexual fantasies and preferences, while understandable in exactly the same terms as any other aspect of the mind, have certain unusual features. One is that they are very difficult to give up or change.

I can and do certainly help my patients feel less ashamed of their thoughts and wishes. Often, when patients better understand their fantasies as creative and adaptive solutions to problems of safety, their self-esteem is enhanced, and they then are able to share their daydreams and wishes with their partners without shame or fear of rejection. Many patients have found that the result of this increased communication is a better sex life. They discover that their partners are willing and sometimes eager to participate with them in enacting their fantasies.

Other times, increased awareness and understanding of the mental mechanisms behind a sexual preference may make it more flexible, less obligatory and rigid, and more open to compromise and negotiation. Perhaps a "top" becomes willing sometimes to be a "bottom," a man fixated on Asian women becomes willing to consider others, a woman who wants to be thrown on the bed and ravished becomes more willing to reciprocate, or a man who can get aroused only by penetrating a woman from the rear becomes able to get aroused by the missionary position. People change the form and content of their sexual lives in response to psychotherapy all the time.

Nevertheless, I think that, in general, the core conditions required for maximum sexual arousal are very difficult to change significantly. Although people may become less ashamed, more communicative, and more flexible about the fantasies that turn them on, it is unusual that they give them up completely. The man who prefers to be dominated sexually by women rarely becomes a man who *prefers* to be dominant. He may be better able to enjoy playing the dominant role, but he won't enjoy it quite as much. The man who is especially preoccupied with young women may become more able to get aroused by his wife or women his own age, but he will still usually have a "thing" for youth. The woman who enjoys seducing men in authority may, as a result of analyzing the meanings of this scenario, become sexually responsive to someone "ordinary," but she will still be likely to gravitate toward powerful men in her choice of partners. The woman who finds herself especially drawn to men who have a rough or even a mean "edge" to them may work through her guilt enough to enjoy the love of a kind man, but it is equally likely that she will still choose a partner who has an edge, albeit a much softer one. In others words, as a result of understanding the meanings of their sexual fantasies, as well as working through the pathogenic beliefs that these fantasies are designed to overcome, people may become much more varied in their sexual repertoires, but they don't give up their old fantasies completely.

Further, while insights into the meaning of their fantasies might be put to good use by patients in changing their lives outside the bedroom, their secret preferences inside the bedroom usually don't change as much. After one man I knew came to understand that his pleasure in being tied up by his wife during sex reflected an attempt to undo his image of women as sad and weak, his guilt toward women in general was reduced, and he was able to assert himself more in his marriage and at work. His primary sexual preference, though, was still to be restrained and dominated by a woman.

What accounts for the relative intransigence of sexual excitement to change in psychotherapy? Why can people turn the rest of their lives around, sometimes radically, as a result of understanding their pathogenic beliefs, while at the same time they hold on to the private sexual scenarios that turn them on?

It is not as if, as a therapist, I don't frequently see patients whose psychology changes very little in therapy or who may improve one part of their lives and not others. Personality, after all, is relatively stable over time. Radical transformation is the exception and not the rule. Patients who tend toward shyness at the beginning of therapy, while becoming more assertive over time, will usually still be relatively mild-mannered at the end. Type A personalities, people who are obsessively driven to work and succeed, can be tremendously helped to relax and reduce their perfectionism by psychotherapy, but it is relatively rare for such a person to become a laid-back Type B after treatment. Sometimes, I see people in therapy whose progress is not only slow but tediously so. If someone consults me who happens to be paranoid, suspicious of my motives, skeptical about the ability and willingness of other people to help him or her, that patient's treatment will proceed very slowly. The intransigence of certain personality traits and problems is a common finding in psychotherapy and one that most therapists come to accept. People get formed in the crucible of the interaction between their families and their genes and, once formed, are not infinitely mutable. Therefore, the fact that sexual fantasies don't tend to dramatically change should not be surprising.

Yet, to me it still is. Why do sexual preferences endure despite the fact that the underlying psychological reasons for their creation may be eliminated? Why do patients manage to change a particular pathogenic belief and, as a result, reduce their work inhibitions, improve their marriages, and become more creative but still strongly prefer a sexual fantasy that arose as an attempt to master that same pathogenic belief? *The main reason that sexual fantasies and preferences don't tend to change much, even as the motives for their creation do, is because they're pleasurable.* Here is one example. A woman who was treated by a colleague of mine had sexual fantasies that were primarily exhibitionistic in nature. She liked to imagine that she was the object of the sexual lust of a group of rough male construction workers. In her fantasies she drove them wild with desire and eventually succumbed to some kind of group sex with them. In the real world this woman also invested a great deal of time, energy, and money into looking sexy and enjoyed the feeling that she was being admired by men wherever she went.

Upon analysis it turned out that her fantasies were arousing because they overcame feelings of shame and rejection that she had felt growing up. Because of particular experiences in her family, she had always struggled against the belief that she was undesirable. As the object of intense sexual attention and adoration, however, she momentarily disproved this belief and was therefore able to get safely excited. After the understanding that she acquired in therapy, she became more interpersonally confident, felt worthy of better relationships, and worried a bit less about her appearance. Yet her primary sexual fantasies remained roughly the same: she was the object of intense, uncontrollable male sexual desire. She still felt a special thrill at the attention she would attract in her real life as well. While other aspects of her life had changed quite a bit, her erotic predilections had barely changed.

Why should they? We usually don't have an investment in altering the scenarios that arouse us. While it is true that the same pathogenic beliefs that give rise to sexual fantasies also produce inhibitions in other areas of our lives, the difference is that sex feels good, while frustrated ambitions and conflicted relationships feel bad. We not only have little incentive to transform the conditions under which we feel excitement but, even if we wanted to, changing them would be difficult. It is as if a certain image, body type, sexual position, or script has always "worked" to produce excitement for us, and there is little reason to change it. Pleasure is a powerful reinforcer and helps cement the desirability of particular sexual fantasies early in life. Pleasurable sexual fantasies are more than a simple habit but less than a compulsion.

The fact that sexual preferences persevere even as their psychological foundations may change does not mean that their meaning and function change. Sexual preferences are still based on a need to establish conditions of safety so that excitement can emerge and flourish. A man who prefers to be rough and dominant in bed because his partner's sexual arousal reassures him against his pathogenic belief that his aggression is highly destructive may use therapy to understand and lessen his irrational tendency to feel guilty, expand his sexual repertoire to include a gentler mutuality, and free up the rest of his life considerably. He still may prefer a dominant sexual role and for the same reasons: to master his guilt, but a guilt that is now a whisper rather than a roar. The fact that his domination scenarios have provided so much pleasure in the past ensures that they will be his preferred scenario in the future. His guilt has been mitigated enough to change his life, but it is still enough to trigger his time-tested and successful solution.

Sometimes, of course, patients might be highly motivated to change their preferred sexual fantasies because, while they may provide pleasure, they are also accompanied by pain. If this man's partner doesn't get aroused by his rough sexual aggression, then his relationship will suffer as a result, and he might be motivated to use therapy to change his preferences. Or if someone's sexual interests feel anxiety ridden, compulsive, or are socially dangerous (as is often the case with Peeping Toms, exhibitionists, pederasts, or even Internet sexual addicts), then there might be enough distress for someone to want to interrupt his or her normal channels of sexual arousal.

Sexual fantasies are used to deal with idiosyncratic versions of universal human conflicts. Who among us hasn't felt restrained by some form of guilt, worry, shame, rejection, and helplessness in our lives? Who among us hasn't felt guilty about having more satisfaction in life than our loved ones have? Who hasn't felt some form of separation guilt? Who can say that he or she has never felt inferior or had doubts about his or her worth? These are inherent aspects of contemporary life and continue to exist in some form regardless of how well psychotherapy succeeds in tempering and dampening their toxic effects. Therefore, even after someone is "cured" in therapy, underlying conflicts still exist that imperil sexual excitement. Thus, his or her favorite routes to the safe experience of pleasure, reinforced countless times over countless years, will always occupy a special place in that individual's sexual repertoire.

A friend of mine recently asked me if there were any sexual fantasies, preferences, or behaviors that I thought were simply immoral or otherwise unacceptable. I had to think for a moment before I answered. I realized that I had two very different responses, depending on whether or not I was responding as a therapist. As a citizen and a human being, I believe that any form of sexual interaction that is nonconsensual is immoral, including any explicitly sexual behavior between adults and children. As a therapist, however, I think and feel differently. If I were treating perpetrators of rape or child abuse, while not forgetting my moral revulsion, I would attempt to put it aside and, instead, understand the processes by which such coercive behavior becomes arousing and the beliefs and feelings that it is attempting to correct. My clinical approach to someone whose fantasies or preferences I personally find bizarre or reprehensible would be identical to my approach to fantasies and preferences that I consider more familiar, morally acceptable, or "normal." In other words, I would focus my attention entirely on understanding and changing the underlying conflicts that gave rise to the behavior that I might personally feel was wrong.

The issue for me as a therapist is not whether a sexual fantasy is bad, immoral, or socially unacceptable, but whether the underlying issues that the fantasy is attempting to resolve are damaging in some way. If a patient tells me that getting whipped turns the person on, or that he or she likes to be urinated on, or someone tells me a fantasy of raping a neighbor or of being raped by the neighbor, I may feel personally bewildered by the appeal of these scenes, but my primary concern isn't that the sexual scenario is pathological (provided it remains a fantasy or is enacted consensually). My concern is that the anxiety or guilt the sex is overcoming is pathologically interfering in the patient's life.

7

The Social Meaning of Sexual Fantasies

Sex divorced from love is the thief of personal dignity.

—Caitlin Thomas

Women need a reason to have sex—men just need a place.

—Billy Crystal

It is impossible to talk about the psychology of sex without also addressing its social, cultural, and political dimensions. Sex isn't simply a private matter. Sexual mores are being fought over in schools, the media, and the political arena. We almost removed a president because of his sexual behavior. Sex is also big business in our society. Billions of dollars are spent in various media in order to arouse us to buy products, watch television shows or movies, or buy publications. Finally, sex is also inextricably entwined with gender roles, with sexual orientation, and with the (seemingly) eternal conflicts in our society between men and women, conflicts that often have to do with power. The social world has an enormous impact on the why, how, and what of sexual fantasy. The purpose of this chapter is to show how social factors interact with the psychological dynamics of the individual and, thus, to place this theory of sexual arousal based on a study of the individual in the context of a study of society.

When we look inside the mind of the individual, we don't find just the echoes of his or her childhood, but the reverberations of the whole world. We are, simultaneously, unique individuals and complete reflections of our social and cultural environment. We experience ourselves as the authors of our own feelings and actions, and yet we are constantly enacting social roles that we had no part in creating.

Consider the cases presented thus far of women who felt so guilty about being too powerful in relation to men that they needed to create a fantasy of being sexually dominated in order to feel safe enough to get aroused. We understood their motivation as an unconscious need to counteract feelings of guilt born of their relationships with weak parents. Their sexual fantasies helped them lift their inhibitions and feel intensely excited.

To the social observer, however, it would be immediately obvious that my patients' guilt about the power of their sexuality to hurt men is common among women. Its explanation, therefore, couldn't possibly lie with their particular families of origin but instead had to lie with something more general that must be built into the social roles of men and women and their relationships to each other. A sociologist would view my patients' belief that men would be threatened by direct expressions of a woman's sexuality as a completely valid response to the social tendency of men in our culture to feel sexually insecure and the social pressure on women to suppress their power in order to assuage these insecurities. Therefore, one would say have to say that the fact that these women had to imagine being dominated in order to feel excited, had to feel restrained in order to express their sexual power safely, reflected a contradiction that owed at least as much to their social role as women as to their childhood experiences with sad mothers and weak fathers.

There is an even deeper level at which the outside world finds its way into our unconscious minds. The pages of this book are filled with the stories of people who grew up with martyred mothers and moody or absent fathers and as a result reaped feelings of guilt, worry, shame, and helplessness, feelings that inhibited their capacity for sexual pleasure and had to be overcome by sexual fantasies. To some extent, such feelings—and, therefore, the fantasies that correct them—are universal. Everyone, after all, has grown up with some degree of survivor and separation guilt, some experiences of rejection, shame, and helplessness. While such feelings can result from being raised by parents with clear psychological disturbances, these guilt and shame-based beliefs are also social in nature. They arise in the context of family relationships that are profoundly influenced by the social world. There are *social* reasons why so many of the mothers depicted in this book felt victimized and disappointed in their lives and why so many fathers were disconnected from themselves and their families.

Our culture has not been—and is not—very kind to families. All the problems that our society faces—sexism, racism, economic insecurity, crime, violence in the media, alienating work, poor education, drugs, cynicism, environmental degradation—intimately affect the lives of parents, influence their states of mind, their self-esteem, their sense of optimism about the future, and the quality of the energy they put into their relationship to their spouse and children. The social context constantly impinges on families, interacting with the particular psychologies that parents bring to their roles and that produce the very environments to which children react with guilt, shame, and helplessness. The more our social world stresses its inhabitants, the more families have to contend with financial, racial, political, sexual, and cultural inequities and conflicts, the more the process of growing up will involve the development of pathogenic beliefs. The reason these pages are filled with the stories of people who are struggling with the residue of childhood feelings of guilt and shame is not only that some portion of this is inevitable in even the best of family situations but because my patients' parents—like all of our parents—were often plagued with frustrations, worries, and inhibitions that arose in response to the problems of the world around them.

The simplest and most profound way that the social and the personal interact is in the natural tendency for children to feel guilty and rejected in response to the mood states of their parents. From the point of view of the developing child, the world appears small, dominated by the authority of a few individuals. As seen through the lens of the child's subjectivity, that world is not "sexist," "deprived," "insecure," or "cynical." It is "Mom," "Dad," or both. But Mom and Dad themselves are the product of their own personal histories, as well as their class, race, religion, gender role, political values, and professional ambitions. Mom and Dad constantly embody and contend with the whole of the outside world. When the patients discussed here formed pathogenic beliefs full of guilt and shame in their families, one might have thought it was only an unconscious response to Mom and Dad, while, in fact, it was simultaneously a response to the influence of a particular culture.

When we look inside the mind, we find the world. At the same time, when we look at the world, we see the complex workings of unique and individual minds. While the sociologist rightly reminds us that most women in our culture have been socialized to feel guilty about being too powerful, the psychologist can just as easily point out individual exceptions to this rule too numerous to count. Many women consciously enjoy exercising their sexual power, do it explicitly with their partners, and don't feel a whit of guilt about it. Many men, on the other hand, enjoy being sexually dominated and feel every bit as guilty as women about being sexually assertive.

These exceptions may not disprove the rule, but they certainly point to its limitations. Neither sex has a monopoly on feelings of power, helplessness, guilt, or shame, nor on the types of sexual fantasies that turn them on. When we look behind social norms and roles, we find tremendous individual variation and complexity.

No single theory, then, can fully explain both the workings of the mind and the world. In order to fully understand sexual desire, we have to look at it from both the inside out and the outside in. When we do so, we will see that not only do culture and history influence sexuality, but the psychology of sexual arousal influences our social environment. It's obvious, for example, that advertisers use sex to sell various products, associating a particular beer, computer, or pair of pants with sexual excitement. Advertising is one of the social institutions that clearly influences our sexuality. However, it is also the case that in order for advertising to successfully stimulate us, it needs to provide us with *just* the right image, *just* the right message. Sexualized advertising "works" only when it resonates with the fantasies of its consumers. The form that these images take is partially determined by the sexual fantasies that they stimulate. The people who design and produce advertisements base them, in part, on their own psychology, on what they themselves find sexually appealing. The relationship between advertising and our sexual preferences, then, is a complicated one. It wouldn't be quite complete to say simply that advertising influences us, that our environment shapes our sexual appetites, because our sexual fantasies also determine the kind of advertising that we see around us. It would also be naive to discount the enormous power of popular culture to shape what we find sexually arousing. Psychology both creates and is created by the social world. Therefore, in sketching out some of the possible areas of confluence and interaction between the personal and the social, we can deepen our understanding of both.

BLAMING THE PARENTS AND THE ABUSE EXCUSE

Nowhere is the interaction between the social and the psychological more salient than in the family. Most of the case vignettes presented thus far have involved patients who grew up with parents who were more or less unhappy. This fact, of course, does not distinguish patients in psychotherapy from the rest of us. Most of us would be hard-pressed to say that our childhoods were so idyllic as to be devoid of negative feelings. The parents on whom we depended and in relationship to whom we forged our earliest identities and belief systems carried with them the burdens of their external social circumstances and internal psychological conflicts. Sure, our parents' difficulties contributed to our own, but what happens to the concept of personal responsibility? Don't *we* have some responsibility here? Are we blaming parents—and especially mothers, who have already been scapegoated by psychoanalysts and other so-called child development experts—for everything?

Children are certainly *not* blank slates upon which parents imprint personality traits and cause distress. They come into the world with a wide array of innate temperaments, sensitivities, and psychological dispositions. We now know that traits like shyness may have a hereditary basis, and we have definite evidence for genetic predispositions to several forms of mental illness, including autism, schizophrenia, and some types of manic-depressive illness. Additionally, we all know people who have suffered terrible childhood trauma and have emerged with great psychological strength, while others with benign origins grew up psychologically impaired. Psychologists still cannot confidently predict, on the basis of analyzing a child's familial environment, how he or she will turn out as an adult. Children are not only *not* passive vessels into which parents pour their values and troubles, it often feels to their parents as if the opposite is true, that they, the parents, are helpless captives of their children! Developmental psychologists often argue that children raise parents as much as parents raise children.

But not quite as much. Children do not affect their parents as much as their parents affect them. Parents have an awesome authority in the lives of their children, not only in the realm of physical survival, but because they have the power to define what is real and what their children should expect from life. Parents define the way things are and the way things are supposed to be. Children are biologically and psychologically primed to take all of these meanings to heart, to internalize the rules of social interaction that they experience in their families. Brain researchers have even shown that many of our most basic neural structures have evolved with the singular aim of figuring out what our parents are thinking and feeling and what they want from us to ensure our survival. Children grow up not only equipped, but highly motivated, to learn about their world. In their early years, that world is primarily the family.

Our families give us our initial clues about how the social world works and why people do the things they do and feel the things they feel. They shape our attitudes toward emotions like pride, anger, love, dependency, sadness, and pleasure. Whether we like it or not, they give us our most basic definitions of masculinity and femininity and of the differences between men and women. How many times have we all caught ourselves—to our amusement or horror—acting like our same-sex parent, unconsciously modeling some behavior, mannerism, or trait that we observed countless times growing up? We may rebel against these unconscious lessons and roles, but they occupy an important place in our psyches.

In addition, the development of pathogenic beliefs is formed through inferences that we draw from childhood experiences in our families. They include such unconscious ideas and feelings as, "If I'm strong, I'll hurt my mother," "If I'm needy, I'll burden my father," or, "If I'm too happy, my parents will feel rejected and left out." While biological factors may contribute to our temperament, the response of our childhood environment primarily determines our view of ourselves and our world. The parent/child relationship may be a two-way street, but the traffic is decidedly heavier in one direction.

Despite parents' "faults," it is also true that children sometimes develop pathogenic beliefs that are distorted or incorrect. Children's thinking tends to be egocentric, and their ability to accurately gauge cause and effect is limited. One woman I treated, like so many of my patients, grew up with the unconscious conviction that becoming assertive and independent was damaging to her father, who seemed to react with anger and defensiveness whenever she disagreed with him. She felt guilty about making him lose control and as a result developed a tendency as an adult to placate and defer to men. While it was true that her father had a short fuse and easily felt frustrated when opposed, it was *not* true that her father was deeply wounded by his daughter's self-assertion. He had always been rigid and re-active in this particular way, and while this trait reflected a signifi-cant psychological problem, it had not crippled his professional or love life. The reality, in other words, was that her father was *not* actually traumatized every time she opposed him.

It is also true that children are often highly sensitive observers of the psychological weaknesses of their parents, who are often sur-prised at how well their children can read their moods and accurately deduce what is going on with them, despite efforts at concealment. This capacity of children is often suppressed by the children them-selves, a form of denial that may create its own difficulties. One of the most vexing problems with which many of us struggle growing up is our difficulty consciously believing what we unconsciously know to be true, in particular, our parents' flaws. This difficulty creates a roadblock to self-love because it makes it hard to recognize and accept our own helplessness and innocence as children. Someone, after all, has to be responsible for our psychological pain. By not facing our parents' flaws, we have to exaggerate our own. Even children who are severely abused regularly defend their parents and blame themselves for their own mistreatment. All of us have a need to idealize and protect those caretakers who are responsible for our security and emotional survival. Unfortunately, we will sacrifice even our own capacities to tell right from wrong, to judge reality accurately, and to register psychological pain in the interest of maintaining our attachment and loyalty to our parents.

The result of this process is that many of us tend to become harshly critical of ourselves and unduly forgiving of our parents. We are unable to develop self-compassion. We can't feel appropriate sympathy for the child we once were. Instead, we internalize the way we were treated. We come to feel that it was deserved, that *it was perfectly understandable* that our parents didn't understand us, or were preoccupied with their own problems, or lost their tempers, or hit us, or blamed us a lot, or were impatient, jealous, seductive, or threatening. We may complain about it publicly, but privately we often suspect that our suffering was ultimately our own fault.

So which is to blame: biology, culture, or our parents? Are we exaggerating the effects of our families on our psychological development or underestimating them? How much responsibility do parents have for the psychological wounds with which children grow up?

The answers depend on the purpose of the questions and the vantage point from which they're asked. If we're struggling in therapy against the irrational belief that we were the cause of our own unhappiness growing up, or that we were primarily responsible for the unhappiness of our parents, it might be therapeutic to emphasize the fact of our innocence, to appreciate realistically our impossible predicament as helpless children faced with a stressful family environment. Locating responsibility in our parents would be both a more useful and more accurate version of our childhood realities than the self-blaming account from which we might have been suffering.

However, if we are parents struggling with stresses in our own lives, worried and guilty about having harmed our children in some way, then it might be most useful to remind ourselves of the *resilience* of children, their tendency to *misunderstand* the meaning of our actions, the contribution of their inborn temperament as to who they become, and the limits of our own omnipotence. It might even be more appropriate to see ourselves, in this case, as victims of our own backgrounds, of our own families, and of our own social milieus. We, as parents, were once children ourselves and deserve as much sympathy and compassion as our own children for the ways that we were—and are—shaped by forces outside our control. Parents, from this particular point of view, are as "innocent" as their children.

Responsibility, guilt, innocence, and blame—these are all highly loaded concepts with multiple levels of meaning, which in turn both overlap and collide. To take an extreme example, should a parent feel guilty and responsible—and be regarded as such by others— if he (the appropriate pronoun, since most sexual abuse is perpetrated by men) molests his child? The question, of course, sounds absurd. The moral issue is clear: the adult is guilty, and the child is innocent.

The psychological issues, however, are not as clear-cut. The molester may be guided by the twisted notion that he is actually *loving,* and not hurting, the child, or the equally twisted belief that the child invited his sexual attention. Although completely false, these beliefs may make psychological sense within the subjective world of the perpetrator. Psychology is not the same as morality. *To make sense of something isn't the same as excusing it.* Since defendants in criminal cases often get psychologists to explain their behavior on the basis of childhood trauma, the impression generated in our culture is that understanding someone's subjective world means sanctioning that person's external behavior. Nothing could be further from the truth. Excusing one's morally corrupt behavior on the basis that it makes psychological sense is wrong because it mixes two different levels of meaning. One can condemn a behavior and still believe that it makes psychological sense.

The "sense" that abusive behavior makes is located in the abuser's own childhood experiences and the pathogenic beliefs they generated. Usually, we find that the sexually abusive parent was molested himself as a child, and he is attempting, in his sexual interactions with his child, to find some kind of relief from intolerable psychic wounds of his own. Looked at from his point of view, the victimizer, even one guilty of the most morally reprehensible of actions, was himself a victim and was almost certainly not responsible for his own victimization.

If a child molester has some kind of claim, however remote, on our compassion, what about normal parents? What about well-meaning parents who love their children but don't always express it perfectly, aren't always attuned, are sometimes moody, distracted, sick, depressed, withdrawn, self-pitying, or angry? Can any of us say that as parents we've never felt these things or communicated them to our children? Wouldn't it make sense, then, to acknowledge that parents may indeed hurt their children's feelings, inflict some kind of psychological strain on them, or even inadvertently traumatize the very children they love and protect, without blaming and vilifying them as "bad" parents? Can't we say that even good parents sometimes fail, and that these failures have psychological consequences for their children, while, at the same time, compassionately acknowledging that these parents also love their children, want them to be happy, and do the best they can to make it possible?

In some situations, in fact, the parents' good intentions themselves are the problem. In her book *Spoiling Childhood*, Diane Ehrensaft discusses at great length how parents today inadvertently hurt their children through a confusing combination of attempting to gratify their every whim while actually providing less and less time for authentic interaction. Neither this excessive gratification nor deprivation flow from ill will but from certain conflicts built into modern family life.

When we look at the parent-child relationship, we need to maintain multiple perspectives on the issues of blame and responsibility. We must directly look at the psychological harm that parents can, and regularly do, inflict on their children from overt child abuse to mild patterns of rejection, neglect, shame, overdependency, indulgence, and guilt. Obviously, some types of damage are worse than others, but all contribute to the creation of pathogenic beliefs that to some extent hurt the child and interfere with some aspect of his or her development. As parents, we raise children without a safety net, and all of us stumble and fall in some way.

It is important to put these potentially unhealthy outcomes of family life in a broader context. The pathogenic beliefs of children often result from their tendency to misconstrue the meaning of a parent's behavior, and as a result the child holds himself back psychologically through no fault of the parent. Further, parents are also responsible for imparting *strengths* to their children. Wherever parents land on the spectrum of good to bad child-rearing practices, they themselves are always deserving of the same understanding and compassion that we extend to their children. Parents not only carry psychological baggage from their childhoods that was not of their own making, but they exist, as adults, in a social world that consistently constrains and intrudes all of the time on their well-being and ability to parent.

We must be careful not to accept the child's point of view inadvertently about his or her parents as either realistic or complete. Children grow up without the ability to appreciate the ways in which their parents have outside lives, lives involving complicated webs of social interaction, pressure, conflict, longing, disappointment, and gratification that have absolutely nothing directly to do with their children. Children, dependent as they are, naturally view their parents through the lens of their own egocentric needs. It is a tremendous developmental achievement for them to even recognize and accept that their parents have *any* life apart from them, much less to appreciate its extent and importance.

It is crucial, then, to distinguish between the world according to the child and the world according to the parents, between the child's experience of a family environment that constitutes the *whole* of his or her emotional world, and a family as seen through the eyes of parents whose lives include multiple environments. The psychoanalyst Alice Balint once distinguished between the child's "love for the mother," a love that is absolute and connected to the child's need to survive, and normal "mother love," the love felt by a parent that is ultimately only relative. By "relative" she meant that the mother can, in principle, leave, replace, or otherwise emotionally survive without her connection to the child in a way that the child cannot possibly do without the mother.

This simple and obvious fact of emotional life is sometimes forgotten by psychologists, who often seem to blame parents for the mistakes they make and for any personality deficiencies that cause their children psychological hardship. As children our "absolute" emotional dependence on our parents leads us to selectively exaggerate their faults. Our emotional well-being, after all, is primarily dependent on theirs. As parents, however, many things can affect our state of mind. As parents we are separate and complex people unto ourselves, with childhoods that were filled with promise and pain, marriages that are happy or troubled, educations that were more or less useful, financial strains that are often not of our own making, and good or bad jobs within which we, spend most of our days. Losing a job or a divorce might affect our emotional well-being far more at a given point in time than the state of mind of our children.

Both vantage points are "accurate," in the sense that each one correctly describes one aspect of reality. Parents do create the environment, for better or worse, within which we, as children, learn about who we are and what we're supposed to be and do. Whether or not we are able to adequately judge cause and effect, to evaluate the true intentions of our caretakers, or to appreciate the complexities and extenuating circumstances of our parents' lives, the emotional fact remains that our parents profoundly shape who we become. Our subjective point of view as children is limited, but it is the only point of view possible at the same time, and it is the one that matters most in the earliest formation of our personalities.

Another crucial way that the social context of parents influences the formation of personalities is that we do not have generic "parents," but male or female ones, with all of the pressures, pleasures, and problems that go along with gender roles in our society. Women are still primarily responsible for raising children and still do so in the absence of significant support from their husbands, extended families, or society. This is a social fact that affects mothers, puts strains on their psyches, and powerfully influences the psychological experience of their children. Here we see with particular clarity the way in which the pressures of the external world ripple through the internal life of a family.

Our unconscious minds, which seem intrinsically personal, are actually profoundly social as well. The mothers we feel guilty about hurting with our independence are mothers who might have reluctantly given up their dreams of a career in order to get married because that's what women were expected to do. The mothers about whom we irrationally felt responsible might have seemed tired and strained all the time because they had to hold down a job as well as be the primary parent, a double duty that was the product of economic hardship, the absence of child care, or the lack of support from their husbands. Either way the child would encounter an unhappy mother who might be overly invested in her children's loyalty and dependence and might have, in fact, been easily hurt by their separation and individuation. Or perhaps some of these mothers might have been simply perceived as unhappy by their children, who then irrationally and without invitation felt guilty and responsible for them. Such children might experience the psychological conflicts that led to their separation and survivor guilt in intensely private and idiosyncratic ways, but these conflicts might have been ultimately provoked by the broadest of social forces, namely, the economic and social subordination of women.

The personal and the political intersect time and time again. Many of the patients described thus far had fathers who were either rejecting or unavailable. As a result, children struggled with feelings of shame, inferiority, and helplessness. But while these feelings were formed in response to intimate exchanges with unique flesh-and-blood fathers, these children were on another level reacting to an entire culture in which fathers primarily work outside the home and have a limited involvement in child rearing. This is a social arrangement, not a fact of nature, but its consequences ripple through the psychological lives of everyone involved. The fathers may also be alienated at work and burdened by the expectations and anxieties that are connected to masculinity in our culture and so are, not only often detached from their children, but emotionally handicapped when they are connected. Their children, however, can't possibly understand that their fathers' absences and moodiness aren't a reflection on how lovable they are and so are likely to internalize these moods and feel bad about themselves. The social again becomes highly personal.

The mechanisms through which societal pressures affect families have changed over time, as have patterns of child rearing, sex-role expectations, and the demographics of family life. Women used to suffer as a result of the social isolation of full-time mothering—the kind of suffering described by Betty Friedan in *The Feminine Mystique*—while today they suffer in a different way by having to work outside the home and still remain primarily responsible for all of the work inside the home.

The brief sketches presented here of disappointed and tired mothers or unavailable fathers do not come close to doing justice to the range of family experience that people actually have as children. My aim here is not to critique the American family—others have done so extensively—but to show how we can study sexual fantasies from the point of view of our inner world while not neglecting the outer world in the process, how we can even look into the most private recesses of our unconscious minds—the places occupied by our fears, conflicts, and pathogenic beliefs—and find the reverberations of society and culture. When we create sexual fantasies in order to feel safe, we are attempting to deal with conflicts that are both psychologically universal and socially constructed.

GENDER DIFFERENCES IN SEXUAL FANTASY

Few social facts impinge on our psyches more than gender. (For a good review of the research on sexual differences in the style and content of sexual fantasies, see Szuchman and Muscarella, eds., *Psychological Perspectives on Human Sexuality*, pages 283–308.) Therefore, we would expect that sexual fantasies inevitably bear the stamp of the complicated social rules and arrangements that define masculinity and femininity. In fact, common wisdom has it that women and men approach sex differently. Women, so this wisdom goes, have a greater tendency to link sex with love, preferring to feel sexual excitement only in the context of a relationship, while men tend more easily to divorce sexual pleasure from emotional satisfaction and pursue sex "for its own sake." To the extent that these gender differences exist, they ought to appear more sharply in the realm of sexual fantasy than in overt sexual behavior because, presumably, sexual behavior is subject to external prohibitions and compromises, while fantasies are private and uncensored. In other words, fantasies should offer the most accurate snapshots of our true sexual desires. They do. Men's fantasies, it has been found, are often more visual and graphic than those of women, while women's fantasies involve more tactile and verbal stimulation. Men's fantasies tend to push the action toward climax more quickly, while women's fantasies tend to involve a longer buildup and more foreplay. Men tend to focus on specific body parts and sexual acts, while women's fantasies put more emphasis on the personal characteristics of their partners. Interestingly, research has shown that, with the obvious exception of the sex of the imagined partner, gender differences in sexual fantasies are as observable among homosexuals as heterosexuals.

Gender differences seem to carry over to the erotica and pornography enjoyed by each sex. Pornography, after all, represents both a cause and effect of sexual fantasy; it is consumed only to the extent that it reflects the sexual preferences of its consumers, while at the same time, it provides images that these consumers then incorporate into their fantasies. Male pornography is primarily visual, focused on specific body parts and actions, and relatively devoid of narrative or relationship complexity. Such pornography has never been successfully marketed to women, whose pornography, or "erotica," has traditionally taken the form of romance novels. In the romance novel, sex is always subordinated to relationships and is usually marked by intrigue, innuendo, and seduction rather than direct sexual activity. The qualities of the hero's character are at least as important as his physique.

These patterns are further repeated in the new world of cybersex.

According to Alvin Cooper and his colleagues, recent research on the use of sexually explicit material on the Internet suggests that men preferentially visit the traditional pornography sites featuring pictures and videos, while women tend to visit sexual chat rooms, where their fantasies can be enacted in relation to other people.

The difference between pornography and erotica is controversial. Some people differentiate the two by defining pornography as sexually explicit material that includes elements of force or degradation, while erotica is defined as material intended to arouse sexually but without depicting force or degradation. At their extremes this distinction is easy to make. Pictures of women in bondage would be pornography, and depictions of consensual sex would be erotica. This distinction can potentially break down on a number of levels. For example, it is often argued that any depictions of women as sexual objects are inherently degrading. On the other hand, consensual sex itself often contains elements of playful domination and submission.

In addition to gender differences in the form of sexual fantasies, there also appear to be differences in the content of these fantasies. Academic researchers have demonstrated what common sense and simple cultural observation tell us, namely, that the fantasies of both sexes tend to involve representations of women as the objects of desire and men as desirers (see Szuchman and Muscarella, pages 238–308). Women, in other words, are "done to," while men are the "doers." There are other distinctions. Men's fantasies are more likely to be voyeuristic, while women's are more exhibitionistic. And further, when a sexual fantasy explicitly depicts a relationship of dominance and submission, it seems more likely the man is dominant and the woman submissive. These themes are so embedded in our culture—and, thus, in our minds—that they are sometimes difficult to separate out and see clearly. Whether it is in pornography, fashion trends, advertising, television sitcoms, movies, comic books, or novels, women are portrayed as the object of the male gaze. Their sexual agency derives more from their ability to attract and hold a man's attention than from asserting an active desire of their own. These fundamental role relationships are embedded in our unconscious minds and therefore are regularly expressed in our sexual fantasies.

The finding that gender differences in fantasy content are consistent with sex-role stereotypes and culturally sanctioned sexual mores is not surprising. If we are inundated with images of women as the objects of male desire, then it is not surprising that many fantasies of both sexes would incorporate this portrait. What *is* surprising, however, is the extent to which gender-based differences in the form and content of fantasies are repudiated or contradicted in real life, the degree to which sexual "rules" are systematically violated.

Many men, for instance, often have fantasies of being sexually dominated. In the case of gay men, the preference for being a "bottom," the one being penetrated, is quite common; and although being a "bottom" does not always mean the same thing as being dominated, the two experiences are closely related. Studies by Kenneth Davidson and Bing Hsu have estimated that anywhere from 6 to 33 percent of men have fantasies of being "forced" into various sexual activities, estimates that are undoubtedly low since they are based on the self-reports of men who would likely underreport an interest in such a nonmasculine role. Two researchers, Denise Donnelly and James Fraser, even reported that men tend to prefer masochistic, as well as sadistic, sexual fantasies more than women. Nancy Friday, in *Men in Love*—her groundbreaking book on male sexual fantasies—argues that even though most men won't admit it, "In fantasy, men want exactly what women want: to be done to." It is certainly true in my clinical experience that it is not rare for heterosexual men to get aroused by fantasies of being tied up or being sexually submissive to a strong woman. Because these fantasies violate social norms surrounding masculinity and femininity, they may well be experienced as more forbidden and shameful in men than they are in women, but their prevalence is indisputable.

The importance of fantasies of sexual surrender among men is further illustrated by the recurring images of sexually powerful women in our culture—the so-called dominatrix or phallic woman who is sexy precisely because she is dominant. These images riddle both mainstream fashion advertising and heterosexual male pornography. In both genres men are being aroused by women appearing in spiked heels, leather, or latex, with pointed breasts, or ruthless facial expressions, all of which suggest power, self-assertion, and sexual dominance. The fact that these depictions of strong women frequently appear in male fantasies should make us cautious about any generalizations regarding the centrality of fantasies of dominance to men. Themes of submission or surrender frequently coexist with the fantasies of domination in the sexual daydreams of many men. In this sense the male psyche contains the same split as that of the wider culture. The sexually exciting image of the sexually powerful woman has long existed in popular culture side by side with the image of a woman as sexually receptive and submissive— Marlene Dietrich and Lauren Bacall alongside Marilyn Monroe and Brigitte Bardot, Madonna side by side with Pamela Anderson.

Corresponding to the high incidence of male fantasies of submission is the significant frequency of female fantasies of dominance. Clearly, the image of the dominatrix is not only appealing to many men but to many women as well. Evidence for this comes not only from scientific surveys, but from the prevalence of these images in contemporary fashion advertising. These images of women who are tough, sexy, and dangerous are meant for women, who are, after all, the primary targets of much of this advertising. In my clinical experience many women identify, consciously or unconsciously, with such dominant sexual roles not only because these images are attractive to men, but also because they make women feel powerful. Whatever the motive, it is by no means rare for women to imagine sexually dominating their partner, although it might be uncommon for women to admit it.

Attempts to generalize about the special nature of women's sexual fantasies are fraught with other difficulties as well. While it might seem intuitively true that women tend to prefer to situate sex in relationships rather than pursue it "for its own sake," these conventionally female dimensions of sexual fantasy are often contradicted in reality. If one peruses Nancy Friday's extensive collections of sexual fantasies, the differences in the form and content of men's and women's fantasies are often quite minimal. In Friday's collections of women's fantasies, we can frequently see foreplay quickly advance to the sex act, with relatively little in the way of seduction or emotional complexity. And this "action" is often described with the same crude, lustful, and salacious language and details as one finds in Friday's collections of male fantasies. Further, the women fantasies in these collections seem to focus as much on body parts—their own, those of other women, and those of men—as the male participants in Friday's studies.

For heterosexual men and women, admitting that they get turned on by fantasies that contradict social norms can be problematic, a fact that introduces an inherent bias into all empirical research that relies on self-reports to establish gender differences in sexual fantasies. Men are not supposed to want to be taken by force nor women to be the takers. These apparent role reversals are equated, consciously and unconsciously, with homosexuality and are inhibited by homophobic fears and disapproval. The reality is that there is no intrinsic relationship whatsoever between sexual orientation and preferences for dominant and submissive sexual roles. It is socially acceptable in the gay and lesbian community for a man to want to be sexually submissive and a woman to be dominant. The homophobic embarrassment that heterosexual men and women might feel admitting to fantasies at odds with traditional gender roles has less to do with the real sexual practices of gay people than with anxieties about straying from culturally rigid definitions of masculinity and femininity.

The question of gender differences in sexual fantasy, then, does not have an easy answer. In the world of the unconscious, social roles can be turned on their heads: men can link sex with intimacy, while women can split them, women can be dominant and objectify men, while men can surrender and submit to women. Our imaginations resist categorization. People tell social researchers one thing about their sexual fantasies and their therapists quite another.

Nevertheless, despite all of the contradictions and ambiguities that mitigate the role of sex differences in sexual fantasy, differences do seem to exist. However much these differences may be exaggerated, there is clearly some truth to what both scientists and everyday experience tell us, that men tend to more frequently objectify women's bodies and fantasize about sex for its own sake, while women more commonly tend to prefer sex in the context of an emotional relationship and value a man's personal qualities as much as his physical ones. While the adage that "men use love to get sex while women use sex to get love" overstates the case, it does capture something important about the different sexual psychologies of men and women.

Each psychology has a strength and a weakness. At the broadest level of generalization, men are allowed to be uninhibited about pursuing sexual pleasure but have a hard time being intimate, while women can be intimate but are not supposed to be lustful and aggressively pursue sexual excitement for its own sake. Sociologists and feminist theorists have described in great detail how our patriarchal culture socializes children into these stereotypical attitudes toward sex and how these different roles damage both men and women.

Like sexual fantasies, stereotypical sexual attitudes represent psychological strategies for emotional safety. Gender differences can be understood as the different strategies men and women employ to deal with different kinds of pathogenic beliefs and feelings. These special strategies serve the same psychological purpose as the details of our sexual fantasies. Men objectify more than women because something in the process of objectification must help them feel safe from certain psychological dangers that are more salient for men. Similarly, women tend to get more sexually excited if sex is merged with love because such an attitude must mitigate the effects of certain pathogenic beliefs that women especially experience.

"WHAM, BAM, THANK YOU, MA'AM"—THE PSYCHOLOGY OF OBJECTIFICATION

How does the capacity of men to pursue sex for its own sake, split off from its connection to intimacy and love, as well as their tendency to objectify women, provide a sense of psychological safety? The answer must somehow lie in the meaning of intimacy to men. In particular, the beliefs and feelings evoked by emotional closeness must open some kind of door to special psychological dangers that male sexuality attempts to negate. As we saw with sexual fantasies, if we understand the pathogenic beliefs with which someone is struggling, we can better understand how a particular form of sexuality evolves. Since most pathogenic beliefs are formed in childhood, it follows that those involving intimacy began there as well. The first woman with whom every man was intimate was his mother. Therefore, something that men commonly experience in their early relationship with their mothers, something *different* from what women experience, must generate pathogenic beliefs that men seek to counteract through objectification and a tendency to divorce sex from intimacy.

There are several problems in boys' early relationships with their mothers that give rise to the pathogenic beliefs that later influence male sexual attitudes. Some of these problems are common in both sexes, while others seem to be exaggerated in boys. One of the most important difficulties that boys share with girls is a problem that featured prominently in our discussion of sexual fantasy—namely, guilt. Like all children, boys often have difficulty psychologically separating from their mothers because they feel guilty about hurting them with their independence. Separation guilt of this sort can include the fathers as well as the mothers, of course, but since mothers are usually our primary caretakers, leaving home is more often unconsciously registered as leaving our mothers. As we have repeatedly seen throughout this book, children unconsciously worry that their mothers will feel excluded, left behind, depleted, or otherwise injured if their children truly become independent. Often, mothers do give their children just such a message and consciously or unconsciously provoke and exacerbate this separation guilt. However, other times children misinterpret their mothers' feelings about their growing up and feel guilty without a rational basis. Either way, the result is the development of a pathogenic belief that psychological separation and independence will hurt the mother.

In addition, children of both sexes often have to contend with the relative emotional absence of their fathers, who, by choice, emotional disability, social role, or economic necessity, have ceded the primary caretaker role in the family to the mother. Children often leave home without the benefit of paternal support, role modeling, and love. The net result is that the intrinsically desirable developmental goal of independence becomes fraught with guilt and conflict.

While boys and girls have to navigate these same emotionally treacherous waters in the course of growing up, boys have an additional burden. They have to grow up and become masculine and *not* feminine. They have to give up their identifications with their mothers, identifications that inevitably accompany the extreme closeness of early childhood, and enter the world of men, a social and emotional world in which femininity is renounced, rejected, and often devalued. This is in contrast to girls, who, like boys, need to give up their dependence on their mothers, but who do *not*, in the process, also have to renounce their identifications with their mother's gender. The *difference* between the boy and his mother—a difference that is meaningless when the boy is little—becomes increasingly important as he grows up. The boy, in other words, not only has to become less dependent in general on the caretaking of his mother, but he simultaneously has to develop a gender identity that radically diverges from hers. He must not only push away his mother but her gender. The process of separation becomes inextricably intertwined with becoming masculine.

Normally this process isn't terribly tortuous. It is promoted by such factors as subtle biological imperatives, the mother's active wish for her male baby to become masculine, the father's encouragement of the same goal, and the ubiquitous forces of socialization found in peer groups, school, and the media. Nevertheless, the boy's journey is different from the girl's. He has to both leave the nest and renounce his identification with his mother. This double duty creates special strains in his psychology.

Encouraged by our culture, the boy seeks to deal with these strains by erecting boundaries intended both to establish his independence and shore up his masculinity. Because these boundaries protect both his sense of self and masculinity, they often tend to be more rigid than that of girls, not only emphasizing the *differences* between masculinity and femininity, but their different *value*. One way men reinforce their separateness from women is to devalue femininity. These defensive processes are often most clearly seen in the behavior of young boys and adolescents who mock girls and all things feminine in the interest of cementing their masculinity and peer group identifications. It is as if they have to reassure themselves they're "one of the boys" in order to avoid the danger of being "one of the girls." In fact, much of the hostility and contempt that men appear to feel toward women functions to maintain psychological distance, to reinforce boundaries that feel weak, and to prop up a masculine identity that may feel precarious. This "us versus them" mentality is certainly seen in both sexes, but it is more salient among boys.

Fathers can help or hinder their sons. If the father welcomes and supports his son's independence and budding masculinity, the boy will have an easier time of it. He can learn to value his own masculinity without having to devalue his mother and push away so hard. If the father is emotionally or physically absent or rejecting or weak and plagued with his own insecurities, the boy's efforts to leave his mother and enjoy his masculinity are hindered because, in part, there are no healthy masculine role models with which to identify.

Since boys face the special developmental challenge of counteracting both their dependence on and identification with their mothers, it is inevitable that they should develop special fears and acquire special pathological beliefs. The belief in male superiority is one of these. Reinforced by our culture, it also arises as an attempt to solve an internal problem. In an effort *not* to identify with their mothers, boys defensively put them down. If these mothers are unhappy in their own lives, this belief is then strengthened because reality is confirming the boys' unconscious misogynistic view of femininity. Feeling contempt is a way to help the boy separate from his mother.

Unfortunately, misogyny also leads to psychological problems of its own. Many boys, and later men, feel guilty about feeling superior to women. Under these circumstances the normal enjoyment of one's masculinity becomes unconsciously equated with denigrating femininity, as if pride in being a boy means devaluing girls. The boy might come to believe that his mother—and, later, women in general—actually feel inferior to men, devalued by the mere presence of masculinity and envious of its privilege. There are other pathogenic beliefs involving the father, of course, but these conflicts about women are particularly debilitating for a boy and interfere with his attempts to leave home. In other words, guilt is a big problem for boys.

We can see clearly that the problems of guilt, ruthlessness, and identification—problems that obviously affect both sexes, and that sexual fantasies so elegantly remedy—can often have a different spin in the minds of men and women. Given the guilt that boys feel about leaving their mothers and enjoying their masculinity, and the special urgency with which they have to establish clear boundaries, it should come as no surprise that intimacy with a woman is potentially dangerous to men. Intimacy not only opens the door to feelings of guilt and responsibility, it exposes a man to the danger of losing his hard-won boundaries and consequently merging with his partner. Differences begin to collapse. This normal process of identification is intensified for men by feelings of separation guilt and responsibility because such feelings lead them to feel ambivalent about their independence. In reaction to guilt, they feel compelled to reassure women that they're loyal, that they're both in the same emotional boat. Once men feel a pull to be in the same boat as women, however, they begin to feel trapped. Guilt promotes identification, and the closeness associated with identification threatens men with anxiety.

Identification, empathy, merger—all are emotional states that, to some degree, accompany normal emotional intimacy. But all pose a special threat to men. Unlike women, men grow up linking independence and autonomy with masculinity. They thus are more likely to experience normal dependence and intimacy as threats to their masculinity. From a man's subjective point of view, he has more to lose by getting too emotionally close to a woman than she does by being close to him.

In the unconscious minds of many men, lowering their emotional guard in this way means they'll feel small again, weak, even feminine, and will not ever be able to be independent. At their heart these are fears based on pathogenic beliefs, the same feelings of guilt, shame, and merger that we explored in our study of sexual fantasy. In addition to these familiar pathogenic beliefs, men also carry around other ones that are more gender specific, including such beliefs as these—that men are supposed to be the polar opposite of women, that femininity is inferior to masculinity, that being dependent or emotionally connected means you can't also be independent. These beliefs are false, but men have acquired them "honestly," in the sense that they arose in the context of growing up in a particular context, both social and familial. As a result, to widely varying degrees, most men experience intimacy as unconsciously problematic.

It's easy, therefore, to see why men have less trouble than women separating sex from love. Love and intimacy open the door to guilt, identification, and merger, feelings that produce anxiety in men and, therefore, are antithetical to their sexual arousal. Sex for its own sake guarantees a feeling of difference and of emotional distance. By separating sex from intimacy, men can safely experience sexual ruthlessness and negate any potential attacks from their consciences or threats to their sense of separateness. That's precisely its point. They can get "in and out," so to speak, without the danger of becoming entangled with the real feelings and needs of their sexual partner.

Our theory of sexual fantasy can also be used to understand the special tendency of men to objectify women and their bodies. Objectification is one aspect of sexual ruthlessness. Another way to understand ruthlessness is to see it as the psychological ability to "use" the other person without him or her feeling used. "Used," in this sense, means that, on some level, the other person is experienced as a means to an end, that in order to become maximally aroused, we have to be able to take our partner's welfare for granted and not be overly worried about it or even attuned to it. At the same time, of course, sexual excitement also depends on the opposite of ruthlessness—namely, empathy. The paradox of sexual arousal is that in order for us to experience it intensely, we have to be able to both connect with our partner and to take him or her for granted.

Sexual objectification—the experience of another person as if he or she were only a body or a part of a body—is employed by men in the interest of achieving psychological safety. Like ruthlessness, objectification momentarily eliminates a woman's emotional life, a life for which men expect to feel responsible and with which they will feel drawn to identify. If they are connecting only with a body and not a whole person, then they can "use" that body without worrying about the emotional consequences. A body isn't sad or hurt, doesn't have needs or make demands, and isn't a cauldron of feelings with which the man might identify and, as a result, lose his boundaries and masculinity.

Instead, objectification promotes ruthlessness, which increases sexual excitement. The psychological reason that this is more salient for men than for women is that while sexual ruthlessness is inhibited by guilt in both sexes, it is especially threatened in men because of the ever-present dangers of intimacy, identification, and merger. Because their ego boundaries tend to be more rigid than those of women, men unconsciously feel more imperiled by closeness as well. As a result, they have to go to more elaborate lengths to shore up their defenses and their sense of separateness. The more they exaggerate their separation, however, the more threatening closeness becomes. Objectification helps men (momentarily) secure a safe and secure vantage point from which they can get sexually excited.

Women, on the other hand, also use objectification for the same reasons—to overcome guilt and merger—but since their gender identities are less threatened by closeness and merger than those of men, they have to resort to less objectification in order to feel safe.

WILL YOU STILL LOVE ME TOMORROW?— PATHOGENIC BELIEFS AND THE IDEALIZATION OF ROMANTIC LOVE IN WOMEN

Almost every study of gender difference in sexual attitudes (at least among heterosexuals) concludes that women do not like casual sex as much as men but instead prefer sex in the context of a relationship. Without the reassurance of an emotional connection, many women report feeling vulnerable before, during, and after having sex. Additionally, women appear to use objectification less than men, often getting aroused as much by a man's character and personality as his physical characteristics. Yet, as with men, there are frequent exceptions to the rule. Many women *do* like sex for its own sake and *are* drawn, as much as men, to the body parts and appearance of their sexual partners. Further complicating the issue is the fact that there is often a wide discrepancy between the fantasies that women may have and their actual behavior. It is not uncommon that a woman will chafe at having casual sex in reality, while enjoying elaborate fantasies of it in private.

Notwithstanding these contradictions, generalizations about the sexual attitudes of women in our culture are still credible and therefore need to be explained. The general rule is that sex tends to be a more serious and personal proposition for women than it is for men. This cultural fact has been explained by critics in a number of ways. The fact that women have historically been economically dependent on men in our society means that they are highly vulnerable to the possibility of abandonment. In fact, in the 1980s, the term "the feminization of poverty" was coined to describe the growing plight of single mothers who were downwardly mobile and disadvantaged as a result of abandonment by their husbands. It was, and is, economically true that when a man leaves his wife, the wife's standard of living eventually goes down, and the man's standard of living eventually goes up.

According to this analysis, the economic vulnerability of women provides the social context within which anxieties about abandonment arise. This danger influences women's attitudes toward sex. Linking sex with love is particularly important to women because it strengthens their relationships and therefore ensures their security. This special need for security and fear of abandonment underlie the adage that women "trade sex for love." As we saw so often in our study of sexual fantasy, safety is necessary for sexual arousal. For women in our culture, love represents both an objective and subjective sense of safety and security and thus tends to be more of a prerequisite for sexual pleasure than it is for men.

A related explanation of women's attitudes toward sex comes from the work of evolutionary biologists and psychologists. The laws of evolution, this argument goes, ensure that traits that increase the likelihood of survival and reproductive success (defined as the probability of passing on one's genes to future generations) will be selectively reinforced over thousands of generations. It is said that this process favored the development in our evolutionary past of different attitudes among men and women toward sex and commitment. Since women produced only one egg each month and were fertile for only a brief period, and since they were highly vulnerable and increasingly dependent during pregnancy—as were their children during their early years—it was in their interest, and those of their offspring, to secure a mate who had the strength and social status to protect them and to find ways to ensure that mate stayed close during her fertile period, pregnancy, and the early years of child rearing. Reproductive success for women, in this view, depended on the survival of the relatively few children that she was capable of producing and therefore on the proximity and commitment of a male.

On the other hand, evolutionary theory dictates that for the male, reproductive success was enhanced by inseminating as many women as possible, because the male's best chance to pass along his genes was to make use of his biological ability to father a huge number of offspring, not to nourish any particular one of them. Thus, in this evolutionary narrative, we have one possible origin of the antipathy of women toward casual sex and men's attraction to it. Sex outside the context of a relationship did not do anything to enhance the reproductive success of women and, thus, wasn't a tendency that was reinforced by natural selection. Over thousands of generations, evolution ensured that the need to link sex with emotional loyalty became wired into women's psyches, even though the subjective interests of any individual woman might diverge from this pattern.

Other theorists attempt to connect more closely the external with the internal forces that shape female sexual desire by emphasizing the powerful effects of socialization, role modeling, and social reinforcement on the particular sexual style of women. This model argues that girls are raised in a patriarchal culture with the expectation that they will emphasize relationships over lust, passivity over assertiveness, and domesticity over hedonism. They are constantly exposed to images of women who are desired as objects, but never as desiring subjects, and to cautionary tales of sexually confident women who "get what they deserve" when they do "flaunt" their sexual appetites. Although feminism has wrought monumental improvements in the choices women have in the last thirty years, there are still powerful social prohibitions against women pursuing sex for its own sake, prohibitions that bear the stamp of the "madonna/ whore" dichotomy that has dominated Western culture for centuries. Women, in this view, are degraded—though also covertly desired—if they are too sexual. Ultimately they internalize these social expectations and come to feel guilty if their sexual impulses are too directly expressive and powerful—too "masculine" in the eyes of the culture—or otherwise don't fit into their appropriate gender role.

These social explanations of the peculiarities of sexual desire in women are important but incomplete. I think that the model with which we understood sexual fantasy can be used to flesh out the psychological effects of these social pressures on female sexuality, the complicated and often unconscious mechanisms by which women actively desire what they are supposed to desire and actively prohibit what society tells them is forbidden. In my view, the key psychological mechanism shaping the special form that female sexual desire takes in our culture is guilt, various blends of separation and survivor guilt that women experience growing up that specifically target their desires and capacities for sexual arousal and pleasure. As a result of guilt, women often experience lust and sexual ruthlessness—both their own and that of their partners—as dangerous and thus opt for the safety that a traditionally "feminine" sexuality provides them. Psychological safety for women dictates the centrality of emotional commitment in the bedroom while psychological safety for men often means leaving commitment at the door.

Girls grow up in our culture with a different set of issues in relationship to their parents than do boys. While boys have to develop a radically different gender identity than their mothers in the process of separating from them, girls do not. While boys have to identify with their father's gender, becoming *like* the father, girls in our culture are supposed to take their fathers as their heterosexual love objects. Not only do boys and girls usually want to grow up in these different ways, but their parents actively help them do so. Girls not only identify with their mothers as their primary role models, but mothers often have a special and reciprocal investment in their daughters. Mothers tend to see themselves in their daughters more than in their sons. This isn't to say that mothers don't identify with and invest a lot in their sons, or even that they don't at times see their sons as extensions of themselves, but that there is a greater tendency for mothers to project who *they* are, for better and worse, onto their daughters.

This greater sense of sameness that develops between a girl and her mother as a result of these reciprocal identifications can have important psychological consequences. As the object of these especially strong projections, girls can have particular problems leaving their mothers. The separation process, difficult for boys because of the need to switch gender affiliation, can be difficult for girls because of the greater and more explicit pull of identification with their mothers. Identification isn't intrinsically a bad thing, of course. It is how girls learn about femininity, how to be women in our culture. But the special identifications that exist between mothers and daughters can also predispose girls to feel greater separation guilt than boys because of their sense that their mothers have more of an investment in their staying connected. The daughter may come to imagine that her mother experiences the daughter's separation and differentiation as if she is losing a part of herself. This type of common fantasy creates a pathogenic belief that separation is especially harmful, a belief that makes the daughter feel particularly guilty and worried about moving away from the mother. It is often compounded by the fact that mothers frequently convey just such a message to their daughters, that the separation *is*, in fact, a special kind of betrayal and loss. When reality confirms a pathogenic belief, that belief is strengthened.

In addition, because of the special bond between mothers and daughters, girls also grow up particularly susceptible to various forms of survivor guilt, the pathogenic belief that having more pleasure, success, and strength than the mother is hurtful. Many modern women who rejected the constraints of their mothers' traditional female role and went on to develop careers and achieve success in a traditionally "male" world found that they had to struggle with feelings of conscious and unconscious guilt about surpassing their mothers and leaving them behind. Even when these mothers had encouraged their daughters to succeed, the daughters often were left with irrational feelings that they were doing something forbidden and disloyal. In addition, these same women may also have had to contend with their fathers' ambivalence toward their daughters' rejection of traditional feminine roles, further exacerbating their guilt. For some, laying claim to the freedom, opportunity, and successes that eluded their mothers seemed to challenge their fathers' sense of authority and lead these women to feel that they were hurting *both* parents.

The survivor guilt evoked by surpassing and/or threatening our parents by our success is a good example of how social prohibitions are mirrored by more intimate ones, how the political becomes personal. In this case, the social constraints on the social advancement of women acquire a very private face in the form of the real and imagined reactions of their parents. A father might feel threatened by his daughter's strength, and a mother might feel left out and betrayed by her daughter's sense of entitlement to have a life that the mother had been denied.

In my clinical experience treating women, survivor and separation guilt often powerfully affect their sex lives. Women come to feel guilty about unadulterated expressions of sexual desire and excitement because they unconsciously believe that such pleasure, if too intense, is more than they're "supposed to have." Simply put, many women feel guilty about having more sexual pleasure than their mothers. Intense and uninhibited sexual excitement, like professional advancement, symbolizes a type of "success" that can and does easily trigger the pathogenic belief in a woman that she is hurting her mother. If a woman can feel guilty about making more money than her mother, then having more fun in bed is not likely to be something she will feel free to enjoy. Indeed, many women feel as if they were dancing on their mothers' graves.

Sexual guilt can also often be a product of relationships with fathers whom daughters experience as threatened by their sexuality. Many girls grow up unconsciously worried about their fathers because they infer that these fathers can't tolerate their strength and, in particular, their sexual assertiveness. The daughters worry about being "too much" for their fathers. In some of these cases, the father may attempt to control a daughter's sexual expression, a repressive response the daughter perceives as defensive and weak. In a related scenario, the father may withdraw from his daughter when she enters puberty and starts feeling her oats as a woman; again, a reaction about which the daughter feels guilty because of the belief that she has driven her father away with the force of her sexuality. While each of these scenarios usually contains elements of both objective truth and subjective distortion, the outcome is the same. The girl develops the pathogenic belief she's hurting or overwhelming her father with her sexuality.

Another way in which paternal vulnerability can contribute to a girl's guilt is if the father responds to his daughter's sexuality by becoming overly stimulated and inappropriately sexual in response. Whether or not this response results in actual sexual abuse, the girl's experience of an aroused father is of a father who is out of control. Such loss of control, besides being frightening in and of itself, is often experienced as *weakness* by the daughter, who then blames herself and feels guilty for driving her father into such a pathetic state. There are obviously many other traumatic aspects to father-daughter relationships that are overly sexualized, but my intent here is to underline the one that involves guilt. Daughters who feel that they can seduce their fathers, whether literally or symbolically, are liable to unconsciously feel too powerful and therefore guilty.

The girl responds to this guilt by keeping her sexuality in check. She represses her urges to enjoy sexual pleasure for its own sake. Many of my female patients have an unconscious expectation that they'll be punished if they have too much fun because it means that they're happier than their mothers and threatening to their fathers. Certainly, such women have difficulty being sexually ruthless because their guilt and worry about hurting others make them so attuned to the inner states of their partners that they are unable to let go and surrender to the rhythms of their own excitement.

Women who are struggling with this issue require the safety of a committed relationship in order to lower their sexual inhibitions. Only in such a context can they feel reassured against their guilt; only in such a context can they feel psychologically safe. Such safety can be understood as deriving from at least two sources. First, if the women are in a stable and secure relationship, they are not laying claim to being totally independent and free sexual agents. Second, in the context of a relationship they can take care that their partners aren't overwhelmed or hurt by the force of their sexual feelings.

In this way, a woman's guilt over being more sexually exuberant and gratified than her mother and about hurting or overwhelming her father is mitigated. Her sexual vulnerability and dependence on a man unconsciously put her in the same boat as her mother and keep her one down in relation to her father.

THE PERSONAL FINALLY MEETS THE POLITICAL

I've been emphasizing the central role of guilt in the genesis of the sexual styles of women because, in my experience, sexual guilt is more consciously prominent in women than in men. I am *not* arguing that were women *not* to feel guilty, they would therefore prefer casual sex just like men. Similarly, I am not arguing that were men *not* to feel unconsciously worried about identifying with women and losing their boundaries, they would require a committed relationship just like women.

In my view the ability to be sexually ruthless, to experience sexual pleasure with joy and abandonment independent of a committed long-term relationship, is a healthy capacity. Similarly, the human need to integrate sex with love, to experience sexual excitement as a route to greater intimacy and connection, is also a healthy need. The fact that men are better at the former and women at the latter is a function of the complex interactions between the social and psychological processes discussed in this chapter. From the point of view of the sociologist, the problem is patriarchy because patriarchy defines the different kinds of outlets that men and women have for sexual pleasure and emotional intimacy and seems to encourage the development of personality characteristics in each sex that match these outlets. From a psychological point of view, however, men and women—each gender in its own different way—emphasize certain dimensions of sexual desire and pleasure and deemphasize other dimensions in the interest of psychological safety. From the point of view of my model of sexual fantasy, the key to understanding the subjective experience of sexual differences is to look at how the special pathogenic beliefs of each gender produce their own solutions in the form of these very differences.

The relationship between social and psychological theories of sexuality is complex. We all experience ourselves as independent centers of initiative and meaning, not as vehicles for social rules and forces. Whether we fantasize about being dominated by a tall, dark, and handsome man or a dominatrix in spiked heels, being seduced by young, nubile women or seducing the president of the United States, we are all obliged to insist that these are the private productions of our own idiosyncratic minds, not the end products of cultural stereotyping, socialization, or patriarchy. Our experience of our sexuality is, on one level, always irreducibly subjective. On the other hand, it requires only the slightest shift of perspective, the smallest change in the power of the lens through which we're viewing ourselves, to be confronted immediately with the influence of the social environment on our most intimate psychological moments.

Viewed from this vantage point, our fantasies inevitably borrow sexualized images from the culture, value what our culture values, and attempt to work out problems that our culture creates. In a culture that rigidly separates masculinity and femininity, fantasies arise that play with breaking down these distinctions. In a culture that creates anxieties and insecurities in order to sell commodities—such as selling diet supplements to women who are made to feel irrationally too fat, or fast cars to men made to feel anxious about their masculinity—fantasies inevitably arise in which the weak become strong, the introverted become extroverted, the sexually repressed become hedonistic, the ashamed become exhibitionistic, and the guilty become ruthless. The function of sexual fantasies is to redress and correct anxieties and conflicts that are often social in origin.

The deepest level at which the world and the mind meet is in the family. Minds, with all their innate wiring, temperament, and potential, are formed in families. And families are the first incarnation of society, the place where children first encounter the rules and expectations that govern the broader social and cultural world in which they will have to function. It is not only that our families transmit how we're supposed to think about such "big" issues as politics, race, or gender, but they shape the more intimate confines of our psyches as well, the places where we learn whether we're supposed to be angry, strong, dependent, competitive, or tender; whether we're supposed to take responsibility for the moods of our partners, or whether we're allowed to be selfish, whether we think that life is supposed to be happy or hard. We acquire not only our strengths and virtues in our families, but our pathogenic beliefs as well. These beliefs will shape who we think we are and who we imagine we can become. These pathogenic beliefs also deeply shape our experience of our masculinity and femininity and the form and content of our sexual desire. They influence boys to seek sexual safety in objectification and girls to seek it in relationships.

The family, then, is both the birthplace of the psyche and a mirror of the stresses and conflicts of the social world. It is both the place in which the pathogenic beliefs that give shape to sexual desire are first formed, and the primary window through which the social world enters our lives. The space where these two vectors meet is in the psyches of our parents. The parents whom we worry about overpowering are the parents whom the social world has weakened. The mothers whom we feel guilty about leaving are the mothers who are overly invested in their children as a compensation for what is missing in the rest of their lives. The fathers who emotionally abandoned or rejected us are the fathers whose social roles have taken them out of their families and into alienated work environments. The family, in other words, is where the personal and the political make their most intimate acquaintance.

The Future of Sex: Final Reflections, Unanswered Questions

"Love looks not with the eyes, but with the mind
And therefore is wing'd cupid painted blind."
  —Helena, William Shakespeare *A Midsummer Night's Dream*

Sex: The thing that takes the least amount of time and causes the
most amount of trouble. —Edmund Burke

PRIVATE FANTASIES AND SEXUAL BEHAVIOR

The human imagination is capable of creating an almost infinite variety of images, stories, and scenarios to produce sexual pleasure. It weaves together elements of culture and childhood, past and present, psychology and biology, in endlessly creative ways to achieve the maximum amount of pleasure in the safest possible manner. It informs our private daydreams and public actions. It shapes what turns us on about other people and what turns us off. It can serve our most altruistic desires to bring pleasure to others and our most selfish desires to use others for our private gain.

As we have seen throughout this book, some of the most interesting, as well as puzzling, expressions of the human imagination are to be found in sexual fantasies and behaviors that diverge from social convention and sexual norms. I would include in this category various forms of sadomasochism or dominance and submission, involving such behaviors as whipping, spanking, piercing, bondage, the wearing of special vinyl or leather costumes, master/slave role playing, asphyxiation, humiliation, rape simulations, urinating or defecating, as well as extreme forms of voyeurism (e.g., Peeping Toms), exhibitionism (like male "flashers" and female fantasies of being a stripper or prostitute), and fetishism (like a sexual fixation on shoes). The fact that these things can excite some people is a testament to the creative power of the human psyche to provide itself pleasure in the most unusual of ways, while keeping itself safe.

More unusual than the fact that some people fantasize about such things is the fact that some people actually do them—act out these unconventional, even bizarre, scenarios in the service of sexual satisfaction. Many of us might be willing to suspend disbelief and accept something unusual or "kinky" when it comes to *private* fantasies, stipulating that, in principle, there might be "different strokes for different folks" when it comes to sexual arousal. When people actually seek out real experiences in which they're tied up, whipped, or urinated on; or in which they play out the roles of a slave, prostitute, or stripper; or set up hidden cameras to look up women's skirts, our disbelief usually reasserts itself, or turns to shock and disgust. To many people, the difference between someone being "kinky" in fantasy and reality is enormous. The question arises: why do some people act out fantasies that other people keep to themselves?

The answer may disappoint. Nobody really knows for sure. Like most therapists, I can often understand retrospectively why a patient developed a particular sexual fantasy or practice, but rarely can I say for sure why he or she either acted it out or simply kept it at the fantasy level. Our inability to definitively explain this difference is part of a broader limitation of much psychological theory. For example, no one has ever been able to study a child in the present and, on that basis, predict his or her future personality. We can explain how it was created after the fact, but not why it had to be this particular personality and not some other personality. We can spot trends, tentatively identify stress points and vulnerabilities, and make educated guesses about the types of psychological issues with which someone likely will struggle, but we are unable to predict exactly how that person will manage these stresses, vulnerabilities, and issues, or the extent to which he or she will be successful doing so.

On the level of sexual fantasies and preferences, our predictive power is even weaker because the forms of sexual desire are so private and the workings of human creativity so idiosyncratic that there is no way to predict, for example, that a person with a particular pathogenic belief will attempt to overcome it with a particular sexual fantasy.

Based on my clinical experience, however, I can offer some educated guesses about several factors that might contribute to the tendency in some people to act out unconventional fantasies. First of all, action runs in the family. If we grew up in a family in which parental impulses, particularly sexual impulses, were routinely acted out or openly displayed, then such behavior would come to feel familiar as, not only the way things were, but the way things were supposed to be. Acting on our impulses might even come to feel unconsciously like a way of being connected and loyal to our family. If children are chronically exposed to impulsivity in their families, such as unpredictable and frightening displays of anger, physical abuse, hyperemotionality, or humiliating losses of control often fueled by alcohol, they will often develop personality styles in which action takes precedence over thought. Similarly, if children are chronically exposed to public and intrusive displays of parental sexuality (including such things as nudity, having sex within sight or earshot of the children, frequently bringing home sexual partners, and so on) or are the objects of direct sexual abuse, then such patterns of overt sexual impulsivity may be incorporated into their adult sexual practices. In general, we identify with our parents' coping styles, and we tend to use the models of behavior and impulse control around us to construct the scenarios that we need in order safely to become excited. Action breeds action.

To say that an impulsive and action-oriented family environment might contribute to the fact that some people act out unusual fantasies isn't to say that such people are necessarily more "pathological" than those who keep such fantasies private, or that extreme forms of sadomasochistic sex are always the result of extreme family pathology. Sadomasochism or dominance/submission scenarios are attempts to deal with unconscious guilt and worry and, less frequently, with feelings of neglect and rejection. Many different types of families—those full of chaotic and sexually explicit behavior and those that are not—engender these feelings in children and contribute to sadomasochistic fantasies and preferences. Furthermore, sadomasochistic fantasies *or* practices are not pathological on the face of it. Their function is no different than that of any other sexual fantasy or preference, namely the creation of a state of psychological safety. Practitioners of S-M can and do live lives that are as full, productive, and high-functioning as other people's lives. Still, if our families tended to express feelings, including sexual feelings, primarily in action, then we might grow up with a tendency to resolve our sexual conflicts by resorting to action as well.

Another factor that might contribute to the need some people have to enact their fantasies in elaborate and extreme ways involves the power of the pathogenic beliefs against which such people are struggling. If, as we've seen, the elements of a sexual fantasy are intended to counteract beliefs and feelings that make sexual arousal dangerous, it follows that if these beliefs and feelings are powerful enough, we might need to resort to more extreme measures in order to disprove them. A private act of imagination might not be enough to do the job because the anxiety or guilt being opposed is too great. We may unconsciously decide that only by acting out the fantasy, only by making an imaginative act into a real one with real consequences, can we get the reassurance needed to transcend the chilling effects of our conflicts. To counteract the potential guilt about hurting others with our sexual power, it might not be enough simply to *imagine* a sadomasochistic scenario in which our partner gets aroused by the pain we inflict. It might be necessary to find a real person with whom we can enact these elaborate scenarios of bondage and domination. The reality of the excitement of a real person would be necessary, in this instance, to convince our unconscious minds that we're not hurting him or her with our power. Some people need more tangible evidence than they can get from fantasy that their pathogenic beliefs are, indeed, false. The more elaborate and extreme the sexual practice actually is, the more evidence is being collected that our worst fears are not being realized.

What determines the strength of our pathogenic beliefs? Again, as a therapist, I usually can answer this question only in retrospect and only in regard to a particular person, not in terms of general rules. Many different family constellations can produce the same irrational feelings and beliefs that sadomasochistic behavior and fantasies attempt to correct. In general, we might say that the greater the psychological trauma, the stronger the resulting pathogenic beliefs tend to be. Profound and prolonged states of helplessness, neglect, rejection, or worry are likely to result in powerful negative beliefs about ourselves and others. Trauma, however, can't easily be defined from the outside. The degree to which a family situation is traumatic is subjective and depends on countless factors, including the child's innate temperament, age, and birth order, and the availability of alternative sources of emotional support. We can perhaps make only the broadest distinctions when it comes to predicting the effects of trauma. If a child is sexually molested by a parent, for example, she or he usually is more traumatized than if the parent merely subjects the child to sexual innuendo. In the case of actual abuse, the child's irrational belief that he or she is responsible for the parent's loss of control and is therefore "bad" is likely to be stronger than in the case of more subtle parental seductiveness. If a mother is chronically depressed and unavailable, it is usually more traumatic than if that same mother is only occasionally withdrawn. The greater the maternal absence, the greater the child's sense of unworthiness is likely to be. Aside from obvious distinctions, we are hard-pressed to rank the severity of someone's childhood hardships, and thus we are limited in our ability to predict the strength and nature of his or her later pathogenic beliefs. While it is probably true that our tendency to act out our sexual fantasies is somehow related to the strength of the negative beliefs we are trying to counteract, we can't really make any good generalizations about precisely what factors make one of these beliefs stronger than another.

CYBERSEX: AN ADAPTIVE ILLUSION OR DANGEROUS ADDICTION?

Nearly 400 million people in the world have access to the Internet, using it every day to send one another E-mail and visit the millions of sites that currently make up the World Wide Web. The development of the Internet has been intertwined with sex from its beginnings. In the late 1990s, it was estimated that 10 percent of the commerce conducted on the Internet was related to pornography or the sex industry. Moreover, in its early years, the technological development of the Internet itself was fueled by sex because the most sophisticated advances in web site design, video, and interactive technologies originated in the world of X-rated adult entertainment.

People frequently use the Internet to express and gratify their sexual fantasies (it is estimated that up to 33 percent of Internet users have visited adult web sites) as well as to learn new ones. There are two broad areas of Internet usage that involve sexual fantasy.

First, there are many sites that basically mirror traditional pornography, providing their visitors and subscribers with access to erotic pictures and videos. Sometimes these sites feature live videos of women or, in the case of gay web sites, men stripping or performing sexual acts for the viewing audience. In general, these sites transpose the traditional pornography of magazines, videos, and peep shows onto a computer format and are mainly visited by men. Every fantasy found on the shelves of adult bookstores can be found in cyberspace.

The second place that sex resides on the Internet is in the worlds of chat rooms, bulletin boards, and E-mail. Chat rooms, in particular, provide a forum in which people can sexually interact with one another in real time, often providing meeting places in which people make connections with each other that they then take into more private areas of cyberspace. They can then, with the help of software modalities, such as "Instant Messenger" or "ICQ," conduct private, one-on-one sexual conversations—in real time—or they can develop private E-mail relationships where participants post and receive messages. Internet bulletin boards provide a less immediate and private connection but still enable erotic relationships to develop between real people.

Chat rooms and bulletin boards, of course, are places where all sorts of interactions can and do occur. Much of the time these interactions are not sexual. People meet in these venues to exchange information, share common interests, conduct research, form friendships, and find romantic partners. They also meet there to have cybersex, which usually occurs in one of two forms: interactive masturbation or interactive fantasy construction intended to arouse both parties. In the first, the participants instruct each other on how to touch themselves in order to get excited and have an orgasm. In the second, the two people mutually construct an erotic story or fantasy that is intended to arouse both of them, sometimes resulting in orgasm.

Cybersex is increasingly popular. Women, traditionally uninterested in ordinary pornography sites, are starting to visit chat rooms and engage in cybersex in greater numbers (although the majority of visitors are still men). Given the fact that the sexual fantasies of women tend to be more verbal and interactive, while those of men are more visual, this trend makes sense. But what accounts for this growing interest in cybersex in general? Is it healthy or unhealthy? Is a person who has cybersex with a stranger being unfaithful to his or her real-life partner? What about reports of the growing incidence of cybersex addiction? Isn't someone who spends twenty hours or more a week having cybersex psychologically disturbed? Isn't there a danger that electronic relationships will replace real ones? How might we understand the dynamics of cybersex using our particular model of sexual arousal?

If it is true that the only way we can get sexually excited is if we feel psychologically safe, then the explosion of interest in cybersex is immediately understandable. Sex over the Internet is the ultimate safe sex, not only in the literal sense that viruses can't travel through phone and cable lines, but in a psychological sense because cybersex is usually completely anonymous. Anonymity on the Internet is ensured not only by the use of pseudonyms, but by the absence of any visual or verbal contact. We can be whatever and whoever we want to be without any fear of exposure and therefore without the shame that people feel about their sexual urges and fantasies. A recent *New Yorker* cartoon perfectly captured this special dimension of cybersex. Two dogs are huddled over a computer keyboard, and one dog says, "On the Internet nobody knows you're a dog." Anonymity can mitigate the pain of rejection, as well as the guilt over rejecting others, worry about other people's welfare, as well as concerns over their opinions about us. In cyberspace, we can don any identity we want, as well as any name, and easily locate someone who shares our precise sexual interests. If my theory is correct that psychological safety is required for sexual arousal, then the Internet will be of compelling sexual interest to many people.

When it comes to its psychological meaning, cybersex often occupies an ambiguous middle ground between masturbation and actual sex. When two people, using pseudonyms, instruct each other on their computer screens about how to masturbate, or create a sexually arousing story together, the resulting experience for each person is neither entirely private nor entirely public, neither fully imaginary nor fully real. The other person is both an actor in our private fantasy and a partner in a real-life interaction at the same time. Contradictions like this abound in the world of cybersex. Since the two people are usually interacting with each other using fictitious identities, the sexual relationship that is created can hardly be called intimate. On the other hand, since computer-generated anonymity creates a sense of safety, people can often express deeper feelings and longings than they could possibly do in person.

Using the Internet, people can find others who fit *exactly* into their fantasies. Tops can find the perfect bottom and bottoms the perfect top. A man or woman looking to worship at the feet of a woman wearing four-inch spiked heels can find just such a dominatrix with whom he or she can create the precise scenario necessary to get aroused. A woman who gets aroused by the fantasy of joining a heterosexual couple in bed can find someone who gets aroused by imagining him or herself as someone in that couple. Our cyberpartners can be so selectively chosen that it can feel as if that partner has been created, like an actor in a play that we have written. In this way cybersex resembles masturbation in the sense that the participants experience a great degree of control over their partner's actions. That control, though, is not complete. There is no mistaking the fact that we are interacting with a real, separate person. The experience is inherently ambiguous and paradoxical.

Cybersex, while scripted according to the psychological requirements of both participants, does not have to be rote. It can also be a creative process in which, within the broad confines of each person's sexual preferences, stories are constructed that provide each person with new and creative avenues to arousal and pleasure. Rather then mechanical recitations of programmed sexual scripts, sexual interactions on the Internet can involve complicated narratives with surprising plot twists. In this way cybersex is similar to musical improvisation—the presence of a clearly defined overall structure or theme allowing tremendous room for creative and highly varied improvisation. Cybersex doesn't have to be a one-note song.

What can we say then about the meaning of this type of experience, an experience that appears to reside halfway between a fantasy and a real relationship? I would liken it to a form of play or art, not in terms of its psychological importance or social value, but because it shares with play and art a special relationship to reality. When children first learn how to play, they invest their toys and games with a particular meaning. The toy, whether it is a stuffed animal, doll, or some other object, is experienced simultaneously as both a part of the child and as separate from the child. No one has to tell the child that his or her stuffed bunny is not a real bunny. In fact, the environment happily colludes in pretending that the bunny is real. On one level, the child knows the literal truth, while on another level, he or she believes fully in the fanciful truth that he or she has created. Is the bunny imaginary or real? Is the child's experience objective or subjective? The answer is both and neither. The child is able to hold both experiences in his or her mind.

The capacity to sustain the tension between imagination and reality is central to our ability to play, to pretend that something is real while knowing that it is invented, to play games with rules that we create and then treat as if they were an immutable part of the outside world, to suspend disbelief just long enough to enjoy the game, or indeed, the play on the stage. The ability of human beings to create something that they relate to as external to them is a dynamic of artistic creation. Art is both found and created. Michelangelo once described the process of sculpting by saying that he sought to remove those portions of the block of stone that camouflaged the intended form. His creations were simultaneously discoveries. The painter Edvard Munch, traumatized as a child by the sight of his mother's gruesome death, grew up afraid to look anyone in the eye for fear of seeing something traumatic. The only beings with whom he could make direct eye contact were the people in his paintings. He could safely have a real relationship with them precisely because they were not real.

Cybersex, like play and art, is both created and discovered. The people in chat rooms arouse one another by creating something that is entirely fictitious—their names, identities, and sexual scenarios—but endowing this fiction with the force of reality. Unlike a purely private fantasy, however, this reality is grounded in the fact that there are two real and separate people who are fully present in the interaction. But these two real people can mold each other into whatever shape is needed to produce excitement, just as a sculptor can mold a piece of clay and at the end discover a shape that he or she feels has always been there.

Bob is having cybersex with Fred, enacting a scenario in which Bob plays the role of a submissive servant and Fred is a stern master. Both might be creating a story arousing to each of them. Let's say that, according to this story, Bob has broken one of the "rules" and is being punished by Fred by having his bare bottom spanked sharply with a paddle. Both are using pseudonyms, and neither has the faintest idea about the real identity or life of the other person—not his age, income, appearance, personality traits, or even his gender. Both Bob and Fred surrender completely to the fantasy, investing it with vivid emotion and passion, much like a child does with his or her bunny or Munch did with the people he painted. They are real to each other because they each know that there is a live person with a modem on the other end of the phone line. Yet it is crucial to their sense of safety and therefore to their excitement that they simultaneously know it is only a game, it is only cybersex, and no one can get hurt in any way. They have created something that has a life of its own while never losing the quality of being a creation of their joint imaginations.

Of course, likening cybersex to play and art risks glamorizing it and overlooking its drawbacks. To say that the experience of having sex with someone on the Internet shares with art and play certain ambiguities about reality does not mean that it has the same role in someone's mind or the same function in psychological development. Cybersex is often simply an especially enjoyable form of masturbation—quick, formulaic, and completely prosaic in its narrative structure and content. The question arises then: is cybersex psychologically healthy or unhealthy? Again, the answer, like the answers to so many questions about psychological health, depends on the person. We cannot make generalizations because people use cybersex in different ways.

The tension between fantasy and reality that cybersex creates can break down in the direction of either fantasy or reality. Some people cannot tolerate the presence of a real person on the other end of the screen who periodically brings his or her own separate interests and needs to the conversation. Even in cyberspace there is some requirement, however vague and minimal, of mutuality and accommodation that spoils the fun for someone who requires complete control in order to feel safe enough to get excited. Such a person either finds partners with whom he or she can create a simple story and quickly reach orgasm, or else such a person eschews cybersex altogether, preferring to use traditional pornography and erotica, on- and off-line, as the safest route to pleasure. Other people, however, have the opposite problem.

People who cannot tolerate the imaginary dimension of cybersex probably avoid such relationships to begin with. They cannot stand the fact that the reality of their cyberpartner might not match with his or her on-screen persona—the potential for deception is too dangerous. Occasionally, some people push to make the relationship a real one.

The sensationalized cases of adult men going into chat rooms and seducing young girls or boys into illicit and sexually abusive relationships reflect one particularly perverse subset of people who can't tolerate the ambiguities of a cyberrelationship (or, most likely, of a real one). These cases, while extremely rare, are troubling by-products of the nearly universal accessibility of the Internet and the anonymity that it provides. In my view, men who "troll" through chat rooms looking for prey are pedophiles who are merely using a new and effective tool of seduction. The psychological dynamics of Internet use don't, in and of themselves, create or contribute to their impulse to abuse children. The Internet, in these cases, is a means to an end and not the cause of that end.

Unfortunately, when such relationships are made real, they are usually disappointing. Objective reality, while needed, is not as arousing as it promised to be.

Thus, there are many ways in which cybersex can be indistinguishable from masturbation and other ways in which it can lead to traumatic disappointment. There are also people for whom on-line sex can be psychologically healthy. Some people are able to use the ambiguity surrounding the issues of fantasy and reality to explore their sexuality. The safety provided by the fact that it's "only a fantasy" frees them from unhealthy inner taboos, while the fact that on-line sex is interactive makes their experimentation more vivid and liberating. They can try various roles, deepening their experience of certain parts of themselves that have been rigidly suppressed because of guilt and shame. People can explore something of what it's like to be a member of the opposite sex, gay or straight, dominant or submissive. They can learn about different ways of having sex by creatively and playfully rehearsing it with someone on-line. In this sense, cybersex offers a safe playground upon which people can expand their sexual repertoires, deepen their self-awareness, and increase their pleasure.

What about the issues of infidelity and addiction? Most of us have heard of cases in which people, usually men, spend an increasing number of hours in front of their computers, developing relationships with people on-line at the expense of a connection with their partners, friends, and families. These on-line relationships usually become sexual and sometimes lead to affairs, divorces, and the breakups of families. Other times, however, someone may be having an on-line relationship, sexual or not, and still be fully connected emotionally and sexually to his or her spouse and devoted to his or her children. Does that person's cyberrelationship constitute infidelity? Does a sexual relationship with someone who is completely anonymous, whose reality is confined to a computer screen, have the same meaning to the participants and their partners as would a real flesh-and-blood relationship?

The answer to these questions is again: it depends. Cyber-affairs, like affairs in general, may indeed be reactions to problems at home. A person who is unhappy in a primary relationship and who might otherwise be tempted to have an affair in the real world might instead have one on the Internet. In fact, someone who would feel too guilty even to consider infidelity in the outside world may readily seize on the opportunities that the Internet provides. The interaction is easily initiated, conducted, and terminated without having to make undue arrangements to ensure secrecy and without the potential misunderstandings about commitment that can arise in an affair with a real person. The person having cybersex can convince his or her conscience that it's not "real" sex and sidestep the feelings of guilt that would otherwise arise.

The anonymity and accessibility of the Internet create a plethora of opportunities to indulge safely almost any sexual fantasy and, as a result, are particularly appealing to someone who finds him or herself unable to explore these fantasies with a real partner.

Sex on the Internet, then, can have the same meaning as sex in the real world, namely that it can reflect a need to escape from a problematic primary relationship and experience new satisfactions. In these cases it is clearly a sign that something is "wrong" in the person conducting the affair or the relationship from which that person is escaping. "It's only a fantasy" is a rationalization. The fact that cybersex involves two real people is much more important than the fact that their interactions are imaginary.

We could argue that for some people, indulging in sexual fantasizing or masturbation on the Internet doesn't necessarily reflect serious problems in a relationship any more than masturbation, the casual use of pornography, or erotic reveries necessarily do. Surely someone can feel quite sexually satisfied and intimate with his or her partner and still enjoy the pleasure of an erotic reverie that involves a stranger. Such daydreaming does not necessarily imply a critique of the current relationship. Cybersex might function in a way similar to sexual reverie, adding to someone's sexual satisfaction rather than substituting for its absence in the real world. There might be fantasies that our partner doesn't share or can't enjoy that can be safely explored and gratified on the Internet, fantasies that are not necessarily so important that their frustration in our primary relationship reflects a problem. In this sense, the fact that cybersex is primarily the enactment of a private fantasy is more important than the fact that there are two real people acting it out. Having on-line sex in these cases would no more mean that our relationship is in trouble than would having a sexual daydream about someone other than our partner while sitting in a café.

Currently, there is a great deal of public discussion about cyber-addiction, a syndrome in which some people spend a significant amount of time on the Internet—in some instances more than forty hours per week—in a manner that is compulsive and that interferes with their everyday lives, including their relationships with their families, friends, and their work. Such addicts are usually holed up in chat rooms, connecting with other people in sexual and nonsexual ways. Treatment programs have even grown up that attempt to treat cyberaddiction in ways similar to a drug or alcohol addiction, using the twelve-step model of Alcoholics Anonymous.

In my clinical experience, the anxiety underlying addictions often involves feelings of disconnectedness, which the addictive substance is used to alleviate. The addict is "filled up" by the substance, ex-periencing it as a substitute for the missing relationship and, as a result, using it to numb his or her pain. The Internet provides the perfect addictive solution to the loneliness and disconnectedness of the potential addict, namely on-line relationships. Fears or other psychological conflicts creating feelings of isolation in a person, making relationships treacherous or burdensome, are perfectly al-leviated by the anonymous, arm's-length contact readily available in cyberspace twenty-four hours a day, seven days a week.

Even if some of these relationships eventually lose their anonym-ity, the fact that they are mediated by the computer makes them especially safe. One can come and go as one pleases, be as self-disclosing as one wants, present oneself in a form that is free of perceived imperfections, and neatly erase potential feelings of guilt, worry, anxiety, shame, unworthiness, and self-consciousness. On-line relationships enable someone to be connected in a way that is simultaneously highly social and completely under control, thereby maximizing a sense of safety.

Given the soon-to-be universal access to the World Wide Web, should the growing incidence of cyberaddiction concern us? Is there a danger that the addictive potential of on-line relationships will touch all of us in ways that, while less dramatic and personally disastrous than full-fledged addiction, are still harmful overall? After all, more and more of us are spending more and more time on-line. Even if most of us don't become flagrant addicts, perhaps we are all in danger of becoming social isolates, hunkered down in front of our computer screens and video terminals, increasingly using assumed identities to relate to others through modems rather than interacting in a real way with real people in the real world.

In my view, the technology of cyberspace, like many other technologies, is capable of both enhancing and harming us. The fact that computers are designed for individual use doesn't mean that they have to promote isolation. Most people don't become cyberaddicts and are as able to keep their on-line involvement under control as they are their drinking. In fact, a recent study by the Pew Research Center entitled, "Tracking Online Life," found that women who use E-mail made more extensive and frequent contact with their friends and families than did people without E-mail, and that they also made more telephone and personal contact. Direct real-time contact via Instant Messenger and ICQ are also modalities that can and do increase our relatedness to one another, breaking down some of the geographic barriers that keep people apart. People who couldn't afford to telephone each other can now make contact virtually free of charge on their computers. Relationships can now be maintained across continents with an immediacy and depth that were impossible in prior eras. In many ways the world is smaller, and the possibilities for connection are greater, as a result of the Internet.

There is, of course, a downside to the quality of relatedness that cyberspace promotes. Cyber-relationships don't necessarily solve the problems of loneliness and disconnectedness that plague so many people in our culture but may offer the illusion that they do. They may temporarily put cybersalve on the wound, but they don't permanently heal it. In addition, since on-line relationships provide a momentary relief to loneliness, they may cover over and help people deny what really ails them, the true psychological and social causes of personal isolation.

In addition, cyber-relating is an inadequate substitute for real relating. Computer-mediating communication can be inherently frustrating because of its inherent inability to communicate complex emotional states. In addition, because E-mail and electronic "chatting" can be highly crafted, they can promote a kind of pseudo-intimacy in which somewhat sanitized and idealized selves are relating to each other. Real relationships, because they inevitably involve disclosing one's imperfections, are not as safe as on-line relationships. Rather than have to confront and work on the conflicts that arise in these relationships, people may use the psychological safety of cyberspace to avoid dealing with these conflicts altogether.

Ultimately, the only way to ensure that the salutary effects of the Internet are not outweighed by its dangers is to confront the sources of the loneliness and disconnectedness that give rise in the first place to the tendency to use cyberspace as a refuge. In many ways the growing use of the Internet for initiating and maintaining relationships can be seen as both a symptom of our collective isolation and an attempt to transcend it. It is both an escape and an attempt at mastery. On the individual level, people need to deal with the underlying beliefs and feelings that interfere with their ability to connect with each other, a process that might be aided by psychotherapy and by finding ways to experience greater intimacy with others. On the social level, we need to decrease the isolation that so many people in our culture feel as a result of the breakdown of communities, unsatisfying work, and a general ethos of selfishness and individualism that pervades our everyday lives. Only when people don't feel as frustrated in their hunger for connectedness and undeserving about getting it can we feel confident that the Internet will provide us lasting social benefits and not simply a temporary and illusory palliative.

WILL THERE BE SEXUAL FANTASIES AFTER THE REVOLUTION?

If sexual fantasies are attempts momentarily to counteract beliefs and feelings that interfere with sexual arousal, then what would happen if we were cured of all of our psychological conflicts? On an even more utopian note, what if we had a world in which we all had healthy, loving, and responsive parents and did not develop pathogenic beliefs to begin with? Would we still have sexual fantasies? To modify the type of question some of us asked ourselves in the 1960s, will we still have sexual fantasies "after the Revolution"?

In my view, the answer is yes.

There are certain aspects of human development that are universal and that no psychotherapy or social movement could ever change, certain inevitable developmental stresses that will always result in the formation of some type of pathogenic beliefs. Therefore, some version of the problems that sexual fantasy attempts to solve is universal, and human beings will always have both the motivation and the capacity to be the solvers. It is in the very nature of childhood cognition sometimes to mistake cause and effect and to take responsibility irrationally for negative things over which one objectively has no control. Developmental psychologists call this the normal "egocentricity" or "omnipotence" of childhood, and it leads to a universal tendency to feel a measure of self-blame in response to the stress of our caretakers. Because parents, even in the best circumstances imaginable, will sometimes get sick, have mood swings, get distracted, feel frustration, be momentarily unattuned to their children's inner states, or die, children will always feel some measure, however small, of rejection, worry, or loss. And, because of their normal egocentricity and omnipotence, they will always be inclined to feel guilty and to take responsibility for whatever happens to them. Even if parental "failures" are brief and the child is explicitly reassured that he or she is not to blame, that child will secretly believe otherwise. Children are not only emotionally motivated to exonerate parents and blame themselves, but are cognitively unable to do otherwise. Self-blaming beliefs and irrational feelings of responsibility, formed in the cauldron of childhood egocentricity, will, in turn, always tend to put a potential damper on sexual feelings and require a fantasy or special scenario in order to overcome them.

Some form of survivor guilt will probably also always exist and, therefore, will always create sexual inhibitions that fantasies will have to address. Because of our love for and attachment to our parents, our normal and healthy trajectory toward independence inevitably sensitizes us to our parents' weaknesses. Even if our parents are strong and happy, we will be inclined to worry that they're not. This needn't be a significant problem and needn't interfere with our primary longings to grow up and feel a healthy sense of relatedness to others. But the fact that we inevitably move away—emotionally, if not physically—from people to whom we're attached increases our awareness of our differences from those people and of the ways in which we have things that our loved ones don't. This awareness opens the door to survivor guilt.

One of the main things, of course, that children usually have that parents do not is a long life ahead of them. It is an irreducible fact that parents are closer to death than are children. Even in a society in which aging is accepted with grace and dignity, and in which elders are revered and fully integrated into society, children will always have more of a life to look forward to than their parents. The fact that we are always at a different place than our parents on the life cycle, particularly when it comes to the importance and frequency of sexual desire, creates a vulnerability to survivor guilt, a sensitivity to having something that our loved ones don't.

While the fact of survivor guilt is universal, the *degree* of it is not. If children were surrounded by people who supported rather than ignored or resented their growth and success, they would feel far less survivor guilt. If we lived in a world in which people were happier and more fulfilled, children would have less reason to feel responsible and guilty to begin with. Good psychotherapy, furthermore, can dramatically lessen the grip of survivor guilt by correcting, at the deepest level, the irrational beliefs that support it.

Nevertheless, there will always be stresses in our lives, there will always be potential interference in our capacity to become aroused, and there will always be a corresponding need for sexual fantasies to help us. Thankfully, human beings are blessed with the imagination to create them. Our imaginations are like a portable first-aid kit for our psyches, soothing our pain, circumventing our guilt, and helping us have pleasure. The great thing about our imagination is that we don't need other people to make it work. We have the capacity to take care of ourselves, to circumvent danger, create safety, and permit pleasure inside ourselves all the time. We will always use our imaginations in these ways regardless of how much therapy we've had or how much better our social world becomes. Our capacity for sexual fantasy is an enduring aspect of what it means to be human.

THE VALUE OF UNDERSTANDING
SEXUAL FANTASIES

We can enjoy our sexual fantasies without understanding them. And understanding them will probably not affect that enjoyment one bit. Theorizing about sex occurs at a completely different psychological and cognitive level than sexual experience itself. What's the value, then, of grasping the underlying dynamics of sexual arousal? And what is special about the particular explanation offered here?

First of all, there is value in understanding for its own sake. Sexual fantasies are creative and complicated constructions of the human mind, often bizarre in their form and amazing in their vivid theatricality. How can someone possibly get sexually aroused by being tied up and whipped? How did someone come up with an erotic daydream in which she is being sexually ravished by two men on stage while the action is being narrated by a large black man with an erection? Why in the world would a man worship a high-heeled shoe or imagine that he is breast-feeding in order to get excited? That people use such unusual scenarios as their route to sexual pleasure is an intrinsically fascinating puzzle that cries out for a solution, regardless of whether that solution is of any therapeutic or practical value.

Even in the realm of more sedate and so-called normal fantasies and preferences, mysteries abound that demand explanation. Isn't it just as puzzling why some people like to talk a lot during sex in order to get maximally excited as it is that other people have to be blindfolded and spanked with a belt by their "master" while doing it? Aren't such sexual preferences as mundane as a need to have sex in the dark as interesting as the need to have phone sex? Isn't the fact that someone's masturbation fantasy always involves seducing someone in authority as inexplicable as a lengthy plot involving dungeons, slaves, and medieval forms of sexual torture? While the reason for the high degree of theatricality of some fantasies and preferences is a fascinating subject of study in its own right, the fact remains that the dynamics behind simpler and conventional behavior are ultimately just as mysterious. I think that there is an intrinsic value and pleasure in understanding, in solving puzzles about the meaning of human psychology and behavior, whether the subject of study is extremely bizarre or just ordinary.

Self-awareness and self-understanding are inherently of value. The examined life is one that offers us more choices and enables us to enjoy a greater degree of self-acceptance. Since sexual fantasies are created in order to temporarily master nonsexual conflicts involving guilt, worry, shame, and helplessness, understanding their meaning can help us shine a light into the deepest corners of who we are. Such self-understanding can help us become less reactive and more thoughtful about our innermost desires and fears.

Self-understanding, then, helps us more comfortably accept who we are. In particular, it helps reduce our shame and guilt about our sexual thoughts and urges. Rather than view our sexual desires through a punitive moral lens, we can potentially view them through a compassionate one that sees our basic desires as healthy and not pathological. Masochistic fantasies don't necessarily mean that we fundamentally like to be weak or sadistic ones that we primarily want to hurt others. Fantasies about young women and men don't necessarily mean we're pedophiles, and daydreams about seducing the president don't have to mean that we're troubled White House interns. Understanding the dynamics of our sexual arousal frees us from the gratuitous self-criticism and embarrassment that we so often feel about our most personal desires.

For those of us who are therapists, the model of sexual fantasy I have described is of enormous therapeutic utility. It helps us link various aspects of our patients' lives. Because sexual fantasies are attempts to overcome our pathogenic beliefs in the pursuit of pleasure, we can use these fantasies as a way to understand the belief structures that inevitably create difficulties in every area of our patients' lives. Sexual fantasies can open an invaluable door to our patients' unconscious minds, provided that we therapists have a good understanding of how such fantasies function.

Using the model of sexual excitement presented here, we are also better equipped to understand certain social phenomena. We can understand the deeper unconscious dynamics behind pornography use, cybersex, objectification, the erotic appeal of fashion, and the ways in which various forms of sexual repression are internalized in so-called normal psychological development. If we start from the premise that sexual arousal has a deep psychological cause and purpose, then we can investigate these social phenomena without immediately going to the political barricades. If particular sexual fantasies and preferences are the only means that our minds can create to solve the problems of pathological guilt and shame, then we can analyze their social expression with compassion and get to a deeper level of understanding than we can when our understanding stops at the level of moral or political disapproval.

This brings us, finally, to the question of why we should use this particular theory or model of sexual arousal to understand either the psychology or sociology of sexual arousal. The first reason has just been hinted at. A theory of sexual excitement that emphasizes the role of sexual fantasy in overcoming obstacles to pleasure has the virtue of being fundamentally compassionate in the sense that it sees people as problem solvers not as "bad" people who fundamentally enjoy being sick or antisocial. I begin with the assumption that sexual pleasure is inherently desirable, and therefore that the motivation for its pursuit is neither complicated nor mysterious. Many other psychological theories argue that sexual fantasies ultimately derive from the fact that, as children, we have primitive sexual desires that are quite different from those that we will eventually have

as adults. They posit that we are inherently sadistic as well as pleasure seeking, that we have special instinctual desires for oral and
anal stimulation, as well as specific desires to have sex with or destroy
our parents. In this view, these early incarnations of sexuality and
aggression are often directly expressed in sexual fantasies. Sexual
fantasies and preferences, so this argument goes, reflect a disguised
version of these early, more primitive desires.

My view of childhood is different, and so is my view of sexual
fantasy. I don't think that babies are born inherently sadistic, nor
do I think that the aggression sometimes seen in sexual fantasies
ever reflects such basic sadism. When people are aggressive or cruel
in their sexual daydreams or practices, it is not because they are
primarily sadistic but because they are trying to solve a problem.
Some people might imagine having rough and forceful sex, not because they intrinsically derive pleasure from being rough, but to
overcome their guilt and worry. The sexual arousal of their partners
provides just the reassurance they need that they're not hurting anyone. Some people might have a sexualized fantasy in which they
really do hurt their partners, not because they have an innate wish
to hurt, but because they're identifying with someone who hurt
them. It derives not from some innate sadism but from an attempt
to overcome their chronic sense of fear and helplessness. In their
sadistic scenario, they're the victimizers, not the victimized.

Dark childhood passions do not animate sexual fantasies, but
childhood fears do. The important issue in understanding a sexual
fantasy becomes, not to discover and explain the underlying desires,
but to understand why someone's normal pursuit of pleasure requires
a particular scenario in order to be safely experienced.

This is a theory about psychological safety. People get aroused if
and only if they feel safe enough to do so. When something jeop-
ardizes our safety, sexual desire is inhibited. We all want pleasure,
but safety is more important. Guilt and shame jeopardize safety and

make excitement impossible, as do feelings of helplessness, worry, and depression. The things we like to do in bed, read about and watch in our erotica, think about during masturbation, and daydream about when we're driving a car are all attempts to ensure our psychological safety. Our conscious experience, of course, is that this or that image or this or that activity "just turns us on." But on a much deeper level, that image or activity is creatively and brilliantly negating the internal obstacles to our pleasure.

THE EMPEROR'S NEW CLOTHES AND THE MEANING OF SEXUAL FANTASY

I have always had a special fondness for the fable "The Emperor's New Clothes." In the story, the emperor is actually naked, but his fawning courtiers and subjects, afraid that the truth will offend and enrage their ruler, compliment him on his beautiful new clothes. Such flattery convinces even the emperor himself that he must, indeed, be dressed in something magnificent. No one dares speak the truth, until one day a little boy, upon seeing the emperor, points out that he's naked. Everyone is shocked, horrified, and fearful lest the ruler respond with injured pride and anger. Instead, the emperor is relieved and grateful to have someone finally tell him the truth.

This is a fable about the dangers of accepting "received wisdom"—so-called truths that aim to persuade on the basis of appeals to authority and peer pressure—and the importance of trusting one's instincts. I have always been skeptical about both popular and professional axioms about sex. I have never been willing to accept the popular notion that sexual fantasy was somehow a mysterious artifact of the human imagination beyond our ability to understand rationally. Its logic might be unconscious, but I didn't think it was unknowable. Similarly, I was never satisfied with most of the prevailing theories about sexual arousal and fantasy in the literature of psychology and psychoanalysis. So often, these theories seemed to me to violate common sense or else portray people as cauldrons of primitive, chaotic, and frightening impulses. In my view these theories were simply intellectual versions of those new clothes that everyone admired on the emperor—flashy, complicated, and sophisticated, but without any real substance or grounding in social or clinical reality

My aim has been to seek the truth about sexual arousal. I've tried to emulate certain aspects of the little boy in the story of the emperor's new clothes, weighing in against certain popular misconceptions and academic mystifications. People think about and do bizarre things, but their motivations are ordinary and make common sense. Sexual arousal feels biological, but its origins are psychological. Sexual fantasies seem to be instinctual, but they represent the tip of an unconscious iceberg that gives them their shape and intensity. Some people appear to enjoy pain, while the reality is that pain makes them feel safe. Cruelty sometimes looks like it is inextricably intertwined with sexual desire, but the truth is that it is really an attempt to master a trauma in order to safely feel pleasure. Men definitely tend to objectify women, but they do so in order to preserve their masculinity not primarily to hurt women. Women definitely prefer sex in the context of love, but the purpose of this preference is to diminish their guilt as much as it is to establish a higher form of intimacy.

Sexual fantasies have a meaning. Although their meaning can be explained, they cannot be reduced to an explanation. Although they have a hidden logic, they are not simply logical. Although the dynamics of sexual arousal can be deciphered, sexual arousal is not a set of dynamics. After we finish all of the explanations, theoretical discussions, and psychological analysis, there is something about sex that cannot be understood. There is something about the power of the human imagination to rescue us from despair, something about the endlessly creative ways that we get ourselves excited, and something about the very sensation of sexual pleasure itself that cannot be translated into theorems.

Nor does it have to be. We can analyze the meaning of our sexual desire while still surrendering to its passion. We can use our sexual fantasies to illuminate important regions of our psyches while still leaving a great deal in the dark. We can appreciate the centrality of safety in sexual arousal and still feel the thrill of the unexpected in the bedroom. We can make rational sense of erotic life and still enjoy its mysteries.

REFERENCES

Baker, Nicholas. *The Fermata*. Vintage, 1995.

Balint, Alice. "Love for the Mother and Mother-Love." *International Journal of Psychoanalysis* 30 (1946).

Benjamin, Jessica. *The Bonds of Love: Psychoanalysis, Feminism, and the Problem of Domination*. Pantheon Books, 1988.

Bollas, Christopher. *The Shadow of the Object: Psychoanalysis of the Unthought Known*. Columbia University Press, 1987.

Chodorow, Nancy. *The Reproduction of Mothering: Psychoanalysis and the Sociology of Gender*. University of California Press, 1987.

Cooper, Alvin, et al. "Sexual Addiction and Compulsion," *The Journal of Treatment and Prevention*. Quoted in *The APA Monitor* 30, no. 4 (April 2000).

Davidson, J. Kenneth "The Utilization of Sexual Fantasies by Sexually Experienced University Students." *Journal of College Health* 34 (August 1985).

Donnelly, Denise, and James Fraser. "Gender Differences in Sado-Masochistic Arousal Among College Students." *Sex Roles* 39, nos. 5–6 (1998).

Ehrensaft, Diane. *Spoiling Childhood*. Guilford Publications, 1997.

Friday, Nancy. *Forbidden Flowers*. Dell, 1975.

———. *Men in Love: Men's Sexual Fantasies: The Triumph of Love over Rage.* Delacorte, 1980.

———. *My Secret Garden: Women's Sexual Fantasies.* Trident, 1973.

———. *Women on Top: How Real Life Has Changed Women's Sexual Fantasies.* Pocket Books, 1992.

Friedan, Betty. *The Feminine Mystique.* W. W. Norton, 1963.

Hsu, Bing, et al. "Gender Differences in Sexual Fantasy and Behavior in a College Population: A Ten-Year Replication." *Journal of Sex and Marital Therapy* 20, no. 2 (Summer 1994).

Laumann, E. O., A. Paik, and R. C. Rosen. "Sexual Dysfunction in the United States: Prevalence and Predictors." *Journal of the American Medical Association* 281, no. 6 (February 10, 1999).

Lewis, Thomas, Fari Amini, and Richard Lannon. *A General Theory of Love: Love and the New Science of the Emotional Mind.* New York: Random House, 2000.

Person, Ethel Spector. *The Sexual Century.* Yale University Press, 1999.

Stoller, Robert. *Perversion: The Erotic Form of Hatred.* Pantheon Books, 1975.

Szuchman, Lenore T., and Frank Muscarella, eds. *Psychological Perspectives on Human Sexuality.* New York: John Wiley & Sons, 2000.

"Tracking Online Life: How Women Use the Internet to Cultivate Relationships with Family and Friends." *Pew Internet Project* 5, no. 10 (2000).

Weiss, Joseph. "Bondage Fantasies and Beating Fantasies." *Psychoanalytic Quarterly* (1998): 626–44.

———. *How Psychotherapy Works: Process and Technique.* Guilford Press, 1993.

Weiss, Joseph, and Harold Sampson. *Psychoanalytic Process: Theory, Clinical Observation and Empirical Research.* Guilford Press, 1986.

INDEX

ML

1/02